Piaget, Education and Teaching

This book has been written for the Education student beginning a study of Piaget and his relevance to education. It contains those aspects of Piaget's theory which the author believes fundamental to an understanding of the relationship of Piaget's theory of intellectual development to education and teaching. The exposition of Piaget's theory stops short of a consideration of Piaget's logico-mathematical formulations and the reader is directed to other sources should he wish to pursue these aspects. What has been chosen in the realm of theory is that which has been shown, by experience, to be within the understanding of beginning students. It encompasses material which the student can relate not only to the usual problems of curriculum and instruction but also to such allied problems as conventional IQ, development, learning, memory and language and to educational theory as a whole.

Piaget, Education and Teaching

D. W. McNALLY

NFP New Educational Press

TO GRACE; AND TO DOMINIQUE,
GREGORY, JOHN AND MICHAEL

First published by
ANGUS AND ROBERTSON (PUBLISHERS) PTY LTD
102 Glover Street, Cremorne, Sydney

This edition published in 1974 by
NEW EDUCATIONAL PRESS LTD
160 High Street, Lewes, Sussex, England BN7 1XU

© D. W. McNally 1973

ISBN 0 904025 04 7 casebound

Printed in Great Britain by
T. & A. Constable Ltd, Edinburgh

Contents

1 The Background to Piaget's Theory of Intellectual Development   1

2 Piaget's Theory of Intellectual Development: An Introduction   4

3 The Relationship of Piaget's View of Intelligence to Conventional Views   56

4 Piaget's View of Knowing, Learning, Development, Language, Memory and the Relationship of Intelligence to these Areas   66

5 General Implications of Piaget's Theory for Education and Teaching   78

6 Piaget and the Understanding and Teaching of Number 103

7 The Implications of Piaget's Theory for the Teaching of Social Studies, Science and Language 123

Appendix A   Tables 148

Appendix B   Piaget's Position and the..... .....

Oxford Criticism 150

Glossary..... 153

Bibliography 158

Index 163

1. The Background to Piaget's Theory of Intellectual Development

Piaget did not set out to contribute specifically to education and to teaching. In fact the proportion of his total writing which comments directly on education is small and was increased considerably by the publication of *The Science of Education and the Psychology of the Child* in 1971. Nevertheless, Piaget's work has considerable significance for education and teaching and teachers who are prepared to undertake a systematic study of his theory and research will find much that is of relevance to a professional understanding of the process of education and the task of teaching. But to be effective, such a study must be comprehensive enough to reveal the underlying unity of Piaget's theory. Not all of what Piaget has said and done is relevant to education and in the pages that follow it will be apparent what is considered relevant. Nor are all of Piaget's views and the implications for education universally accepted. Criticism is inevitable when one sets up a theory as novel as Piaget's, but, in general, his theory and approach have stood up well under criticism. Although modified in some respects, they appear to be gaining increasing acceptance as having educational relevance and as being a point of departure for others who seek an answer to educational problems in the last three decades of the twentieth century. Where it has been considered that criticisms have relevance to the ideas being put forward, they are discussed and an attempt is made to indicate the status of the criticism in the light of recent research.

Jean Piaget was born in 1896 in Neuchatel, Switzerland. As a boy he showed a keen interest in nature, an interest which developed into an interest in biology which was the focus of his undergraduate and graduate studies at university, and which has been a continuing interest. It was this early interest which gave Piaget his unique biological conception of knowledge and the development of intelligence.

Parallel with this interest in biology went an interest in philosophy; in particular an interest in epistemology which is that branch of philosophy concerned with the nature of knowledge. But influenced by his scientific orientation, Piaget sought to take the question of the nature of knowledge

1

from the realm of abstract philosophy and place it under scientific scrutiny by posing the question: "How does knowledge come about?" which, as he says (Furth, 1969, 255), "implies an attempt to explain knowledge through its formation and development".

Piaget is therefore often referred to as a "genetic epistemologist", that is, one who attempts to get at the problem of the origin and development of knowledge. He also believed that the origin and development of knowledge was open to investigation through the methods of psychology, in particular through what is termed the clinical method. Basically the clinical method, as applied by Piaget, involved exploring the child's thought by asking a question and letting the child's response determine the course of subsequent questions. The aim was to follow the child's own thought in a way which is precluded by the use of standardised test procedures.

But Piaget's conception of "knowledge" is a wide one and differs considerably from the general conception. Knowing and intelligence are seen as two aspects of the one action, and therefore to enquire about knowing and knowledge is also to enquire about intelligence. This particular view of intelligence, with its biological orientation, frequently presents a problem to those used to equating knowledge with facts and ideas, and intelligence with IQ and mental age. Understanding Piaget's view involves taking a new perspective, the development of which must begin with an examination of his fundamental beliefs concerning life itself. As one would expect, Piaget's view of the world reflects his interest in nature and philosophy for he emphasises universal order, suggesting that all things are related. Thus he sees biological, social and psychological systems as related and sees logic as the link. He believes that the logic of the laws governing the physical aspects of the universe, the biological processes, and the processes of the mind are similar. This belief is at the base of Piaget's unique view of intelligence, which he sees as an extension of biological adaptation. He regards the development and functioning of intelligence as just as biological a function as digestion. For Piaget it is the progressive development of logic within the child which enables him to understand the biological, social and physical worlds and it has been one of Piaget's chief concerns to show that the development of intelligence in the child is in effect the ability to apply increasingly more complex and effective logical systems.

The belief in universal order provides an understanding of why Piaget set out to study the development of cognition, intelligence, and not the cognitive development of individuals as individuals. He believed that a study of individuals would reveal the underlying processes of thinking common to all human beings. This explains, to some extent, why in his early work he used small samples which he considered representative. Piaget concluded that if all human beings had this underlying logical system of thinking which evolved over time, then it would only be necessary to examine a small number of subjects in depth to discover the essential structure and function of intelligence. Thus Piaget's studies may be referred to as ontogenetic because he is concerned to discover what is common to his sample rather than what is different. This does not mean that Piaget did not contribute to an understanding of individuals and individual differences. He most certainly did, but such a contribution was not his main aim. It came as a by-product of his fundamental enquiry.

Concomitant with his view of universal order is Piaget's belief that it is necessary to view the development of intelligence in terms of evolution. Human intelligence from Piaget's standpoint is "the end manifestation . . . of a biological process that spans the billions of years of evolutionary history, the thousands of years of human civilization, and the sixteen odd years of individual development" (Furth, 1969, 205). Piaget also sees this evolution manifested in the progressive development of thought in those sixteen years as the child moves progressively through qualitatively different stages of thought. He believes that the individual progressively gives up erroneous ideas for more correct ones or, more correctly, transforms initial inadequate ideas into higher-level more adequate conceptions. The "logic" present in the behaviour of the infant is much more primitive and far less systematic than that observed in the primary school child.

Mental growth is not considered to be determined entirely by innate factors, however, but is seen as the resultant of interaction between the maturing organism and the environment in accord with fundamental biological principles. The way in which this organismic-environmental interaction leads to the progressive development of intelligence in man is the subject of the next chapter which begins by exploring briefly the role of instinctive behaviour in the development of intellect.

2. Piaget's Theory of Intellectual Development: An Introduction

One of the distinguishing behavioural characteristics as one views the animal hierarchy from the simple one-celled organism to the complex primates is the increasing individuality and flexibility of behaviour. At the lower end of the scale "knowledge", or the ability to deal with the environment, is typically the result of heredity and it has been shown that even where such instinctive behaviour is very complex this remains essentially true as, for example, the dance of the honey bee to communicate the distance and direction of a food source. With complex organisms such as man, very little of what is present in the behavioural repertoire of the mature adult is inherited in its final form. Exceptions are, of course, the functions that keep the organism alive, such as heartbeat, breathing and swallowing. The rest develop as a result of complex interaction of heredity and environment.

If the human infant does not inherit ready-made behavioural patterns, what does it inherit which enables it to develop into a complex organism with the ability at maturity to solve abstract and complex problems? At birth the human infant inherits a number of reflexes which can be modified through interaction with the environment. Prominent among these is the sucking reflex about which more will be said later in this chapter. The important point here is that such reflexes can be modified by experience. This is another way of saying that a baby can adapt in response to environmental interaction. This ability to adapt is of course a characteristic common to all life and is fundamental to Piaget's conception of the development of intelligence. Piaget sees in the adaptation of the organism to the environment a fundamental principle which applies to the development of intelligence as much as to any other aspect of development.

But in addition to the principle of adaptation, Piaget postulates another biological principle which is also involved in the development of intelligence: the basic tendency of the organism towards *organisation*. Every adaptive act takes place as part of organised behaviour because all actions are co-ordinated. Adaptive behaviour does not come from chaos and disorder but must be related, through organisation, to the overall system or totality of which it is a part.

At the biological level this organisation is readily apparent when, for example, the pancreas secretes insulin to reduce the blood sugar level. Here the circulatory system and the glands are co-ordinated into an efficient system which is organised to preserve the equilibrium of the body. But it is important to note that this co-ordination or organisation is not independent of the rest of biological functioning but is part of a system of relationships which form a totality of acts of which it is but a part.

Similarly, the tendency to organise is present at the psychological level, and the same principle of interrelationship and integration applies to the development of intelligence. To illustrate with an example from infancy, one can readily observe that at birth a baby can both suck and grasp objects but does not initially co-ordinate these actions. After a time he is able to grasp and suck a desired object. Thus he is able to build up a higher order system from two more rudimentary actions. It is quite apparent from this example that the infant has *adapted* and adapted in an organised manner. Whether it concerns biological or psychological functioning, all individuals adapt to their environment and possess organisational properties which make adaptation possible.

Piaget believes that these principles hold for biological functioning in general, and since he believes that intellectual functioning is only a special case of that, these principles also hold for and define the essence of intellectual functioning. This is one of the difficult concepts of Piaget's theory and in the following pages the specific link between *adaptation, organisation* and *intelligence* is discussed and illustrated.

Piaget argues that we inherit a way of intellectual functioning which operates in interaction with the environment to lead to a progressive development of *intellectual structure*. At this stage we can regard intellectual structures as being strategies, or ways of dealing with the environment. In effect, a structure, i.e., the general form of coping with the environment, is what we have available at each developmental level. Quite obviously, the structures that a typical two-year-old child has available to deal with the environment will be considerably different from those of an eight-year-old. Nevertheless, Piaget believes that the fundamental process (function) underlying the progressive development of each child is identical. Indeed he asserts that the fundamental properties of intellectual functioning remain the same throughout life. They never change but operate whenever there is an exchange between the person, be it an infant, child, adolescent or adult, and the environment. The two basic functions which always operate are adaptation and organisation and to these complementary principles Piaget gives the self-evident name of *functional invariants*, i.e., functions which do not vary.

Further understanding of how the functional invariants relate to intellectual development comes from a closer examination of what Piaget means by adaptation. But this is much more easily accomplished if we expand first of all on the notion of intellectual structures briefly mentioned above because function (adaptation and organisation) and structure are intimately connected.

It has already been stated that intellectual structure may be usefully thought of as that which the individual has available for the interpretation and solution of problems posed by the environment. Just as the body has structures to deal with the world, so Piaget believes that the mind has structures also. Of course, structures are not observable but are inferred from behaviour. They are not considered by Piaget to be a particular part of the mind. Thus the structures of a one-year-old child are considered to be different from a four-year-old child because of the observable differences in behaviour.

Structures change as the result of the interaction of maturation and experience and they always exhibit organisation. Piaget considers that the various aspects or parts of a structure are interrelated and organised and it is this organisation and integration which really defines any particular level of intellectual functioning. Thus an infant whose most advanced achievement is being able to bring the hand into the mouth by a systematic co-ordinated movement has a much less developed structure than the infant who can see a toy, want it, move towards it and overcome a barrier in its path to get it. The name Piaget gave to these interrelated structural aspects or parts was *schemas* (singular: schema).[1]

It is through these intellectual or cognitive schemas that the individual adapts to and organises the environment.[2] Schema is perhaps best illustrated by describing what happens when a child is confronted with a stimulus situation. Typically the child tries to fit the stimulus somewhere. He tries to classify it, to give it meaning in the terms of what he has available for such classification. Suppose a two-months-old baby is given a rattle, the chances are that he will put it into his mouth and suck it because at this stage the schema he has available for dealing with this stimulus is the grasping-sucking schema. The nine-months-old child, on the other hand, may put the rattle to his mouth and suck it but he may also shake it, roll it, hit it or throw it. To the two-months-old baby the meaning he gives the rattle will be in terms of the limitations his schemas impose. His "classification" or "indexing" will be in terms of this intellectual structure or schemas. On the other hand, the nine-month-old child will have a more highly developed structure and in consequence will have schemas available to invest the rattle with a much wider variety of "meanings". He will still most probably apply the sucking-grasping

---

[1] The word "schemas" is preferred by the author to the alternative "schemata" even though in his more recent writings Piaget reserves the word "schema" for the organisation of images and uses the term "scheme" for organisation of actions.

[2] "Cognition: a general concept embracing all forms of knowing. It includes perceiving, imagining, reasoning and judging." (J. P. Chaplin; *A Dictionary of Psychology*, p. 87.) Cognition for Piaget always implies a mode of action, an active connecting process and not a passive connecting of events through external association and repetition, (Kohlberg, 1968). In general the terms "cognitive", "thought" and "intelligence" basically refer to the same thing. These concepts are developed in their specific meaning for this text as the discussion proceeds.

schema but it will be at a different level from the two-month-old child, having been changed (modified or adapted) through the interaction of maturation and experience.

As a further illustration of the concept of schema, consider a child during a car trip through the country who sees some sheep in a paddock and exclaims, "Look at the puppy dogs". Quite obviously the sheep approximated the child's criteria of a dog. When confronted by the stimulus of sheep, the child tried to fit it into available schemas. He saw the sheep in terms of that part of his cognitive structure (schema) which seemed to apply. Thus one other way of viewing the concept of schemas is that they are intellectual or cognitive structures that serve to organise aspects of the environment into categories according to some common property. One very important feature of structures (schemas) is that they change as the result of the interaction of maturation and experience though they consistently exhibit the organisation referred to above.

At birth, the only schemas available to the baby are reflex activities. As we will see when the sensorimotor period (first stage of intellectual development) is discussed, this generalised sucking reflex is soon modified into other sucking schemas which might be labelled the sucking schema leading to satisfaction and the sucking schema leading to non-satisfying consequences. In fact it is from these rudimentary reflexive schemas that the structures of the adult develop through adaptation and organisation. Thus as intellectual development proceeds, the individual's schemas become more *complex, differentiated* and capable of *greater generalisation* to situations yet always organised and integrated.

One of Piaget's chief concerns has been to trace the progressive development of intellectual structures from infancy to maturity. In doing this he has been able to show that there are relatively distinct stages each of which is characterised by certain "logically" similar patterns of thinking. This concept of the relationship of structure to stages of intellectual development is examined in more detail later in this chapter. For the present we return to a consideration of how adaptation relates through intellectual structures to cognitive or intellectual development.

ADAPTATION

Early in this chapter it was stated that adaptation is one of the functional invariants. That is adaptation is going on all of the time. It was also stated that adaptation is a fundamental biological principle and is as much concerned with intellectual as with physical development. For Piaget adaptation has two complementary aspects, *assimilation* and *accommodation*. Assimilation is the intellectual process whereby the individual deals with the environment in terms of his present cognitive structure (schemas). The individual sees something in terms of something familiar.

To return to the example of the child calling the sheep a dog, a child of this age will have many schemas included among which may be one for dealing

7

with small four-legged, woolly animals. The child sees the sheep and applies the schema available. He therefore assimilates (incorporates) his perception of the sheep into his existing intellectual structure. It is important to realise just how this information from the environment is fitted into the existing schemas. In explaining adaptation (assimilation and accommodation) Piaget uses a biological analogy, that of the digestion of food. Piaget notes that in the course of digestion the body incorporates food but it is incorporated according to the biological structure of the particular organism. The form of assimilation of food into the system is dictated by the particular biological structures available to deal with it. Thus the structures of the organism incorporating the food into the system have a fundamental effect on how that assimilation will take place. In the same way when an environmental event is assimilated into the cognitive structure, it is not just a mechanistic trans-action, the assimilating cognitive structure imposes its own "organisation", "meaning" or "interpretation". As Flavell says, it is the "bonding of a reality event to the template of one's ongoing structure" (1963, 48). Even the simplest environmental stimulation is never passively received and registered because knowledge is mediated rather than copied directly. Interposed be-tween a stimulus and its assimilation is the organism, an *active* organism whose cognitions are as much a function of this activity as they are of the actual physical properties of the environment. Thus the organism is in dynamic interaction and can in no sense be thought of as analagous to a camera copying the passing scene faithfully.

But just as the incoming stimulus (environmental event) is being changed through incorporation by the schema, so too is the schema forced to modify by the demands of the environmental event. As Flavell suggests (1963, 48), even in the most elemental cognition there has to be some coming to grips with the special properties of the thing apprehended. The organism or the schema must accommodate.

When a schema and the environment interact and accommodation and assimilation take place, the schema is always modified because while assimila-ting features of external reality to the schema there must also be accommoda-tion (change) in response to environmental intrusion or pressures.

To illustrate the operation of assimilation and accommodation, consider the example of an eighteen-months-old child who is given a wooden box to play with. Let us suppose that he has played with similar sized cardboard cartons before but never with a wooden box. The wooden box is therefore a novel feature of this environment to which he needs to adapt (accommodate and assimilate). The child first tries to lift the box but in doing so he must accommodate to the box in a number of ways:

1   he has to accommodate visually in order to perceive the box;
2   he must accommodate to the distance between himself and the box;
3   he must adjust his fingers to the shape of the sides and to the texture of the wood; and
4   he must accommodate his muscular exertion to the weight of the box.

Thus, in lifting the box the child is forced to make a series of accommodations and so modify his structures (schemas) to meet the demands of the environment.

But at the same time as he accommodates, the child also assimilates. Prior to being presented with the box the child has already grasped and lifted objects, including cardboard cartons. Therefore he has a well-formed structure or schema of behaviour already. On first seeing and attending to the wooden box he tries in a sense to transform the object into something which is familiar; to respond to the wooden box as he has responded to other similar objects such as cardboard ones. He tries to "fit" the "stimulus pattern" or assimilate the wooden box to existing schemas leading to the accommodations mentioned above.

Thus the lifting of a wooden box by an eighteen-months-old child clearly involves adaptation to an aspect of the environment and, as such, it involves both assimilation and accommodation. Whenever adaptation takes place both assimilation and accommodation are involved and they occur simultaneously. But they do not always occur in the same proportion. When adaptation takes place either accommodation or assimilation can but does not necessarily predominate. Thus when a child is engaged in imitation, accommodation predominates. When a child is playing, assimilation predominates. (This important topic will be discussed more fully when the second stage of intellectual development, the Preconceptual or Symbolic Stage, is discussed in a later section.) But a child of eighteen months has already developed through adaptation other schemas for dealing with a wooden box. Having succeeded in lifting the box and standing it on its end, the child proceeds to turn the box over and stand on top of it. In so doing he is applying the schema of standing on the box and in adapting to this the child will accommodate and assimilate. In his previous experience with the environment, the child has climbed and stood on chairs and other items of household furniture. Soon the child tires of standing on the box, turns it over again and sits in the box, probably in similar fashion to the way he has sat in cardboard cartons. Thus he has assimilated the wooden box to existing schemas. He has invested it with "meaning". But in doing so he has had to accommodate to such things as its rigidity and texture as he feels the stiffness of the box against his back and feet and the roughness of the wood on his hands and on his fingers. In fact all of the child's dealings with the wooden box have been in terms of the *actions that he can apply to it.*

The organism is always active and interprets the environment by the actions that can be applied to it even if this is only mental activity as it is at later stages. In the period that Piaget designates the Sensorimotor Period— from birth to approximately two years—this activity frequently takes the form of overt action. In fact in the period of infancy, Piaget labels schemas by the behaviour sequences to which they refer and speaks, for example, of the schema of sucking and the schema of sight. Yet no two behavioural sequences of the one schema are exactly alike, even such elemental ones as grasping. There is nonetheless a core of similarity that gives a schema the cohesiveness which permits repetition of the schema and its consequent growth. Through repetition the schema incorporates a variety of objects into itself. Its field of application therefore becomes wider and at the same time, because of the variety of the qualities in the objects assimilated, the schema is differentiated also, so that the schema responds differently to the various objects it assimilates.

Reviewing what has been said so far we find that the human infant is born with a number of reflexes which are capable of modification as the infant adapts to the environment. Adaptation applies to psychological (intellectual) development and is always organised and co-ordinated. The two processes which are simultaneously involved in adaptation are accommodation and assimilation. With respect to intellectual development, accommodation and assimilation operate in such a way as to result in the progressive development of intellectual structures (schemas) which may be conveniently regarded as being strategies or schemas of action for coping with the environment. Structures change over time and become progressively more complex and efficient. The principle of adaptation presupposes activity on the part of the organism such that modification of structures is never a passive reception and registration of environmental stimulation. Knowledge of reality is always relative to the intellectual structures of the person who is responding.

EQUILIBRATION AND EQUILIBRIUM

To account for the dynamics of the interaction or exchange between the individual and the environment, Piaget invokes the very important explanatory principle of *equilibration* whose operation leads to a state of *equilibrium*. Essentially, equilibrium refers to a balanced state of affairs within the organism and can refer both to biological and psychological states. For example, a person experiencing a rise in body temperature above typical body heat will automatically attempt to make adjustments in the direction of normality. The process of making the adjustment is what Piaget means by equilibration and the adjusted state is what he means by equilibrium.

Similarly psychological (intellectual) equilibrium can be conceived as the compensation which results from the activities of the subject in response to external intrusion (attention to environmental object or event). In intellectual development equilibrium is the process of bringing accommodation and assimilation into a balanced co-ordination, the result of which is equilibrium. As Piaget puts it "all behaviour tends towards assuring an equilibration between internal and external factors or, speaking more generally, between assimilation and accommodation" (Piaget, 1968(a), 103).

For Piaget, this process of equilibration which he sees operating continuously in all interaction between the developing person and the environment is that which promotes change and adjustment—the motive force behind the "coming into being" of all developing structures. It is most important to realise, however, that equilibrium does not refer to static balance. Accommodation and assimilation come into balance only to prepare the subject for a new disequilibrium.

10

On the intellectual level the balance that is achieved through accommodation and assimilation makes the person ready for further adaptation and modification. This balancing effect is a very necessary part of intellectual development. If the individual assimilated all the time and never accommodated, or accommodated all the time and never assimilated, there would be no patterned development, no stability or integration and very little dependable and consistent behaviour. It is the process of equilibration that ensures that the interaction the organism has with the environment through assimilation and accommodation is balanced.

The principle of equilibrium is involved in another way in intellectual development. Intellectual development that starts at birth and reaches fruition in adulthood consists essentially of activity directed towards equilibrium. Just as the body evolves toward a relatively stable level characterised by the completion of the growth process and by organ maturity, so mental life can be conceived as evolving toward a final form of equilibrium represented by the adult mind.

Equilibration then is the process which seeks to establish equilibrium between accommodation and assimilation in the interests of the individual's progressive development towards more complex and mature forms of mental functioning. Viewed another way it can be regarded as the internal regulatory factor underlying development. For Piaget the organism does not sit around waiting for something to happen but actively seeks interaction with the environment: "Once a structure is present, utilising it becomes a need which is satisfied through exercise or through function pleasure . . ." (Elkind, 1968, xiv). The equilibrium of the cognitive structure is a dynamic one achieved in order that the organism may once again interact and so develop progressively. Piaget does not find it necessary to invoke the concept of needs energised by drives or other extrinsic motivations (as do many psychologists) since cognitive structures are self motivating.

How then does Piaget view motivation, for this is surely a most important question for teaching. To answer this we return to accommodation and assimilation and consider their operation in two extreme examples. Consider, first of all, what relevance differential calculus has for the ten-year-old child and, conversely, what relevance the shaking of a rattle has for an adult. If these examples are examined it can be seen that when a feature of the environment is outside the accommodative grasp of the individual (calculus to a ten-year-old), the individual simply ignores it, for the task is too difficult and too far removed from the current state of his schemas for it to have any significance. It is simply a non-problem. Teachers all over the world can attest to this situation. Similarly, if the task is so easy that the individual can assimilate it easily, he becomes bored and quickly loses interest. Again teachers would heartily concur.

To Piaget, the individual is most interested in that which is moderately novel. That is, interest is highest in that which is neither too familiar nor too novel to correspond to existing schemas. Thus it is not the object as such which interests the child but how the object or experience *relates* to his

11

previous experience and to his current cognitive structures. Thus it may be said with respect to Piaget's view of motivation: that the individual actively seeks new stimulation; and the individual is interested in that which *matches* his current cognitive structure in such a way that it is moderately novel so that accommodation and assimilation will be possible and through the process of equilibration will lead to equilibrium or balance of the cognitive structures at a new level preparatory to the search for new experiences.

This is saying that the individual can only respond to that for which he is ready. Therefore, in so far as he is seeking new experiences which must match the state of his current cognitive structures, the child is literally the architect of his own intellectual development. This is the dilemma of the schools for it clearly points to the need to have each child, at least for a large part of his classroom experiences, working on a problem that is specifically designed for his own state of development. Teachers have long been aware of this and have sought to give effect to it under the general heading of *individual differences*. The problem of matching current cognitive structures with appropriate experiences is so fundamental that much of Chapter 5, which deals with the general implications of Piaget's theory, is given over to its discussion.

PIAGET'S STAGES OF INTELLECTUAL DEVELOPMENT

Implicit in the foregoing discussion has been the all-important point that intellectual functioning is dependent on the cognitive structures available at any one time. These structures develop continually as the individual matures and interacts with the environment. But Piaget has been able to show that their development falls into several clear stages, each defined by a characteristic way of functioning. It is probably this aspect of Piaget's theory which is known best.[3] What follows then is a comprehensive account of the development of these stages preceded by a short discussion of some important general attributes of these stages.

There are a number of ways of classifying these stages, but the one below is preferred because the names are to a certain extent indicative of the characteristics of the thought processes at each of the levels.

Stages of Intellectual Development

	APPROXIMATE AGE RANGE
Sensorimotor Stage	Birth to two years

[3] Piaget's stage concept has been questioned on several grounds, e.g., that it gives the impression that intellectual development proceeds by a series of abrupt movements or that his concept of stages does not indicate the fluctuations that may occur within any one stage. A comprehensive discussion along these lines can be found in D. P. Ausubel, *Jour. Res. Sci. Teaching*, 2, 1964, 261-266. See also Piaget's discussion of the problem of stages in J. Piaget, *Science of Education and the Psychology of the Child*, 1971, 170-173.

Preoperational
    (a) Preconceptual or symbolic   two to four years
    (b) Intuitive or Perceptual   four to seven years
Concrete Operational   seven to twelve years
Formal Operational   twelve to fifteen years

In considering these stages it must be borne in mind that although we speak of "thinking" and "thought" at all levels, true logical thought does not occur in terms of Piaget's criteria until the stage of *concrete operations*.

There are several features of these stages which require comment before each is described in more detail.

1 The stages do exist and have been found to do so by investigators other than Piaget, some of whom were unsympathetic to his point of view when their investigations were made.

2 The stages always occur in the order in which Piaget says they do with the exception that many retarded children fail to reach the final two levels, the highest one in particular. But a child cannot skip a stage. He cannot go direct from the sensorimotor stage to the concrete operational one. Even in some cultures where intellectual development proceeds more slowly, the same sequence prevails.

3 Each stage has an initial preparation period and a final period of achievement as the process of equilibration continuously operates to develop structures at ever increasing levels of functioning. The structures which are developed in earlier stages are incorporated into and built on in the later stages. Intellectual development is a progressive integration of structures from birth onwards.

4 Although a particular developmental span, e.g. the concrete operational stage, is referred to by the one name from onset to consolidation, it is often the case that a cognitive structure which can be applied to a certain task "A" cannot be applied by the same child to task "B", yet later during the stage the child has no problems of application. Without using many of the technical terms which will be introduced later in the chapter, let us look at an example from the concrete period.

A typical problem presented to a child during this period is to show him two identical balls of plasticine and after he has agreed, upon examination, that they are the same, one of the balls is deformed in some way—it may be successively made into a sausage, a snake-like shape and a pancake. The child is asked if there is still the same amount of plasticine in the deformed ball of plasticine when compared to the ball which remains unaltered. A child who is reasoning at the earlier levels of this stage will assert, often quite confidently, that there will still be the same amount of plasticine no matter what is done to it. Yet he will at the same time assert that the deformed piece weighs more or weighs less. Piaget refers to this as *horizontal decalage* and by it he means

13

that the cognitive structure the child has developed does not automatically have generalised applicability but is itself subject to development.

In later chapters the term horizontal decalage is used in a much broader way to mean a failure to be at a particular stage of reasoning, for example the concrete stage for all things. More recently, Piaget has used another term —"overlaps in extension" (1971, 171)—to refer to this phenomenon.

THE SENSORIMOTOR STAGE (BIRTH TO 18 — 24 MONTHS)

The sensorimotor stage, which is the first stage of development, cannot be classified as a stage of "thought" in the sense that later stages can. True thought, in Piaget's eyes, does not exist until the child reaches the concrete operations stage where the child's thinking exhibits a system of logic for the first time. Real thinking for Piaget is logical and follows the rules of logic. Tracing the development of thought is in fact tracing the development of the appearance of more effective logical systems.

A further feature of the development of thought is the gradual progression from a situation where the environment is overwhelmingly in control (infancy) to eventual autonomy of thought, i.e., to a situation where the thought processes respond to the logic of the situation and judgments are made on the logical relationships existing among objects, statements or events and not, as at earlier levels, in terms of what appears to be.

The development of thought may also be conceived as the progressive development of increasingly effective cognitive structures (schemas), the most effective being those that form a logical system.

The Sensorimotor Stage: The Six Sub-stages

It is difficult to imagine what is going on in the "mind" of a newborn baby. Quite obviously he has no "thoughts" as such, yet it has been clearly demonstrated that even the unborn child can learn, if learning is regarded as a change in behaviour as the result of experience. Thus, although the new born child cannot think at birth he does come into the world with the capacity to adapt as the result of experience and with certain structures, reflexes, which are capable of being modified. Piaget believes that the developed mature intelligence in man has its origins in the modification and development of these reflexes. Thus, intellectual functioning at any stage has evolved in a direct way from earlier levels through the progressive development of structures (schemas). The period of sensorimotor development covers the period from reflex activity to the stage where the child has begun to talk and therefore use symbols. The schemas he has available at two years are more sophisticated, efficient and complete than the rudimentary reflexive schemas at birth.

During this period the child makes some notable gains. First, he develops the concept of the *permanence of objects* and comes to recognise that objects have an existence in their own right. This concept eventually extends to include himself as a separate part of the environment. This development is a very important one for the child because, as will be made apparent later, it assists him to relinquish his *egocentric* view of the world. Egocentric as used by Piaget means that the child in his earlier stages of development is unable to see the world from any perspective other than his own. He is not aware of any other point of view because he is incapable of comprehending it. Initially, he has no perception of himself as an object and this must take place before he can finally objectify his view of the world to the stage where he can effectively take the role of another, and put himself mentally in the position of another person.

The development of the concept of the permanence of objects and of himself as one of them is also related to the second important gain that is made during the sensorimotor period, the beginnings of an awareness of cause and effect relationships.

Piaget has divided the sensorimotor stage up into six substages and in the descriptions that follow it should be borne in mind that each substage forms the basis of, and is incorporated into, the next stage as the structures progressively develop in the same way as the integration and incorporation that occurs from major stage to major stage.

1 *General Assimilating* (0 to 1 month)

The newborn child possesses the basic reflexes of sucking, grasping, crying and the movement of parts of the body. Initially the child sucks at anything regardless of what it is and will grasp automatically any object which touches the palm of his hand. This substage is called the generalising assimilation substage because in the first few weeks of life the infant is merely exercising already existing schemas. As Piaget points out, the organism finds this satisfying. During this time the organism does not differentiate between objects and will suck the nipples of the breast, the sides of the breast, his own fingers should he contact them, and even the edge of the blanket. Thus it can be said that the infant assimilates (incorporates) all environmental (stimulus) events into the existing reflexive schemas in an undifferentiated way.

Gradually the infant modifies his schema as accommodations force him to adapt and he becomes adept at distinguishing between satisfying and non-satisfying suckable objects. His behaviour begins to exhibit the first signs of direction as he seeks and searches for the nipple. This pattern of behaviour was not present at birth and it is an instance of the modification of an existing schema into a more efficient form. Clearly the infant who can seek and find the nipple is adaptively superior to one who continually has to be introduced to it. There is no suggestion, however, that the child at this stage is engaging in intentional behaviour.

2 *Primary Circular Reaction* (1-2 to 4 months)

By the end of Stage 1 then, the infant is able to distinguish in a rudimentary way between objects. At the end of this period he will reject, if hungry, an object placed in his mouth which does not produce milk. This pattern of progressive integration and development of schemas is continued in the second stage with the co-ordination of such schemas as thumb sucking and moving the head in the direction of sounds. In each of these the infant co-ordinates existing schemas into more complex ones which were not present at birth, the co-ordinations in the above examples being hand-mouth and eye-ear respectively. Thus we have the progressive development of schemas into organised systems through the operation of accommodation and assimilation as the organism interacts with the environment.

Characteristic of this period is the activity from which the stage gets its name, the primary *circular reaction*. A circular reaction is one in which the completion of the response pattern or sequence is the cue for its repetition and can be seen to operate when, e.g., the child accidentally causes an interesting or satisfying effect and seeks to reproduce and maintain this satisfying state of affairs by repeating it. One example of this is when the child moves his hand across his field of vision and later repeats it. In this way the child repeats the satisfying effects that the exercise of a schema gives, and the process culminates in an organised schema. It is called a *primary circular reaction* because it is centred on the infant's body.

In this stage the child is beginning to move his attention to the environment although the environment is still overwhelmingly in control. He has no sense of the permanence of an object and if an object within his gaze disappears, it no longer exists for him.

3 *Secondary Circular Reactions* (4 to 8 months)

The circular reactions are now directed to objects in the vicinity of the child as well as to his own body. They are secondary reactions because they involve the co-ordination of activities which are no longer reflexive. Thus the reaching and grasping activities and listening to sounds of the primary circular period are co-ordinated into a higher order schema of, e.g., pulling a ribbon on a toy attached to a bassinet so that the attached object will shake. During this stage there is progress towards object permanence. Prior to this stage the child would not make any attempt to search for the missing object when it was removed from his gaze. He simply moved his attention to something else. Now, however, he will make an attempt to search for an absent object, but he does not persevere long.

Associated with the development of the permanence of an object is the development of the concepts of time and space. It is part of Piaget's conception that the idea of space and time are built up gradually as the child matures and interacts with the environment concomitant with the progressive change in cognitive structures.

As the infant becomes more adept at the co-ordination of sucking, hitting, grasping, pulling, seeing etc., he begins to move things about and there now develops an elemental concern for the relation of objects to one another. The infant now begins to become concerned with the positions of objects around him (space) as well as with the actions he can apply to them. Despite progress

16

with respect to object permanence, the child remains egocentric during Stage 3. He is still a long way from the time when he will be able to see himself as a self.

4 *Co-ordination of Secondary Schemas* (8 to 12 months)

The child is now moving towards the end of its first year of life and the co-ordination and development of schemas provide further advances. The concept of the permanence of an object is now fairly well established and the infant comes to see objects other than himself as "causes". At this stage too there is evidence of the development of "intentional" or means-end relationship and the child begins to anticipate events.

During Stage 4, the child clearly indicates that he has an end in view and uses certain means in order to reach this end. The child selects the means intentionally before initiating behaviour. Thus a child will remove a barrier (object) to reach a predetermined goal. The infant is now able to anticipate events in a new means-end relationship. Here, once again, we see the co-ordination of several schemas in one higher order action. Consider the example of an infant who sees a toy he wants on the other side of a large but empty cardboard box. He will crawl purposively in the direction of the toy virtually brushing aside the cardboard box as he quickly grasps the toy. Analysis of this sequence clearly reveals evidence of earlier schemas which have now been co-ordinated into the one action sequence (co-ordination of secondary schemas).

But in reaching the toy the infant has shown a degree of originality, although limited, that was not present before because he is able to develop new means he did not previously have. To Piaget, this intentional behaviour represents *intelligent behaviour*. Furthermore, the actions or co-ordinations that were applied to reaching the toy are now capable of being generalised to other related situations. At this time, too, certain "signs" are recognised as preceding certain actions.

Further development takes place with respect to object permanence parallel with the development of manipulative skill and higher order manipulations. The infant is now able to examine objects more effectively, turning them this way and that as he moves them closer and further away. Through such behaviour the infant comes to realise that the objects remain the same no matter what position they are in. This can be seen clearly when a feeding bottle is presented to the infant the wrong way round and he quickly changes it.

5 *Tertiary Circular Reactions* (12 to 18 months)

Tertiary circular reactions get their name from the fact that the child now actively "experiments" in order to investigate the properties of objects and events whereas primary circular reactions were concerned with the action of the infant's own body and secondary circular reactions with direct actions on the environment.

With the advent of this new stage the child tries different ways of producing satisfying or interesting events through active experimentation. Unlike Stage 3, where the infant tries to repeat the satisfying event by the application of fairly rigid schemas, the child now initiates activities which will lead to variations in the interesting event itself. In addition, the infant behaves as if he is interested in what happens to the object as he acts upon it. Through subjecting the objects in his environment to exploration on a trial and error basis he discovers something of their properties. Through this "experimental" approach the infant discovers new means for reaching goals. When an infant at this stage comes up against a problem which cannot be solved using available schemas, the infant will experiment and develop new means for the solution of the problem.

The child is now able to adapt to unfamiliar situations and, through accommodation and assimilation, develop new means. At this stage Piaget would not refer to this new found ability as the ability to think, for thought is the application of logical structures and comes much later. He does, however, regard the ability to solve new problems as an indication of intelligent behaviour.

During this stage, the infant is making considerable progress with respect to the concept of object permanence. The child is now able to cope with *sequential displacements*. As long as he sees where an object is hidden, he will look for it there. Prior to this the child would look for the object in the place where it was usually hidden. The child, however, is still unable to search for objects which he has not seen hidden. This development comes with Stage 6.

There is evidence too, at this stage, of parallel development in the concept of causality both with respect to other persons and to objects. This is apparent in the case of persons when the child looks to another, usually an adult, to assist when, for example, he cannot open a box. He may even go to the extent of placing the adult's hand on the box, thereby indicating that he realises that he depends on the adult to execute the actions he finds too difficult. Objects, too, are now seen as causes of action that are outside the child. One example occurs when a child is presented with a new toy which is placed on the edge of the table. In this situation the child will grab the toy, anticipating that it will fall. Thus the child's concept of the permanence of objects and his appreciation of causality both show a considerable advance on previous stages.

6 *Beginnings of Thought* (18 to 24 months)

Stage 6 may be regarded quite properly as the transition between the sensorimotor stage and the preconceptual or symbolic stage (Preoperational). Quite marked advances occur during this period as the child is now able to represent objects mentally (internally) and to use this representation in the solution of problems. Whereas previously the child solved problems by experimenting actively to develop means for problem solution, the development of new means during this stage is attained without active experimentation. The child is capable of finding new means by internalising action. When faced with a problem, such as opening a box, the child does not now run off all the actions that can be applied but "he stops the action and attentively examines the situation after which he suddenly slips his finger into the crack and succeeds in opening the box" (Piaget, 1969, 12). Unlike the previous stage, experimentation is now interiorised and the sudden solution to this sensorimotor problem indicates that the solution was arrived at internally through the co-ordination of schemas and was independent of external experience.

This is a distinct advance, for whereas "thought" in the previous stage was characterised by the experimental combination of actions that could be applied, "thought" in Stage 6 is representational, for the child can now represent and combine actions internally which is a much more rapid and efficient way of dealing with the environment. It is the culmination of two years of progressive development.

At Stage 6 there is a further development in the child's concept of the permanence of an object as the child is now able to search for and find objects which he does not see hidden. This means that the child is now able to "keep in mind" an image of an object and to realise that no matter where the object is it still has permanence. Not only can the child internalise actions in solving problems, but he can internalise images of objects and evoke that image when searching. This superior ability to represent objects "mentally" has a significant effect upon the child's development of notions of causality. In Stage 6 a child frequently demonstrates an appreciation of cause and effect. This can be seen clearly when a child engaged in pushing a box around a room gets it stuck between a lounge chair and the wall and is unable, through his own cramped position, to pull the box clear. Almost immediately the child moves around the chair to the other side of the box and pushes the box out. Clearly the child, through internalisation, has invented the means to the solution of the problem. He thereby demonstrates an understanding of cause and effect.

THE PREOPERATIONAL PERIOD

The preoperational period extends from approximately two years to seven. Several methods of classification have been employed by commentators to outline this period, but the one favoured by the writer is the twofold division of: Preconceptual or Symbolic Period (2 to 4 years); and Intuitive or Perceptual Period (4 to 7 years).

This classification is preferred because the labels used define, to a certain extent, the characteristic mode of thinking which prevails during the particular period. It is, however, difficult to talk exclusively about the Pre-conceptual and Intuitive phases because inevitably an aspect raised in one phase has connections with the other. In general, discussion will be confined to the one stage and if, during this discussion, it becomes necessary to refer to connections with another stage this will be made explicit in the text.

Preconceptual or Symbolic Period (2 years to 4 years)

Symbolic Function

The most significant advance during this period is the development of the *symbolic function*. By symbolic function is meant the ability to represent something such as an object, event or conceptual schema by what Piaget refers to as a *signifier* (1969, 51). This can be language, a mental image or a symbolic gesture. One important aspect of this new development is the ability to represent, by using words, mental symbols etc., something which is not present. This is an important progression because it frees the child from dealing with the present only, in the sense that he is not now confined to acting on things in the immediate environment. He can evoke the past and his thinking is now much more efficient than previously. Briefly reviewing the development of thought to this stage, we have the interpretation of the environment by the action that can be applied to it, followed by the internalisation of actions which allowed sensorimotor problems to be solved without direct action and now this further development where the child can form mental symbols of objects and events. Thus, besides extending the scope of the child's thinking, this new development also speeds it up and in that particular sense the child's thinking is more efficient.

The Formation of Mental Symbols

For Piaget the formation of mental symbols can be traced directly to imitation which begins in the sensorimotor period. Piaget (1969, 53) gives the example of a sixteen-months-old girl who sees a playmate become angry, scream and stamp her foot. The child has not seen this happen before but an hour or two after the departure of the playmate, the child imitates the scene, laughing. Piaget refers to this as *deferred imitation* which he believes constitutes the beginning of representation. Thus the sixteen-months-old child was able to witness a sequence of behaviour, represent it to herself in some way and at a later stage imitate the behaviour. Piaget also notes with this example that it is a good illustration of the beginning of a *differentiated signifier*. The representation the child had of the behaviour of her playmate referred to the behaviour not perceptible at the moment. The child thus demonstrated that some of the signifiers she now had (signifier being that which stands for something) referred to absent objects and events as well as to present objects and events.

In typical fashion, Piaget shows how the child's early sensorimotor imitation, which is in effect overt imitation, gradually becomes internalised until it becomes possible to speak of internalised imitation as a mental symbol. As an example of overt sensorimotor imitation, Piaget cites the occasion on which one of his children, Lucienne, having observed that her father's bicycle moved back and forth, swayed in imitation of the bicycle's movements. To this infant, signification or representation of the bicycle was by the action of swaying.

But the child moves on from this stage to where the amount of action or movement becomes very slight until the only movements discernible are the almost imperceptible movements of the muscles. The amount of overt representation (action) at the end of the sensorimotor period is considerably reduced and the older child may simply imitate the bicycle by slight muscle movement. Internal imitation eventually becomes so efficient that it is very difficult to detect overt behaviour at all.

Symbol representation by internal imitation is extended by Piaget to cover visual imagery as well. Piaget maintains that visual perception is just as much an activity as causing the body or parts of the body to imitate an object or event. In perceiving an object such as a book, the child has to make a series of eye movements and bring into operation the complex nervous system which integrates eye and brain. When at a later stage the child gets a visual image of the book he will, according to Piaget's theory, go through the initial process of perception (action) in an abbreviated form, just as he did in forming the symbol of the open box, or of the bicycle. Thus the visual image is another version of internal imitation and as such constitutes a symbolisation of the object. The visual image is thus a mental symbol originating in basically the same way as the other cases of internal imitation referred to above.

There is however a very important aspect which must be noted in connection with the symbol. From the foregoing it can be easily seen that the *symbol* (mental symbol) is formed personally. A symbol, that is the way it represents what it represents, is unique to the individual and it is formed through accommodation. It is formed through accommodation because it is formed through imitation and imitation involves modifying the structure to meet the demands imposed by the environment. Imitation involves accommodation because it involves modifying the structures (schemas) so that they will parallel the behaviour of another person, or the characteristic of an object. This can be readily seen in the cases referred to above, viz., the imitation of the temper tantrum, the imitation of the movement of the bicycle and the imitation of the opening of a box.

Thus one very important aspect of symbolic functioning is the development and use of symbols which are personal to the individual. In addition to the formation and use of symbols which are created by the person himself, there is another kind of symbolic function, *words*, which Piaget refers to as *signs*. Words are arbitrary, conventional, and are transmitted by the culture. Words or signs are received by the child through imitation, but this time as an acquisition of external models. However, the ability to use language emerges at about the same time as the other aspects of symbolic functioning and will be discussed separately later in the chapter.

One very important aspect of the formation of mental symbols is the meaning that is attached to them. Remember that as the child grows older the symbolic function will involve both symbol—what the object means to the child himself—and sign (word), the culturally accepted label.

Piaget is concerned to point out that the signified (by which he means what the word stands for, or the meaning) cannot be the real object. It must always be an intellectual or mental construction of the real object. It must be the way in which the child sees it or understands it. What, for example, does a child's mental symbol of a "billycart" or "go cart" refer to? It depends on the child. For one it will represent a four-wheeled cart-like object which careers down hills at great speed and provides considerable enjoyment. To another child it is also a four-wheeled cart-like object, but it signifies for him something to be feared. Although each child could quickly point to a "billycart" and identify one from a group of other wheeled objects, each has assimilated "billycart" to a different schema. Billycart therefore refers to the particular understanding that, through assimilation, each child has constructed. The schemas which provide the meaning (the thing signified) have been formed as the result of the interaction of the child with the environment. The resultant meaning has come about through accommodation (change in response to the environmental pressures) and assimilation (the incorporation into existing schemas).

Internal imitation then is basically accommodation as the child is forced to modify his structures as he represents an aspect of the environment. This leads to the formation of symbols which are developed as meanings through assimilation into the personal mental schemas of the individual. Words, which are signs, are acquired through imitation too. But they are initially imitations that are external to the child. The meaning of a word is largely decided by the culture or sub-culture to which the child belongs but it does have a common or shared signification (what it stands for) from which it derives its usefulness in communication.

Play

In Piaget's opinion *symbolic play* "is the apogee of children's play". Symbolic play, or the game of pretending, is another facet of symbolic function which Piaget (1969, 53) says is unknown at the sensorimotor level. By symbolic play, as the name suggests, Piaget refers to the way in which young children use one object or situation to stand for another while playing. Thus Piaget observed one of his own children using the corner of a tablecloth to represent a pillow at the sensorimotor stage. When the child is older the symbolic play becomes more sophisticated. Piaget (1969, 59) reports that a child some time after hearing a church bell, and enquiring at the time as to how the bell worked, stood stiffly beside her father's desk. Upon being told that she was bothering her father she replied, "Don't talk to me, I'm a church!"

Once again in these examples it is clear that the child is using deferred imitation. In the case of the church bell example she uses a symbol (signifier) to stand for the church. The child knows perfectly well that she is not a church but she has structured a symbol to substitute for it and through assimilation (incorporation) to existing schemas this symbol is given the meaning she expressed by imitating or playing that she was a church.

For Piaget symbolic play has considerable significance for intellectual social and emotional development and it is worthwhile to explain this in some detail. He observes that symbolic play is an essential function in the life of the child (1969, 57). The child is forced "to adapt himself to a world of adults whose interests and rules remain external to him, and to a physical world which he understands only slightly".

It is therefore impossible for the young child to adapt to reality as a fourteen-year-old would. The schemas he has available for modification, and the structure he has available for dealing with the world, are so poorly developed and undifferentiated that a great deal of the stimulation he encounters just washes over him. It is once again the problem of matching experiences to the level of the cognitive development. What the child needs is some way of incorporating or assimilating the demands and events of the world, in which he must live, to the existing schemas he has available. He wants something which will transform reality by assimilation (incorporation) into the needs of the self. He requires something which will match his present needs with his present ability. To Piaget this is supplied by *play*, symbolic play in particular. Play, then, is largely assimilation, while imitation is largely accommodation.

Piaget observes that the essential instrument for social adaptation, language, is not of much use to the young child because it does not permit him to express his needs or his living experience of himself; his emotions. What the child requires is a means of self expression in which the meanings are constructed by himself and which is capable of being moulded to his wishes. For Piaget symbolic play fulfils this role because in it the child uses the symbols (meanings) he has borrowed from imitation to serve as a symbolic "language" which thus serves the function of what for an adult would be internal language. To illustrate this point Piaget cites the example of the young child who observed, with deep interest, a plucked duck she had seen on the kitchen table. Some time later the child was found lying on a sofa in such a manner that she was thought to be ill. As Piaget reports, at first she "did not answer questions; then in a faraway voice said 'I'm the dead duck!' " For Piaget this was more than simply recalling an interesting event in that the child was using direct symbolism to relive the event.

Between two and four years symbolic play forms a large part of the child's activities and is of considerable assistance to the child in handling the frustrations and conflicts which come when he is forced to conform to a set of social rules, and obey commands whose purpose he does not comprehend and which frequently cut across his own needs and desires.

Piaget observes that during this period symbolic play is concerned primarily with affective conflicts: ". . . if a child has been frightened by a big dog when it comes to a symbolic game things will be arranged so that dogs will no longer be mean or else children will become brave" (1969, 60). By using symbolic play in this way the child is able to compensate for unsatisfied needs, as well as resolving conflicts, and can also mentally reverse the roles of obedience and authority as, e.g., when a girl makes her doll finish an unwanted meal. Thus the child through symbolic play is able to adjust to reality by interpreting it in her own terms and thereby providing an essential instrument for the maintenance of emotional stability.

Drawing

In his work on symbolic function, Piaget draws attention to drawing which, like symbolic play, gives the child pleasure and also assists him to interpret the world by imitating the real. For Piaget, drawing is imitative accommodation. As the child draws and tries to represent an aspect of the environment, he is forced to modify his schema.

Initially, at two to two-and-a-half years, the child merely scribbles and, as Piaget notes, this is pure play. But soon after this the child begins to represent forms and drawing may be said to have begun.[4] Piaget favours Luquet's classification of stages and interpretation and he has shown that until about eight or nine the child's drawing is realistic in intention but the child initially draws what he knows about persons or objects long before he is able to draw what he sees. Thus the child does not represent (draw) what he perceives but reproduces what he has constructed through the operation of accommodation and assimilation which is of course dependent on the stage of development he has reached.

Luquet shows how the realism of drawing passes through several different phases. The first phase occurs when the child sees in his scribble drawing some kind of meaning so that the meaning is discovered in the act of making the scribbled drawing. To this phase he gives the name "fortuitous realism". The next phase is that of "failed realism" and in the drawings of this phase the elements of the picture are not co-ordinated into a total picture. Thus the child is likely to draw a man with the buttons alongside the body. The picture lacks integration. This is also the stage of the "bodyless" man when the typical drawing of a man consists of a head with arms and legs attached to the head.

This phase is followed by the phase of "intellectual realism" where the drawing is now co-ordinated but the child includes in the drawing all of the things that ought to be there rather than what can be seen from a particular perspective. Thus a drawing of a man standing behind a paling fence will have the legs visible even though this was not possible when the scene was viewed from the position from which it was drawn. "Intellectual realism" is succeeded at about eight or nine by "visual realism" which is a distinct advance for two reasons. First, the drawing now represents only what can be seen from the position of the artist. Perspective also appears in the drawings. Second, there is an overall plan in the arrangement of the drawing and clear evidence of an appreciation of proportion.

This developmental sequence of the ability to draw has very interesting parallels with intellectual development of later stages, particularly in the transition from the intuitive to the concrete levels of reasoning soon to be discussed, and which the writer believes have definite implications for the teaching of art in the infants school. The intellectual developments referred

---

[4] The discussion of this aspect of child development (drawing) will encompass a much wider period than the preconceptual and will trace development from approximately two to ten years of age.

to are the ability at about seven to appreciate the "permanence" of spatial relationships both in two and three dimensions, and the ability to see things from the perspective or physical position of another. This point will again be raised when the intuitive-concrete stage is discussed.

Language

Language provides a fourth element or aspect of symbolic function and as indicated in the discussion above concerning signs, quickly becomes established in the preconceptual period. The child is first able to use words in the sensorimotor period but does not use words in a symbolic way. The meaning of words to very young children is not constant and the child at this age responds to words in a way that indicates meaning is personal and does not represent any socially shared meaning.

The child begins in the sensorimotor period by using "one word" sentences and by the end of the second year has usually progressed to two word sentences. From two to four years the use of language expands rapidly and the child gradually masters the rules of syntax while his understanding of the spoken word also increases. During this stage the child gradually attains the ability to use words to stand for absent objects or events as well as for actions and wishes that are immediately present.

Piaget notes (1969, 86) three differences between verbal and sensorimotor behaviour:

1 Sensorimotor patterns, because they must follow events at the same speed as action, are not nearly as rapid as verbal patterns which can represent a long chain of actions very rapidly.

2 Unlike sensorimotor adaptations which are tied to immediate space and time, language enables thought to range over vast stretches of time and space.

3 Thought, through language, can represent simultaneously all the elements of an organised structure. This new-found ability is of course a great step forward in the development of the child.

Thus for Piaget, language, along with the other symbolic functions mentioned above, serves to detach thought from action and this symbolic function as a whole becomes the source of representation. Language, however, plays a particularly important role among the symbolic functions because it brings with it a socially elaborated system of classifications, relations, meanings etc. for use in "the service of thought".

Piaget, however, has very firm views about the relationship between language and the development of thought in terms of its relationship to the development of logical thought or operations. This is a matter of some controversy and will be taken up again in Chapters 4 and 7. For the present it is sufficient to say that Piaget does not attribute as much importance to language in the early stages of the development of thought as do theorists such as Bruner, Luria and Vygotsky.

Reasoning

In this segment attention is directed to the typical style of reasoning exhibited in the Preconceptual Stage. The reason for the use of the name Preconceptual as a label for this stage is discussed.

When a teacher uses the word concept in the sense of referring to concept formation, he usually means that the child has abstracted a generalised notion from a series of particular examples. For example, the concept of a tree would be formed from experience with various types of trees such as pines, gums, willows and even dead trees. The important point here is the *generality* of the idea he has formed concerning a tree. A teacher intent upon developing the notion of area in children of about twelve years of age could proceed by using either *deduction* or *induction* or most likely both. Deduction refers to reaching conclusions about a specific case from an understanding of a general rule or principle. Thus, given the area of a rectangle as "length by width", the child applies this to the problem of finding the area of a rectangle four inches by three inches because he can see that this specific case fits the general principle. Induction refers to the development of a general rule or principle from a series of specific instances. The child arrives at the concept of the area of rectangles from experience with calculating the area of specific rectangles.

But a child of two or three cannot reason either inductively or deductively but instead reasons *transductively*. In transductive reasoning the child goes from particular to particular without any apparent logical connection, as when Piaget reports that on an afternoon when Lucienne did not take a nap she said: "I haven't had my nap so it isn't afternoon". Similar reasoning can be seen in the young boy who wanted a lolly from the corner grocer shop after it had closed for the day. He stoutly maintained that the shop was not closed but his mother insisted firmly that it was. A few minutes later the child rushed into the house and said, "The grocer's shop is open because the grocer just walked past our house". There is of course a certain logic in the thinking of Lucienne and the boy wanting to go to the grocer, but it is not a logical connection in the usual meaning of that term and is far different from the logic that can be applied by a twelve-year-old. At this preconceptual stage thinking is related to the wishes of the child as can be seen in the above example of the boy wishing to go to the grocer's shop. The child's desires distort his thinking and in a sense the child's reasoning is aimed at achieving a personal goal.

Transductive reasoning prevents the child from forming true concepts because he cannot cope with general classes. He is unable to distinguish between "all" and "some". Piaget (1950, 127) gives an example of this when he notes that a young child did not know whether the slugs encountered in the course of a walk constituted a single slug which kept on appearing or a class of distinct individual slugs. Preconcepts are schemas which remain midway between the generality of the concept and the individuality of the elements composing them without arriving either at one or the other. They are as yet not true logical concepts.

To illustrate this inability to form concepts, consider the following example which comes from the author's research with children. Several three-year-old children were shown some of the attribute blocks which are part of the structured material of the "Triad Mathematics Laboratory" for Kindergarten (Plate 1). They were asked to hand the experimenter some blocks that were alike. One child handed the experimenter in order a blue circle, a blue triangle, and a red triangle. The child had linked a blue circle to a blue triangle (by colour) and then the blue triangle to the red triangle by shape. A five-year-old presented with the same problem handed the experimenter a red and a yellow triangle. When asked for some more that were alike he handed the experimenter another red and another yellow triangle. When the experimenter put these four triangles on the floor and asked the child to point to some more that were alike he was shown a red and yellow triangle again. Another child of six handed the experimenter all the blue triangles that were in the pile. In the case of the three-year-old child no true concept was formed. With respect to the five- and six-year-old children, both were able to abstract to generality although one had abstracted at a higher level than the other.

The Intuitive (Perceptual) and the Concrete Operational Stages

The intuitive stage extends and develops the progress in thought made in the preconceptual period. In this sense it can be regarded as an elaboration of the preconceptual period and in fact it has already been stated that it is common for writers to discuss these two sub-periods under the one heading of preoperational, and to make no distinction at all. This is a matter of preference, but it is true that the distinction between preconceptual and intuitive is by no means as clear nor as dramatic as the distinction between the intuitive and concrete periods. Discussion proceeds, therefore, by first noting some general points about thought in the intuitive period and continues by contrasting the thought of the intuitive child with that of the child who has reached the level of concrete operations. It is impossible to discuss the intuitive stage adequately without reference to the concrete stage.

The Intuitive (Perceptual) Stage (4 to 7 years)

It is clear that at this stage the child has made considerable progress. His thought has developed to the stage where he can give reasons for his actions and for his beliefs. He is able to classify at a "higher" level, e.g., sort coloured shapes either by colour or by shape, but not initially by colour and shape. Language too progresses rapidly and assists internalisation of behaviour through representation which acts to speed up the rate at which experience takes place. Yet thought at this stage is restricted in quality and effectiveness by two things. It is dominated by immediate perceptions, by the dominant aspect of what is attended to, and by the fact that he is unable to keep in mind more than one relation at a time. These limitations have important consequences and clear implications for those who deal with pre-school and infants school children.

Teachers and parents of children in this stage frequently note that the child seems to contradict himself without any real concern for the facts. This is certainly true from the point of view of the parent for if the successive views of the child are compared by adults they quite often do contradict. This is not so from the point of view of the child because, unable to keep in mind more than one thing at a time, he forgets what went before. Consider the following example. A six-year-old child went recently to the Agricultural Show and on his return drew a picture of what he had seen. In the centre was a large pavilion on each side of which he had drawn a sign covered with wriggly lines to indicate printing (see Fig. 1). Asked to describe the picture the child said that the left hand sign said, "Go in Here" and the right hand sign said, "No Dogs Allowed". The child switched attention immediately to the left hand sign again and said, "That says vegetables but not plants and grass" and pointing to the right hand sign said "That says Chips and Drinks". Ten minutes later the teacher said, "I have forgotten what your signs said, could you tell me what they said again?" The child replied, "That one [left hand sign] says 'In' and that one [right hand sign] says, 'Out' ".

Figure 1

Figure 2

The child here made no effort to stick to his original opinion and was quite unconcerned about the whole matter. To him there was no contradiction.

The same drawing provided a further illustration of thought in this period when the child was asked to say how he travelled to the show, what he did and saw and how he came home. His reply was "I got a mask at the Royal Easter Show. When I went there I saw Mary. My brothers brought me home a present when they went to the show. I went on the Ghost Train at the show."

The task given to this young child would, of course, tax the ability of much older children but nevertheless there is in this reply clear evidence of a lack of direction in thinking—successive, unrelated, in the sense of unordered, explanations. In response to the question of "What makes a car go?" the same child, on the same day, replied, "The wheels. The motor. The petrol. By the steering wheel." Here the child has put together a set of explanations, which although related to the movement of a car do not constitute an ordered explanation. The ideas are merely put side by side as they were when describing his visit to the show. In his earlier works Piaget used the term "juxtaposition" to describe this phenomenon which in effect involves an inability to see any relation among the parts which constitute a whole (Piaget, 1928).

Paradoxically, young children also engage in a type of reasoning in which they tend to connect a series of separate ideas into a confused whole and

29

assign to quite different things a similarity which to the adult is illogical. To this type of reasoning Piaget gives the name *syncretic*. The child reasoning this way perceives the whole but does not see the differences within this whole.[5]

On the surface it would seem that juxtaposition where the child ignores the whole in favour of the parts and syncretism where the child can ignore the parts in favour of the whole are irreconcilable. Analysis shows, however, that both effects are instances of the child focusing on one aspect of the situation at the expense of the other. The child is unable to attend to differences among things and to their similarities at the same time. Each is a special instance of the child focusing upon only one aspect at a time.

It is this characteristic of focusing on one dimension, of attending to a dominant feature, which is characteristic of thought at the intuitive stage. In his later work which was more experimental, Piaget looked at this phenomenon in great detail and it is the results of this work in the form of the various stages of thinking which are perhaps best known. Certainly such results have had a considerable influence on education and teaching in the last twenty years. Discussion proceeds by looking at the key concepts of Piaget's later views on intuitive thinking. It does so by first of all describing two typical experiments that Piaget conducts to determine whether the child is still at the intuitive stage or has progressed to the concrete operational stage. This provides a reference point for a discussion of the properties of thought characterised by these two periods.

A typical experiment of this kind is to present to a young child, say a six-year-old, two equivalent balls of plasticine. When the child agrees that the balls of plasticine are equivalent, one of them is distorted by being rolled into a sausage whose length is approximately three times the width. The child is then asked whether there is more, less or the same amount of plasticine in the sausage as in the ball. A child at the intuitive stage is likely to say something like, "There is more plasticine in the sausage because it is longer", or "There is less plasticine in the sausage because it is thinner". The child who has reached the stage of concrete reasoning might say, "There is still the same amount because you could roll the sausage up again and it would make a ball again", or, "There is still the same amount because you didn't take any away".

A similar experiment requires the experimenter to present the child with two beakers in which there are equal amounts of water. After the child agrees that they are equivalent, the contents of one beaker are poured into a tall thin glass and the child is asked whether there is more, less or the same amount of water in the tall glass as there was in the original beaker. The intuitive child says something like "There is more because it is taller" or "There is less because it is thinner".

[5] It should be noted that these findings with respect to young children's thinking belong to Piaget's earlier period where he was more concerned with analysis of verbal responses (op. cit., 1928).

These two descriptions of experiments represent only part of each experiment. In the plasticine ball experiment the ball is typically deformed into a long snake, a ring, a cake, a flat pancake and frequently cut into many pieces. In the water experiment which is an experiment in the conservation of continuous quantity, the water is frequently poured into a number of smaller glasses. When the experiments are extended in this fashion it is usual to find three stages, not two as indicated above. The succession of stages is from intuitive, through a transition where a child may believe the sausage is the same as the ball but not believe the snake is the same, to conservation where equivalence is unhesitatingly asserted.

There are, of course, obvious similarities in these answers which give insights into the child's reasoning. First there is what Piaget refers to as *centration*. The child centres on one aspect of the situation. In the case of the plasticine ball test it is the shape of the sausage. The specific aspect he attends to is the length or width. He does not attend to both at the same time. In the case of the water in the long glass he attends to the shape again. He centres on the glass's height or thinness but is unable to take into account the reciprocal influence of both. In Piaget's terms he is unable to *decentre* his attention so that it becomes clear that height compensates for width and the amount of water remains the same. The child bases his judgments on what seems to be, on intuition.

It also becomes clear from these illustrations that the intuitive child focuses on successive states. He attends to the plasticine ball in the first instance and then to the subsequent shape. What he fails to take into consideration and what will be a feature of his thinking in the concrete period is the *transformation* between the state of plasticine ball to the state of plasticine sausage. The intuitive child cannot assimilate this because he does not attend to it. His attention is restricted to the particular perceptual event. First it is the plasticine ball that claims his attention, which then shifts directly to the final state, plasticine sausage.

What is required before the child can compensate for the changes described above is the development of a *logical structure* which can be applied to such situations. This is the subject of the next section on concrete reasoning but it is important to mention here that a very important aspect, indeed the key aspect of the development of that logical structure, is the development of *reversibility*. This refers to the ability to mentally return to the starting point of an event, and see, e.g., that the plasticine sausage could be rolled up again into a ball or that the water could be poured from the tall glass back into the beaker and leave the situation unchanged. The intuitive child cannot do this. He cannot shuffle mentally back and forth between the two states. It is this ability above all others which marks the concrete thinker off from the intuitive thinker because it enables him to *conserve*. He is able, by force of his ability to apply a logical structure, to compensate for the biasing distortions of perception.

Once developed and consolidated, this ability to conserve has wide generality of application. The nature of conservation and its relationship to logical thought in the concrete period is more complex than that presented in the preceding pages, and some important elements are discussed in the section on concrete reasoning below. A thorough treatment of the topic in the sense of a detailed examination of Piaget's system of logic as related to thought is, however, beyond the scope of this book. The reader is referred to Phillips (1969), Boyle (1969) and Flavell (1963) prior to reading Piaget's work for a comprehensive introduction to this aspect of the theory.

THE CONCRETE OPERATIONAL PERIOD (7 OR 8 TO 12 YEARS)

The clearest indication that a child has reached the concrete level of reasoning is the presence of conservation. As was seen in the previous section, conservation is basically the ability to reverse internally, to decentre, i.e., to take into account more than one feature at a time and to focus upon the transformation between one state and another.

There is however another important feature of conservation which marks it off clearly from intuitive thinking and that is its wide generality of application. Whereas in the intuitive stage the child could reason successfully along single dimensions, the relations of that period are now co-ordinated into an overall logical system, a general logical structure, whose existence is related to the child's ability to conserve. There are many areas of conception in the concrete reasoning period in which conservation plays an integral part. Researchers and teachers typically explore conservation of continuous quantity, discontinuous quantity, length, two and three dimensional space, area, weight and volume. As was indicated earlier, conservation does not come all of a sudden and apply to every conceptual area. It is typical to find a child able to conserve in one area and not in another. Progress towards conservation is gradual but when it does develop, the underlying logical structure is the same. One frequent finding of Piaget and his co-workers is that there is a definite progression of attainment of conservation with respect to quantity weight and volume. Conservation of quantity appears first, followed by weight and finally, towards the end of the concrete period, by volume. (This particular progression is discussed in more detail later in the chapter.)

The underlying logical structure which is at the base of conservation is what Piaget calls the structure of "groupings".

The psychological existence of "groupings" can be inferred from the responses of the child, for without grouping there could be no conservation. The child who is capable of reasoning with the structure of groupings knows in advance that the whole will be conserved even though it is broken into parts.[6] The five conditions of grouping which form a logico-mathematical scheme are as follows:

---

[6] It should be noted that a grouping combines the attributes of both the *group* and the *lattice*. A discussion of this relationship is beyond the scope of this text and readers should consult, initially, Boyle (1969), Phillips (1969) and Flavell (1963).

1 *Combinativity or closure:* Any two operations can be combined to form a third operation. E.g.: $3 + 2 = 5$; all the boys in the class plus all the girls in the class equals all the children in the class.

2 *Reversibility:* There is for every operation an opposite operation which cancels it. E.g.: $3 + 2 = 5$ is equivalent to $5 - 3 = 2$; all the children in the class with the exception of all the girls in the class equals all the boys in the class.

3 *Associativity:* If three operations are combined it does not matter which are combined first. Another way of putting it is that the same goal can be reached by a different route. E.g.: $(3 + 4) + 1 = 3 + (4 + 1)$; all plants plus all animals plus all rocks equals all animals plus all plants plus all rocks.

4 *Identity:* When an operation is combined with its opposite the result is 0. E.g.: $3 - 3 = 0$; all animals less all animals equals no animals.

5 (a) *Tautology:* Repeating a classification, a relation or a proposition leaves it unchanged. E.g.: all men plus all men = all men; $A < B$; $A < B = A < B$.
   (b) *Iteration* which holds for numbers. When a number is combined with itself the result is a new number ($4 + 4 = 8$; $4 \times 4 = 16$).

When a child has developed the overall structure of groupings he has available a number of important concepts whose existence marks a considerable advance in logical thought and which enables him to reason in a way not possible in the intuitive stage. These groupings which stem from this logical structure are discussed below. They are *classification*, *seriation*, *number* and *space*, all of which are concepts which are of fundamental importance to real understanding in the infants and primary school child.

To this point we have seen that the thinking of the concrete reasoner differs from that of the intuitive reasoner in several ways which can be summed up by saying that he can conserve and that he has available a logical structure which can be applied in such a way as to make his thinking qualitatively superior to the earlier stages. What has not been made clear is why the period is labelled the *concrete operations period*. Operational intelligence or operational thinking is fundamentally the application of a logical system in the service of thought. The operation of the logical system outlined above leads to quite different thought than was possible earlier, in that the child can transform reality by means of internalised actions that are grouped into a coherent, reversible system. The structure available to the child now enables him to compensate internally on a logical basis for, say, the biasing distortions of the plasticine ball test or the water in the jar test. He is no longer tied to surface appearances because his thought is now more autonomous and determined by the logic of the situation. Concrete operational thinking, or more strictly concrete operations, constitutes the first true logical thought.

In Piaget's words concrete operations are called *concrete* "because they relate directly to objects and not yet to verbally stated hypotheses" as they will later. Concrete reasoning proceeds when the objects or the data which are to provide the basis for thought are physically present. (This has important educational implications which are discussed at length in later chapters.) Concrete operations then refer to the child's ability to reason logically about data (objects) which are present, on the basis of intellectual structures characterised by groupings which underlie the ability to conserve and the development of permanent and important concepts such as classification and seriation. In the discussion that follows the development of the concepts of classification, ordinal relations, numerical correspondence, space (including perspective and its effects on egocentrism), substance, weight and volume, area and velocity is explained. The development of these concepts is, of course, at the very base of an adequate understanding of mathematics and science, a point which is taken up in some detail in Chapters 6 and 7.

Classification

Suppose we have:

(a) two solid wooden circles, one red, one blue, one thin and one thick; and

(b) two solid wooden triangles, one red, one blue, one thin and one thick.

If we wish to place these objects into two classes we can put the circles in one class and the triangles in another *or* we can group the red blocks in one class and the blue ones in another *or* we can group the thin blocks in one class and the thick in another.

Examination of these groupings shows:

1   None of the blocks is a member of both classes at the same time. The classes are mutually exclusive or disjoint.

2   Each member of a class is similar in some way. They are either circles or triangles, thick or thin, red or blue. One way of stating this is say, e.g., that redness or thickness is the property which defines the class or is the *intension* of the class.

3   It is possible simply to list the members of the class such as the red circle and the blue circle. A list of the members is the *extension* of the class.

4   It therefore becomes apparent that intension defines extension because if we know the basis on which the class is to be formed we know what can be placed within it.

Piaget has looked at classification developmentally and has found that like other aspects of thought it follows several stages. The rudiments of classification can be found in the sensorimotor period where the child "classified" objects according to the actions that could be applied to them. However it is not classification in the sense of formation of classes, because the sensorimotor child is unable to do this.

Stage 1

But from the stage designated by Piaget as Stage 1, from about two to five years of age, it becomes possible to see attempts at grouping which will gradually develop into classification at later stages. At this stage, the child who is asked to put together things that are alike among squares, triangles, rings and half rings of various colours, will string together objects without an apparent overall plan to guide him. For example, the child will string together a row of circles and squares in no particular order. Sometimes the child will use the objects given him in the experiment to construct a picture or an interesting shape. It is clear that these arrangements do not constitute true classes and therefore the child cannot really classify.

Stage 2

From the ages of about five to seven, children sort objects into groups which satisfy the criteria of class outlined above. When asked to put together things that are alike among circles, ovals, squares and oblongs the child will group first on the basis of all the "round" ones and then on the basis of all the "square" ones and will further subdivide these as shown in Figure 3.

CLASSIFICATION OF GEOMETRIC BLOCKS

Figure 3

At this stage the child seems able to form classes and arrange them hierarchically. Piaget believes, however, that the child at this stage does not understand the relations between the various levels of the hierarchy, i.e., the concept of class inclusion. A typical problem presented by Piaget to test this is as follows. A child is presented with twenty wooden beads, eighteen of which are brown and two of which are white. When the child agrees that all are wooden he is asked which would make the longest necklace, the one made out of the wooden beads or the one made out of the brown beads. A child in Stage 2 frequently answers "The brown beads because there are more brown beads than white beads". The explanation for this is again in terms of centration because the child who gives this answer is centring on the biggest part "brown beads" and ignoring the whole "wooden beads". He is unable to go back and forth mentally and see that the brown beads are a subordinate class of the superordinate class wooden beads.

Stage 3

When a child from about seven years onward is presented with the same problem he is more likely to answer "the wooden beads". Such a child is now able to construct hierarchical classifications and comprehend class inclusion, as e.g., the classification illustrated in Figure 4.[7]

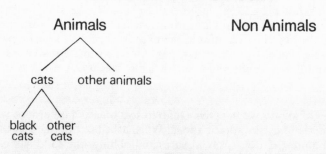

Figure 4

What is apparent at Stage 3, however, is that as with all thought in the concrete stage the child understands class inclusion relations pertaining to objects he can see. But he is not at all sure when asked to classify absent objects. This is a further instance of the difference between verbal and concrete reasoning. In explaining classification Piaget shows how it depends upon the five elements of grouping stated above. A consideration of this is however beyond the scope of this and the reader is referred to Flavell (1963). Classification is an important aspect of the child's understanding of numerical concepts and this relationship will be discussed fully in the chapter relating Piaget's theory to an understanding of number.

Ordinal Relations

In general when we refer to ordinal relations we are referring to the process of ordering numbers, objects, sounds etc., according to size. Thus the numbers 18, 25, 3 and 36 may be ordered going from the smallest to the largest as 3, 18, 25, 36. The absolute size makes no difference. Piaget has studied the child's ability to construct orderings and to establish ordinal relations and has found that here too there are three stages.

[7] A number of investigators, including the writer, have failed to establish the same age range as above for the beads class inclusion test. It seems to be a much more difficult concept than would seem indicated from the above. For example, in some research carried out by the writer, 71 per cent of 60 children between the ages of 7 and 7·5 could conserve on the water in the jar test (continuous quantity) but only 33 per cent could answer correctly the beads test. Of children between the ages of 9 and 9·5, 93 per cent could conserve on the water in the jar test but only 61 per cent on the beads test.

Stage 1 (4 to 5)

One experiment which Piaget does is to ask a child to order ten sticks in order of size. The shortest stick is nine cm long and the longest about sixteen cm. They differ in length by about eight cm. The sticks are presented in random fashion and the child asked to select the smallest, then the next smallest and so on. Sometimes the child is asked to make a staircase. The child in Stage one cannot solve this problem. He either puts the sticks in random order or he puts some in order and the rest at random.

Stage 2 (5 to 6)

Children in the second stage generally succeed in ordering the sticks from shortest to longest, but usually with difficulty and often with several mistakes. The child seems to lack an overall plan and his behaviour suggests that his attempts are based on trial and error. If after constructing the correct order of sticks another set of sticks is presented to the child such that they will fit, in order, between the sticks already arranged, the initial difficulties are highlighted. Children at this stage have great difficulty with this problem and few are able to solve it.

In a further problem the child is presented with a set of ten dolls and a set of ten sticks which are shorter but parallel the sequence of dolls. The child is told that he is to match each stick with each doll so that if the doll were going for a walk he would choose the correct stick. Once again the solution presents difficulty and the method seems to be trial and error.

Stage 3 (6 to 7)

By the time the child has reached six to seven years of age he is able to complete successfully all of the tasks described, and in doing so seems to be following an overall plan. Once again, however, the same restriction that applies to classification with respect to the concrete operational child prevails. He can deal with relations on a concrete level only. This has important implications for the teaching of number which will be discussed in the chapter dealing with the teaching of mathematics. Piaget however has done some interesting experiments on the conservation of number itself and this is the subject of the next section.

Number

There are two aspects of number which interested Piaget which will be examined: one-to-one correspondence and conservation.

One-to-one correspondence consists in pairing each member of one set (Set A) with each member of another set (Set B). When any two sets are in one-to-one correspondence then irrespective of the nature of the objects, each set will be equivalent in number. Conservation of number refers to whether or not a set of objects remains constant as to number, irrespective of its physical arrangement. If Set A and Set B in Figure 5 are initially equivalent on the basis of one-to-one correspondence, does rearranging Set B, as in Figure 6, alter the number of elements in Set B?

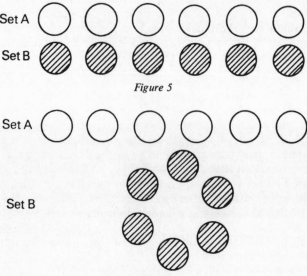

Set A

Set B

Figure 5

Set A

Set B

Figure 6

This is a typical problem posed by Piaget and as with other concepts he found once again a succession of stages. The crucial question being asked is really: what is the process whereby the older child establishes the concept of a set of objects in the same way as the sensorimotor child eventually establishes the concept of the permanence of an object?

Stage 1 (4 to 5 years)

Several problems can be presented to the child to determine one-to-one correspondence and conservation. However, the same example will be used to illustrate the three stages. A child of four years six months was given seven toy egg cups and ten toy eggs. The seven egg cups were placed in a row and the child asked to put as many eggs in a row as there were egg cups. He was instructed to make his own row underneath the egg cups. He put down ten eggs so that the ends of his row matched the ends of the row of egg cups as in Figure 7.

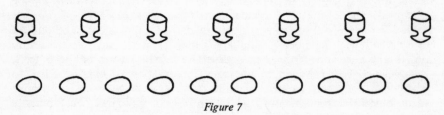

Figure 7

The child was then asked to place an egg in each egg cup so as to make a one-to-one correspondence while the three remaining eggs were discarded. The child has therefore been forced to establish one-to-one correspondence. The child however quickly shows that he does not conserve the numerical equivalence of the two sets because when the eggs are shifted so that they form a longer line than the cups he believes there are more eggs. He fails to conserve because he centres on one dimension and is unable to co-ordinate the two. His reasoning is still tied to perception. He has no logical structure which will permit him to compensate for the bias and distortion presented. It makes no difference to the outcome if the child is permitted to count the eggs and egg cups, for when one set is pushed closer together or moved further apart he asserts inequivalence.

Stage 2
In this stage the child easily establishes two equivalent sets of objects, as e.g. eggs and egg cups but, like one five-and-a-half-year-old tested, fails to conserve when either the eggs or the egg cups are spread out. Thus with reference to Figure 7 the child will say alternatively that there are more eggs because that row is longer or alternatively, there are more egg cups because they are closer together. This is, of course, an improvement over Stage 1 in that the child realises that both density and length are relevant but is still unable to co-ordinate the two perspectives. Reasoning is still dominated by perception as the child fails to decentre.

Stage 3
Between six and seven years of age the child can both establish equivalent sets and conserve. He asserts without hesitation that it does not matter how much one set is changed it is still numerically equivalent to the other. Once again conservation can be explained in terms of decentration and reversibility. The concrete operational child can, in this instance, decentre by co-ordinating the elements of the situation such that if the line of eggs becomes longer than the egg cups then the line of egg cups must be denser. He is able to mentally balance or compensate for the distortion by seeing that density and length cancel one another, which is in effect a form of reversibility because he can see that it is possible to go back to the starting point without altering the relationship. He attends to the transformation or relationship between the sets and not to states exclusively. Sometimes the child may use identity by seeing and saying that as nothing has been added or taken away there must still be the same number of objects.

This ability to conserve sets of objects bears a relationship to classification and seriation, a relationship which is discussed in Chapter 6, but for the present it is sufficient to note that the conservation of a *set* of objects is an important development for the complete understanding of number.

Conservation of area
In *The Child's Conception of Geometry*, Piaget, Inhelder and Szeminska

(1960 262) illustrate the conservation of area with the cows-in-the-field test. In this experiment, the child is presented with two equivalent sheets of green paper to represent fields and a toy cow is placed in each. The experimenter also has a number of wooden blocks which represent buildings. Initially the child is asked: "Which cow has more grass to eat?" and the usual reply is that they both have the same amount. When a building is placed in one field and the same question asked even very young children (e.g., five years) can see that the cow in the field with no building has more grass to eat and that when a building is placed in the other paddock, both cows have the same amount to eat. The picture changes, however, when another building is added to each field such that in one field the buildings are flush against one another and in the other, spread out. When this is done children from five to six years will usually not agree that each cow has the same amount of grass. If more buildings are added, in similar fashion, such that in one field the buildings are placed side by side and in the other spread out, children between the ages of six and seven would frequently agree that the amount of grass was the same up to approximately twelve buildings but when more buildings were added perception dominated and the child believed that the areas were different. From about seven years onward, however, it was usual for the child to assert that the area of grass remained the same no matter how many buildings were added as the child, through the logical operation of reversibility, was able to range mentally back and forth, compensate for the bias and distortion of appearance and realise that area had been conserved.

Conservation of weight and volume

It is usual to include the discussion of the conservation of weight and volume with the discussion of the conservation of substance. Piaget maintains that there is a definite sequence with respect to conservation of substance, weight and volume such that the conservation of substance (5 to 7 years approximately) precedes the conservation of weight (7 to 9 years) which in turn precedes the conservation of volume (10 to 12 years). This is what Piaget refers to as horizontal decalage (cf. Chapter 2), the fact that the child cannot apply his logical structures in all areas at the same time. But before briefly describing an experiment which illustrates the sequence of conservation of substance, weight and volume, it is clear that although the bulk of evidence supports Piaget's contention with respect to the sequence, some studies, e.g. Hyde (1959), did not find this sequence.

Perhaps the best way to illustrate this sequence is to continue with the plasticine ball example. In an extension of this experiment one of the balls of plasticine is cut up into sections and the child is asked whether the pieces weigh as much as the original ball. Piaget claims that the children go through three stages: (a) they say it will not weigh the same; (b) sometimes they agree that it weighs the same but sometimes disagree (transition); and (c) assert unhesitatingly that it weighs the same and give valid reasons for their conviction.

Conservation of volume is tested by repeating the original plasticine ball test of rolling one of the balls into a sausage and dropping it into a jar of water. The child who is unable to conserve volume will either say that the sausage will take up more space than before or he will believe that less space is taken up.

There are several other tests which explore the conservation of volume and one which is frequently cited is that which calls for the child to build a house with as much room as a model 4 cm by 3 cm by 3 cm which he is shown. The task requires the child to build a new house from cubes of side 1 cm on bases of varying sizes. As was stated above, it is typical to find the ability to conserve volume consolidated at about twelve years of age and, as there is usually a sizeable overlap with respect to age ranges in the achievement of all these tasks of conservation, it can reasonably be assumed that there are many children aged twelve for whom the meaningful calculation of volume would present problems.

Concept of velocity

The preoperational child, e.g. a five-year-old, judges the speed of two objects in terms of the order of their arrival at an end point. He has no conception of velocity or speed as a relationship between time and distance travelled. Piaget (1946) demonstrated this by an experiment in which two dolls were moved through parallel cardboard tunnels simultaneously. The cardboard tunnels were of different lengths and the dolls entered their respective tunnels at the same moment and emerged at the same moment at points, designated, for exposition, X and Y. The five-year-old child admits that the tunnels are different in length but maintains that the dolls move at the same speed. In answer to questions he supports this by saying that they move at the same speed because they arrive at X and Y at the same time. If the tunnels are taken away and the dolls are made to run the same distance under the same conditions as before, but in full view of the child, he will now admit that one doll is going faster than the other.

Analysis of the reason for the change in the child's opinion reveals that the child believes that the doll that travelled the longer distance travelled faster because it caught up with and passed the other just beyond XY. The child's concept of velocity at this age is therefore in terms of change in relative position. One car is going faster than another if it overtakes the other, while the one overtaken is going slower.

Overall then, the young child's conception of velocity is intuitive in the sense that it is tied to what he perceives, to what appears to be. Later, which is for Piaget between seven and eight years and for Lovell (1971) in his research between eight and nine, the child comes to understand velocity as a function of distance and time, i.e., when logical structures are available for the co-ordination of these two variables.

Space

The concept of space develops parallel to, and in synchronisation with, the logico-arithmetic operations. The operations connected with the concept of space are called "infralogical", but this is because they relate to another level of reality and not because they develop earlier (Piaget, 1969, 106). In fact the concept of space becomes consolidated during the concrete operational period though slightly later than number. In the discussions that follow, space will be interpreted widely to incorporate such things as perspective. It will not be confined to, but will include, conservation of two-dimensional and three-dimensional space.

Piaget's initial work on space is contained in *The Child's Conception of Space* (Piaget and Inhelder, 1956) and *The Child's Conception of Geometry* (Piaget, Inhelder and Szeminska, 1960). Piaget quite clearly considers that the development of the representation of space is intellectual development so that conceptions of space are built up through the organisation of actions that are applied to objects in space. As with other aspects of intellectual development the very beginning can be traced to the sensorimotor period leading with progressive integration and internalisation to an operational system in the concrete period. The accent as in all developing intellectual structures is on progressive construction, for like other concepts, the concept of space is literally built up through the interaction of maturation and experience and as will be seen from the experiments described below, follows fairly clearly delimited stages.

One of the interesting findings of Piaget is that the development of an understanding of topological space takes place before the acquisition of projective and Euclidean concepts. The three geometries emerged historically in mathematics in the order Euclidean, projective and topological. The logical order is different in that the most general and inclusive system is topology with Euclidean and projective geometries being special cases within topology.

Topological properties relate to such things as continuity and enclosure, that is open or closed space. A good example of what topological space means appears in Figure 8.[8]

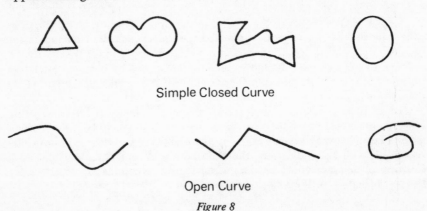

Simple Closed Curve

Open Curve

Figure 8

[8] Taken from the *Guide Book, Triad Mathematics Laboratory for Kindergarten*, p. 50.

Young children meet topological space in the form of open and closed space when they concern themselves with enclosing toy farm animals with toy gates and fences or see a fly buzzing in an empty bottle. The question of open or closed space, in these instances, revolves around the question for the child as to whether or not the sheep can get out of the paddock or the fly out of the bottle. It will be much later before they are concerned to draw a rectangle fifteen centimetres by ten centimetres and very much later before they are concerned with space in the sense of the theorem illustrated in Figure 9.

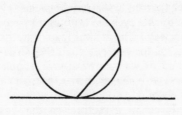

Figure 9

Theorem: An angle between a tangent to a circle and a chord drawn to the point of contact is equal to any angle in the alternate segment.

Piaget's studies show that topological relations are consolidated by about seven years but that Euclidean and projective properties are not integrated into an operational system until about nine or ten years. There is at present some questioning of Piaget's contention with respect to topological and Euclidean space, e.g., Lovell (1971, 102-104). Having reviewed the evidence relating to this question, the writer believes that Piaget's main thesis is tenable at this stage and agrees with Lovell (1971, 103) that more experimental evidence is necessary. One very real difficulty is the dispute concerning the meaning of *topological*.

Some Experiments on Spatial Concepts. For many years, psychologists have been using tests such as the Goodenough "Draw a Man Test" to determine the developmental level of the child. This test does this by comparing a child's drawing of a man with certain standardised versions that have been developed over the years. Psychologists have come to realise that at successive developmental stages the child will be able to reproduce more and more detail and make progressively better attempts at realistic representation. In an earlier section on *Symbolic Function*, it was shown that Piaget believes that what the child constructs in his drawing depends on his current cognitive structure and that he draws what he knows about a person long before he draws what he sees. These earlier representations of the child are, of course, closely connected with the development of the concept of space. If we examine the two drawings of a six-year-old child reproduced in Figures 1 and 2 (pp. 28, 29), several interesting observations can be made with respect to spatial relations. The drawing of "The Easter Show" discussed earlier with

43

respect to the preoperational period contains a typical feature of children's representation of space at about this age, the absence of anything between the representation of the sky and that of the ground. When this child was asked what the gap was there for the child said "It's nothing. That's the sky and that's the ground and that's the big shed." When asked how he could get to the sky the child replied: "You would have to get in an aeroplane or a rocket ship." The drawing of "The Duck" shows similar features. The ground and sky are clearly represented and there is the space between the sky and the ground. In this drawing however, the profile of the duck's face shows the two eyes represented in the one plane.

The child does not see (perceive) this gap between sky and earth in real life nor does he see that the duck's eyes are both on the one side of his face. Why then does he draw it this way? The answer from Piaget's point of view is that his drawing is in terms of his current cognitive structures with respect to spatial representation and as was shown above, topological space develops first and this is concerned with shapes, being together or separated. It is only at later stages that the child can take into account perspective and co-ordinate the various objects in a picture, so that each is seen in proper relationship. The stages through which these various concepts of space develop have been traced by Piaget in a series of experiments and some of these are presented in outline below.

Co-ordination of Horizontal and Vertical. Children are shown two narrow-necked bottles, one with rounded and one with parallel sides, each of which is one quarter filled with coloured water. The children are asked to guess the position the water will assume when the bottle is tilted. Younger children are asked to indicate this on empty bottles of the same shape and size with certain precautions being taken by the experimenter to ensure that he gets the true intention of the child. In general, children over five are given outline drawings of the jars at various angles and asked to draw the position of the water corresponding to each position of the bottle before they see the experiment performed. The children are also asked to draw the edge of the table so that they have a horizontal plane to assist in judging the position of the liquid. When the child has made his drawing he compares it with the experiment which is then performed, and is asked to correct it or produce a new drawing.

During the experiment with water level a small cork with a match stick inserted in it vertically is floated on the surface of the water and the child asked to draw the position of the "mast" of the "ship" when the jar is tilted to various positions. In another version the child is asked to plant posts upright on a model of a mountain, at the top on the slopes or on the ground nearby. The child can also be asked to draw houses, people and trees on the sides of the mountain. Care is taken to discover what the child means by straight and sloping. It should be noted that although certain distinct stages are indicated here Piaget makes it quite clear that development is gradual and continuous.

Stage 1. This lasts until about four to five years and both with respect to water level and to the representation of trees on the sides of mountains, it is clear that children are unable to distinguish planes as such. The liquid is not shown as a surface but as a "quantity" inside the jar as, e.g., in Figure 10.[9]

Figure 10

The representation of people on the side of the mountain shows similar features as e.g., in Figure 11.

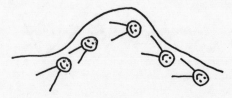

Figure 11

Here it can be seen that the people are placed roughly parallel to the contour of the mountain. Figures 10 and 11 indicate that the child is not thinking in terms of Euclidean concepts such as planes or inclinations but in topological terms.

Stage 2. In general, the child can establish the surface of the liquid as a plane and locate trees on the mountainside. However, when he draws the objects he cannot orientate the water in the tilted vessel or the trees on the inclined slope, despite the fact that at the more advanced level of this stage he can place houses and trees vertically on a model mountain.

An example of the progression in representation at this stage is given in Figure 12. The first set of drawings indicate the earlier phase of this stage where the child believes that the water will move towards the neck of the bottle but will stay parallel to the bottom of the jar. The trees and houses are at right angles to the slope of the mountain. The second set of drawings indicate that the child is on the way to realising that the water will remain horizontal to the table by drawing the water line as a part curve and at least part of one of the objects on the mountain vertical to the horizontal plane.

Stage 3. In this stage the child gradually develops the ability to apply the concepts of the vertical and horizontal to all situations and in the final sub-stage of Stage 3 can do so as soon as the problem is presented. This usually

[9] The drawings which follow have been adapted from Piaget and Inhelder, *The Child's Conception of Space*, 1956.

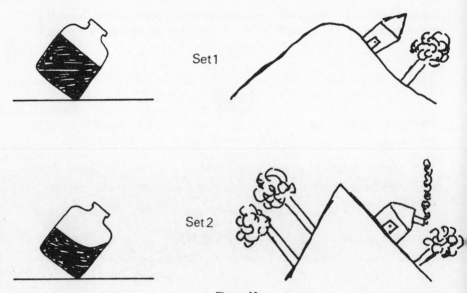

Set 1

Set 2

Figure 12

occurs around about nine years, with the final achievement being as represented schematically in Figure 13.

The ability to co-ordinate vertical-horizontal axes is constructed in the same gradual way that other cognitive structures are developed. The mere fact of living in an environment which incorporates horizontal-vertical frames of reference is insufficient to ensure the development of the structuring of Euclidean space. Piaget and Inhelder have dispelled the notion that just

Figure 13

because: (a) a child spends a good deal of his early years in the horizontal position; and (b) learns in his second year to stand upright and spends a good deal of time in the vertical position, he automatically orients himself in space and has a thorough appreciation of it. What is clear is that children need experiences introduced at the appropriate time to permit this sequential development of co-ordination of vertical and horizontal.

Measurement or Length

Two simple experiments illustrate the difficulty that intuitive reasoners have with length. They both illustrate that the intuitive child tends to estimate the length of an object by the interval between its boundaries, thinking in terms of whether the ends match up.

Measurement (Length) Experiment 1. A straight stick and a wavy length of plasticine is put in front of the child with their end points level as in Figure 14.

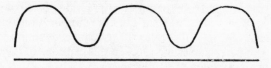

Figure 14

After preliminary tests to determine whether the child can estimate equality in straight sticks, the child is asked to compare the lengths of the two lines. Younger children of four to five estimate that they are the same length. Between five and six most children agree that they differ in length, although children tend to go through an intermediate period where, e.g., it is necessary for them to run their fingers along the lines before giving the correct answer.

Measurement (Length) Experiment 2. Two straight sticks of equal length are lined up so that their ends match. One of the sticks is moved forward as in Figure 15. The children are asked whether the sticks are the same length.

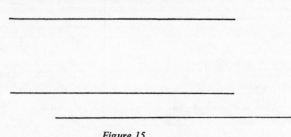

Figure 15

As with the previous experiment, intuitive reasoners attend to the extremities and in this case centre upon one aspect only—the part which protrudes. These children assert that the stick which has been moved forward is longer. After a period of transition the child from about six to seven years onward declares that the sticks are the same length despite any movement which

47

might be made. In this experiment, as with other instances of conservation, the conserver decentres in that he attends to the transformations and not to the beginning and end states exclusively. He can compensate logically and perception no longer dominates.

Perspective

This final section outlines an important experiment performed by Piaget and Inhelder on perspective. The experiment is important in its own right because of what it reveals about the child's conception of space, but it is also of considerable significance because it serves to illustrate wider achievements in development. It clearly indicates changes in egocentrism which in turn have important implications for social, emotional and cognitive development and of course for education. The experiment is presented briefly and is followed by a separate section which looks at the other implications mentioned.

The experiment reported illustrates the gradual growth in the appreciation of the relativity of perspectives in space. In this experiment the child is shown a model of three mountains as in Figure 16.

The child sits at A and a doll is placed in the various other positions at the table and the child is asked what the doll sees. He can indicate this by drawing what the doll sees, by constructing the doll's perspective with cardboard cut-outs or by selecting which of a number of drawings represents what the doll would see. In the intuitive phase, children are incapable of such representative co-ordination of perspectives. Children at this stage imagine that the doll's view of the mountains is the same as their own. In the early phase of the concrete operations period, at about seven or eight years, children can make a number of correct arrangements and assessments, but remain confused about others. It is not until the later phase of concrete operations at

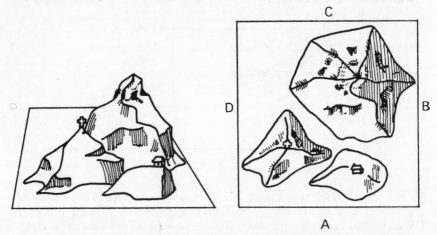

Figure 16. The Three Mountains
(*Adapted from Piaget, J. and Inhelder, B.*, The Child's Conception of Space, *1956*)

48

nine to ten years of age that they achieve complete relativity of perspectives and can anticipate with certainty, how the mountains will appear to another, who views it from a different perspective.

This experiment, along with others discussed on spatial conceptions, brings out repeatedly the difference between and the developmental lag between conceptual space and perceptual space. There is little doubt that preoperational children *see* the mountains as well as the older concrete reasoners. What they do not have is the operational intelligence to co-ordinate the relationships necessary for the formation of adequate conceptions in space.

Perspective and Egocentricity

The development of perspective is of fundamental importance to the cognitive growth of the child but it is also very closely connected to its social and emotional development. The achievement of the co-ordination of perspectives is fundamental to the development of mature interpersonal relations. These depend solidly on the ability to put oneself in another's place, and to view the world and ourselves from his perspective.

One of the consistent themes of this chapter has been the progressive development of the child from the stage where he is completely dependent upon action and perception to the stage of relative autonomy of thought processes. One of the achievements of the child has been the development of the notion that objects have permanence despite re-ordering and rearrangement. The child takes a strong forward step when he realises that not only do objects have permanence but that objects can be other people and that he himself is in a real sense an object. This becomes established as he progresses from the sensorimotor stage, through the preoperational stage and becomes consolidated at a new level in the concrete operations period, when in addition to regarding himself as an object he becomes able to put himself in the place of another and imagine things from their perspective. This development was foreshadowed in discussions of the sensorimotor period where it was stated that this ability to take the point of view of another is necessary if the child is to relinquish his *egocentric* view. In a very real way the discussion of the concrete operational period has already been stressing this process because it is part of the general ability or logical process of decentring that has been evident in the operations necessary for conservation, classification etc. Very young children cannot view things objectively at first because things are only relevant if they concern their own private preoccupations. The ability to view objects or environmental events from another viewpoint comes slowly in association with the capacity to decentre attention more and more away from the child's own thoughts and desires to other objects in the environment including other persons. In this respect the relinquishing of egocentrism is an important correlate of cognitive development.

Social development as a whole, and the development of social acceptance in particular, depends to a great extent upon the ability to assess how the other person feels about you. In other words it depends on how well the social signs are read. Reading of social signs is facilitated, with respect to personal acceptance, when the child is able to take the point of view of another and, as it were, look back on himself and assess his own behaviour from the other's viewpoint. In a very real way, then, the development of social acceptance is dependent on the co-ordination of perspectives which comes during the period of concrete operations.

Likewise, Piaget has shown that moral development is tied to the child's intellectual development. This aspect of Piaget's work is discussed more fully in the section dealing with his theory and the teaching of social studies. For the moment it is sufficient to indicate that the ability to take the role of another is of crucial importance to the ability to follow rules. Young children are incapable of following rules if they regard them from an egocentric position. Genuine co-operation demands that the rules be viewed as consistent from each participant's point of view.

THE FORMAL OPERATIONS STAGE (12 TO 15 YEARS)

Despite the impressive gains made during the concrete operations period, there are nevertheless limitations in the quality of thinking in that period. Probably the most significant limitation resides in the fact that the logical structures of the concrete operational child relate directly to objects and relations between objects with the result that the "logical organization of judgments and arguments is inseparable from their content" (Piaget and Inhelder, 1969, 32). The concrete operational child does not yet possess a unified logical system which will explore systematically abstract relations, independent of content, be concerned with the non-present, or with hypothetical relationships. In essence the concrete operational child is concerned with organising and interpreting that which is immediately present, although he gives evidence of limited concern for the non-present or potential.

Characteristics of Formal Operations

What follows is a verbal description of some of the chief characteristics of formal thought. It should be kept in mind, however, that a complete understanding of formal operations as a logical system requires a knowledge of Piaget's logico-mathematical model which can be found in Inhelder and Piaget (1958), Flavell (1963), Boyle (1969) and Phillips (1969).

The fundamental difference in the approach of concrete and formal thinkers to the consideration of a problem can be summed up in the phrase, the real versus the possible. No longer concerned exclusively with the data, the formal thinker proceeds by envisaging all of the possible relations implied by the data and attempts by logical analysis and enquiry to make a judgment as to the truth or falsity of each of the possibilities advanced. In consequence that which is real is conceived as but one aspect in the total set of possibilities and remains a possibility until analysis and enquiry confirm its reality, acceptability or truth. This significant change in orientation carries with it certain clearly identifiable modes of thinking.

1 *Thinking is hypothetic-deductive in nature*
The ability to conceive of the real as but a subset of the possible is really another way of saying that the adolescent proceeds by setting up hypotheses to be subsequently tested and confirmed or denied. In successively testing, confirming or denying these hypotheses, the adolescent is engaged in reasoning which is *hypothetico-deductive* in nature. This is, of course, the procedure characteristic of the scientific method and represents a distinct advance on concrete operations where the child certainly discovers relationships but is tied to the immediate reality before him.

2 *Thinking is propositional*
Formal thinking is pre-eminently *propositional* thinking. What the child or adolescent manipulates in his thinking are assertions or propositions about the data. The formal thinker can follow the form of an argument independent of its concrete content and in fact manipulates the relationships which might exist. It is this ability to follow the form of an argument and to disregard the content that gives the stage its name of formal operations. Hunt (1961, 232-233) illustrates this by citing the concrete and formal thinker's responses to the following nonsense sentence devised by Ballard: "I am very glad I do not eat onions, for if I liked them I would always be eating them, and I hate eating unpleasant things". The concrete operational child concentrates on the data and says, e.g., "Onions are not unpleasant". The formal thinker accepts the data and concentrates on the contradiction apparent between "if I like them" and "onions are unpleasant".

3 *Thinking is combinatorial*
A further characteristic of formal thinking which adds to its force and effectiveness is the ability to systematically isolate all of the variables inherent in a problem with all the possible combinations. This *combinatorial analysis* has the effect of ensuring that the variables of a problem will all be examined and their influence either alone or in combination will be considered when the possible relational effects are considered.

Overall, then, formal thinking can be distinguished from earlier stages because it is characterised by hypothesis testing, the isolation of all relevant variables and their possible combinations, and the ability to reason with assertions or propositions about the data rather than with the "raw reality" data themselves. These three aspects are, of course, interdependent in the formal reasoning process. Hypotheses are set up on the basis of propositions which take into account the respective variables. This is illustrated below in the analysis of an example which in addition provides an illustration of the application of formal thinking.

In their book *The Growth of Logical Thinking from Childhood to Adolescence*, Inhelder and Piaget (1958) illustrate the differences between concrete and formal operations through a variety of problems one of which is the *Combination of Colourless Chemicals* problem. In this problem the child is presented with four similar bottles of colourless, odourless liquids which cannot be distinguished by sight. They are numbered 1, 2, 3, 4. One of the bottles, number 2, contains water. Another bottle with a dropper is also provided and identified as g. The chemicals are such that $1 \times 3 \times g$ will produce a yellow precipitate. Number 4 added to the yellow precipitate will remove the colour. The subject is presented with two glasses, one which contains 1×3 and the other, 2. The substance g is added to both and 1×3 turns yellow. Following the demonstration, the subject is asked to reproduce the yellow colour using bottles 1, 2, 3, 4 and g as he wishes. At the stage of concrete operations the subjects "spontaneously and systematically associate the element of g with all others but without any other combination" (ibid., 111).

Two major changes appear when the formal thinker approaches this task. He uses all of the combinations systematically and understands that the colour is due to the combination which produces it. Analysis of this experiment and part of one of the answers to the problem (ibid., 117) will serve to illustrate the relationship between hypothesis testing, propositional thinking and combinatorial analysis.

Cha, a 13-year-old, responded to the problem in part as follows: "You have to try all the bottles. I'll begin with the one at the end (from 1 to 4 with g). It doesn't work any more. Maybe you have to mix them (he tries $1 \times 2 \times g$, then $1 \times 3 \times g$). It turned yellow. But are there other solutions? I'll try" (ibid., 117). (He then tries all the other two-by-two combinations.) Examination of this response shows that *Cha* has set up three hypotheses: (a) "You have to try all the bottles"; (b) "Maybe you have to mix them"; and (c) "But are there other solutions?" When these are put together *Cha* is in effect saying, "In order to get the correct solution you have to try all the combinations of the bottles and there may well be more than one solution to the problem".

It is also evident from *Cha's* response that not only has he set up hypotheses but that he tests the hypotheses by *systematic combinatorial analysis*. However, not only does he do this but in saying "But are there other solutions?" he is going outside the actual physical problem indicating formal or propositional reasoning. He has solved the initial problem but has taken the result of his initial operations, as a basis for further reasoning. His reasoning is *formal* because what he has manipulated in this thinking is an assertion or proposition that is, in effect, independent of the concrete content first presented.

This point is perhaps exemplified better in further statements by *Cha* in response to the experimenter's questioning. *Cha* was asked about the role of the chemicals in bottles 2 and 4 and proceeded to discover that 4 added to $1 \times 3 \times g$ cleared the yellow colour but 2 did not. The experimenter then said, "And if I were to tell you that 4 is water?" to which *Cha* replied "If this liquid 4 is water, when you put it with 1 × 3 it wouldn't completely prevent the yellow from forming. It isn't water; it's something harmful" (ibid., 117). *Cha* is here making a proposition about a proposition in that he asserts that liquid 4 is water (Statement 1) which carries with it the implication that such a liquid will not prevent the yellow from forming (Statement 2). Here *Cha* is reasoning by implication, with propositions about propositions. For *Cha* the real is but one possibility among a number of such possibilities.

There is in this example then evidence of the three important characteristics of formal thought: hypothesis making and testing, combinatorial analysis and formal propositional thinking. These are the essential attributes of *scientific method* or *problem solving* the educational implications of which will be discussed in Chapter 5.

Some Comments Concerning the Incidence of Concrete and Formal Operations in the Primary and Secondary Schools

a *The Incidence of Formal Thinking.* The comments on the formal level of thinking are based on research and surveys in Melbourne and Sydney.

In a survey recently completed in Melbourne, Dale (1970) came to the conclusion, as did Lovell (1961), that the sample of Geneva children tested by Piaget must have consisted of "able children". Dale's comments refer specifically to his replication (repetition) of Inhelder and Piaget's "Combination of Colourless Chemicals" experiment which was briefly described above. His results indicate that his sample of Melbourne children were much less successful in solving the problem than were the sample used by Inhelder and Piaget (1958). Dale (ibid., 284) reports that "At age 11-12 years, approximately 10% of the Melbourne sample completely solved the problem and approximately 25% were successful at age 15". However, while Dale's findings are at variance with those of Inhelder and Piaget with respect to the age at which the problem is typically solved, he notes that his findings support the theory of the development of thinking with age and in particular, the development of combinatorial thinking with age (ibid., 285).

The Sydney surveys on formal thinking were carried out by the writer (McNally, 1970, 1971). In the Sydney surveys an entirely different technique was used based on the work of Peel (1959, 1960, 1966). Basically the method involves the presentation of simple, but logically similar, stories to children, who having read the stories answer questions. The answers are then classified. Peel (1959) originally classified the responses as intuitive, concrete and formal, but later dropped this classification in favour of a literal classification in terms of the quality of reasoning in the answer. The present writer (McNally, 1968) has, however, made out a case for the retention of the intuitive, concrete and formal classification and the results reported below are based upon such a classification. On the basis of the combined results of three stories, the results by grade are as indicated in Table 1.

53

TABLE 1

Percentage of Intuitive, Concrete and Formal Thinkers in a Sample of Sydney Children and Adolescents

| GRADE OR FORM | STAGE OF THINKING | | | N |
	% Intuitive	% Concrete	% Formal	
6th Grade	0·5	95·5	4·0	246
2nd Form	0·0	77·0	23·0	112
4th Form	0·0	42·7	57·3	157

These are composite results. Sixth grade incorporates five co-educational classes in three schools drawn at random from the Sydney Metropolitan Area. Form 2 is a complete second form from a girls high school. Fourth form consists of a complete fourth form from a boys school and a girls school. The mean ages of the groups when tested were: sixth grade 11·5, second form 14·1, fourth form 15·5.

Despite the considerable differences in technique, the results of the McNally studies support the contention of Dale and Lovell with respect to the approximate age at which children reach formal reasoning. The McNally studies also indicated, with respect to the technique used, that the attainment of formal thinking is a gradual process without any apparent abrupt change from concrete to formal thinking.

b *Incidence of Concrete Thinking.* The incidence and onset of concrete operations is difficult to determine. There are three reasons for this. First, the concept of concrete operations itself and children exhibit considerable unevenness with respect to individual achievement of various conservation tasks. Also, there is no one test which determines when concrete operations have been consolidated which means that results depend on which test or tests were used. Thirdly, the same test is administered frequently with different scoring procedures.

Therefore, the results reported below are based upon the Goldschmid (1967) standardised version of three tests of conservation: substance, continuous quantity, and discontinuous quantity. Research carried out by Goldschmid (1967) and McNally (1971) shows that these three tests have the highest intercorrelation with a Total Conservation score based upon a much larger battery of conservation tests. The correlations with Total Conservation follow with the McNally correlations reported first and the Goldschmid correlations second, in parentheses: Total Conservation and Substance 0·92 (0·85); Total Conservation and Continuous Quantity 0·93 (0·82); and Total Conservation and Discontinuous Quantity 0·92 (0·80).

Table 2 gives the percentage of children classified as conservers and non-conservers for a complete first grade in a co-educational Sydney suburban infants school, October 1971. Average age was 7·1 years.

TABLE 2

Percentage of Children Classified as Conservers and Non-conservers on each of Three Tests (Substance, Continuous Quantity and Discontinuous Quantity) in a First Grade Co-educational Infants School, October 1971

TASK	% CONSERVER	% NON-CONSERVER
Conservation of Substance	70	30
Conservation of Continuous Quantity	69	31
Conservation of Discontinuous Quantity	71	29
N = 69		

It should be noted that although the percentages for each test approximate each other, there were quite a number of instances where children would pass one or two of the tests and fail the remainder. To this extent the results indicate a uniformity which performances did not confirm. Nevertheless, the results indicate that on any one of the three tests approximately 30 per cent of the first grade was not conserving.

3. The Relationship of Piaget's View of Intelligence to Conventional Views

It would be very useful if we could proceed on the basis that everyone knew what intelligence is and that everyone agreed with that view. Then all that would need to be done would be to take that view and compare it with Piaget's. Unfortunately there is considerable disagreement and it is necessary therefore to outline briefly the main ideas and current position concerning conventional intelligence prior to any comparison with Piaget.

Burt (1970) reminds us that the concept of intelligence as a single entity was a gift to psychology from biology when Herbert Spencer in his *Principles of Psychology* discussed the nature, laws and development of intelligence in the animal world and the human individual. The idea of intelligence tests we owe to Galton who, in his book *Hereditary Genius*, distinguishes between "ability" and "zeal", today's counterparts of cognitive or intellectual ability and motivation. Galton also believed that this ability was *general* and to a large extent innate. It was to this notion of an innate, general, cognitive ability that Galton and his earlier followers come to attach the label "intelligence". Furthermore it was also generally believed that this hereditary general ability could be measured. This view has persisted and is apparent in such everyday statements as "He is not very intelligent" and in the general acceptance of the IQ as a measure of overall intelligence.

But differences developed with respect to intelligence in two related areas: the most appropriate way to view or conceptualise intelligence (theory); and the most appropriate way to measure intelligence (psychometrics). This resulted in the emergence of rival theories of intelligence typified by the theories of Spearman (Britain) and Thurstone (United States of America).[1]

Spearman developed a two factor theory of intelligence (initially a one factor theory) of a "g" or general intellectual factor common to all cognitive or ability tests to some degree and a specific factor unique to each particular test. Spearman supported this view by analysing mathematically the cor-

[1] There are, of course, many other theories of intelligence such as those of Knight, Thorndike, Thompson, etc.

relations or relationships between various mental or ability tests in a group of tests. Thurstone developed a multi factor (specific factors) approach to intelligence by applying a different though related method of mathematical analysis to that of Spearman. He came to the conclusion that intelligence was best viewed as a group of Primary Mental Abilities each measuring a different factor and thereby giving a set of measures that would give a good analytic picture of the underlying types of intelligence rather than a general score. Thurstone's Primary Mental Abilities were Number, Word Fluency, Verbal Meaning, Memory, Reasoning, Space and Perceptual Speed. Now if these different theories had been merely alternative ways of looking at the same problem, then it would not matter very much because after all we had intelligence tests which gave a measure of "intelligence".

If you consider the position in Australian schools today and, for example, consider only three of a number of intelligence tests that are employed, the importance of theory begins to emerge. The Lower Grades Primary Mental Abilities Test is based on Thurstone's theory of Primary Mental Abilities, the A.C.E.R. Junior B has a high loading on g, and some loading on the "reasoning factor" suggesting that it strongly reflects Spearman's theory, while the Wechsler Intelligence Scale for Children seems to take cognisance of the work of Spearman, Thurstone and Burt. Thus the items which comprise such tests have been selected to reflect the constructor's view of intelligence, although it sometimes happens that items are chosen more for their statistical properties than for their reflection of theoretical structure.

It is not surprising then, that different tests frequently yield quite different results when applied to the same group of children, to say nothing of the marked fluctuations that sometimes occur when the one test is applied on more than one occasion to the same subject. If different psychologists have different theories and if these theories lead to the construction of different tests which themselves lead to different results, is there any sense in talking about intelligence?

The position is not quite as grim as the foregoing would suggest. When Thurstone's data were reanalysed and data on younger children were obtained it was found that a "second order" factor emerged that was similar to Spearman's "g" and in the latter years of his career, Spearmen came to recognise the existence of group factors as well as "g" and specific factors. This convergence of the different theories is represented in the hierarchical approach of Burt and Vernon who incorporate some features of all views and argue that the best representation of intellect provides for general intelligence, group factors, specific intelligences and detailed skills and task factors involved in each individual task.

As there are data to support all views it is apparent that there are several ways to view intelligence and today arguments about the "true" nature of intelligence have largely gone out of fashion. Experienced users of intelligence tests now decide which of the approaches and which of the tests best suits their purpose and when results are obtained interpret these so as to abstract as much information as possible. This usually includes an examination of the subtest scores, e.g., the various verbal and performance scales of the Wechsler Intelligence Scale for Children, as well as the overall assessment of intelligence obtained from combining subtest scores, all of which is interpreted in terms of the particular test and its limitations.

Nevertheless it has become increasingly clear over the years that it makes most sense to talk of "g" or general intelligence with children, less sense to talk of "g" in relation to adolescents, particularly older adolescents, and very little sense to talk about "g" with respect to adults at all for as age increases specific abilities become more manifest.

Another important concept which is an integral part of the conventional view and which is of importance in any discussion of Piaget's views is that of the concept of Mental Age (MA), originally a concept put forward by Binet as a method of measuring the relative ability of children with respect to mental functioning. Thus if a child was five years of age and could only successfully complete tests up to the three year old level he was retarded two years. In assigning tests to a particular age level Binet proceeded as follows. An item was assigned to a particular age level, for example, the five year old level if from about 60 to 75 per cent of this age were able to perform it accurately, if less than about 60 per cent of four year olds could do it correctly and if it could be done by more than 75 per cent of six year olds. If a child could do all of the five year old tests, failed none of the tests below the five year old level and could do none of the six year old tests, then he had a MA of five years. Later the intelligence quotient (IQ) was devised to give a means of comparing a child of one age with that of another and the relative mental development of the one child from one year to another. The IQ was obtained by dividing MA by Chronological Age (CA) and multiplying by 100:

$$IQ = \frac{MA}{CA} \times 100$$

Modern tests of intelligence such as the Wechsler Intelligence Scale for Children and the 1960 revision of the Stanford Binet no longer use this method of calculating IQ but use instead a deviation IQ based on the child's position relative to his own contemporaries. For example, a child of 7 years 6 months is compared with children in the age range 7 years 3 months to 7 years 8 months on Wechsler Intelligence Scale for Children, and assigned an IQ by comparing his performance with scale obtained from a sample within this age range. It must be noted, however, that a deviation IQ, while in some ways comparable to the earlier concept of IQ, cannot strictly be interpreted in terms of MA. Nevertheless MA has become so closely connected with the interpretation of conventional intelligence tests and is frequently used as an indication of intellectual status that it will be used in the discussions that follow.

This continuing interest in expressing a child's performance on an intelligence test in terms of an intelligence quotient reflects the major difference between Piaget's approach and the conventional one. Piaget's approach can initially be regarded as *qualitative* while the conventional view can be regarded as *quantitative*. In general the conventional view says "How much?" while Piaget says "What is it like?" This is simplification, because those who work in the conventional field would certainly assert that they are also interested in "what intelligence is like", or the nature of intelligence, while some of the work based upon Piaget's view can be considered to examine, at least in part, the question of "How much?" even though this is done in an imprecise way.

In fact, it will be shown in the following pages that while, for purposes of discussion, the distinction between a qualitative and quantitative view is useful, a too rigid acceptance of this view obscures the definite relationship which exists between the conventional view and that of Piaget. One of the great difficulties for those used to thinking in terms of conventional intelligence and the IQ in conceptualising Piaget's concepts of intelligence is the view that the development of intelligence proceeds in a lock step manner in which each particular child gradually becomes more intelligent as he grows older at about the same relative rate each year. That is, if a child has an IQ of 80 then each successive year will see him increase in ability at about 8/10 of the rate of increase of a child with an IQ of 100.

Now it is certainly true that as a general rule the dull tend to remain dull and the bright tend to remain bright and that bright children can solve more complex problems and solve problems more quickly than their less well endowed age mates. But the acceptance of the "steady rate of increase" view of intelligence leads to problems, particularly with respect to the constancy of the IQ and its ability to predict academic success. Study after study has shown that children's IQs can vary quite markedly from one occasion to another. Loretan (1965), for example, reports fluctuations as high as 40 points, while Furth (1970) reports that at age five or six, occupation and educational level of parents have higher correlations with final school achievement than does measured IQ.

There are many reasons for these fluctuations including such factors as the age of the subject, the use of different IQ tests, differences within the individual at different times with respect to motivation, social and emotional adjustment, fatigue and so on. The catalogue of effects is well known and professional test users operate and interpret tests within the limits and constraints which such factors impose. But it is possible to find in Piaget's conception of cognitive development a source of supplementary explanations for these fluctuations particularly at the intuitive-concrete level and in so doing to indicate a more organic relationship between Piaget's qualitative view and conventional intelligence.

Piaget has put forward the notion of developmental stages to explain the different logical structures that a child employs in dealing with the world. The stages that are of concern here are the intuitive and concrete ones. As was seen in Chapter 2, when a child reaches the concrete stage of reasoning or can conserve, he is able to employ a distinctly superior logical structure to that which characterised his thinking in the intuitive stage. Principally, he can decentre (the ability to attend simultaneously to more than one aspect); he has reversibility (the ability to return to the starting point of a problem while still holding the ideas in mind) and logical multiplication (the ability to compensate, for example, a change in height and width as in the water in the jar problem) all of which lead to conservation, the capacity to account for changes (distortions of plasticine etc.) in terms of the logic of the situation rather than in terms of changes in appearance (perceptual cues).

This is of course a distinct advance, for the child's central thought processes are now in command and are able to compensate for the bias and distortions of perception. The important point raised in Chapter 2, however, was that the child did not achieve this all at once. This was referred to as *horizontal decalage* and it meant that for some problems he could conserve and might be said to have reached the concrete stage while in others he could not. Thus what the unreliability of the IQ might be reflecting, in addition to other factors suggested above, is this unevenness with respect to logical development.

Convincing evidence for this variability with respect to conservation in addition to that of Piaget comes from studies by Tuddenham, Dodwell, Elkind and Goldschmid who report low to moderately high correlations between the various tests of conservation. Thus a child who is in the process of consolidating the concrete stage may exhibit conservation with respect to number, two-dimensional space and substance but not discontinuous quantity, length and area. His friend may have a completely different pattern. Therefore a particular IQ test that these children might take could contain items which call for a logical structure favouring one individual pattern rather than another resulting in a difference in performance and, of course, a difference in IQ or intellectual assessment.

It is therefore quite possible that at least some of the inconsistency or unreliability of IQ scores found in the intuitive-concrete developmental period may be linked to differing patterns in the progressive development and consolidation of the concrete logical structures.

This argument does not preclude the possibility of having two children in the one class with the same CA and IQ yet having different patterns with respect to the development and consolidation of conservation for it would depend on their logical structures as these related to the items of the test, and to the operation of other factors that contribute to intelligence test scores not related to conservation at all.

Further evidence to support a relationship between Piaget's stages and conventional intelligence comes from studies by Dodwell (1961), Feigenbaum (1963), Goldschmid (1967), Kaufman (1971), McNally (1971) and Tuddenham (1970) which show for infants and early primary grades correlations ranging from low positive to moderately high positive between mental age, in the case of Goldschmid, Kaufman and McNally, and IQ, in the studies by Tuddenham, Dodwell and Feigenbaum, and overall performance on conservation tasks. Goldschmid found correlations between MA and conservation (giving the correct response) of ·50, between MA and giving the correct explanation ·45 and between MA and the combined scores for correct response and correct explanation ·49. What these results of 102 first and second grade children suggest is that the higher a child's MA the more of the

60

conservation tasks the child responds to correctly.

Taken together then, the results which indicate variability across conservation tasks and a relationship between the degree of conservation and MA suggest that even though Piaget was primarily interested in discovering the logical structures which characterised the operation of intelligence, or the qualitative aspect, available evidence suggests an organic relationship between Piaget's stages and conventional intelligence at the infants and primary school levels.

One of the reasons why this relationship has not been readily apparent is due to the masking effect of assigning points for success or failure on intelligence test items. For example, in the "Similarities" test of the Wechsler Intelligence Scale for Children, a child gets one point if he says a duck and a swan are alike because they both have feathers, but two points if he says they are both birds. This is clear recognition of qualitative differences and in fact in this case the parallel with Piaget's work on classification is not hard to find. The qualitative differences are lost, however, when scores on individual items are summed prior to conversion to a scaled score and eventual IQ.

An explanation for the link between Piaget's qualitative view and the conventional one is suggested by Tuddenham's comment that conservation tasks correlate more highly when conservation items have more in common with respect to content, a contention that is borne out in the fairly substantial correlations among conservation items that characterise Goldschmid's results. Tuddenham concludes that the notion of conservation, that is, invariance under transformations such as seeing that a change in shape does not alter the amount of plasticine, acts as a sort of general factor, a view that was put forward by Hunt as early as 1961.

However a major difficulty arises when thought is given to applying Piaget's theory, and the evidence flowing from it, to the construction of tests which will have relevance to education and teaching in the same way that IQ tests have had. It soon becomes apparent that Piaget-style tests do not apply uniformly to the various areas of concern. For example, when Tuddenham's results are re-examined, it is clearly evident that the correlation between tests of conservation and Raven's Test of Intelligence (Coloured Progressive Matrices) is much higher than that between the same tests of conservation and the Peabody Picture Vocabulary Test. Tuddenham comments, pointedly, that it is not surprising that the items which minimise verbalisation correlate appreciably higher with the non-language Raven than with the Picture Vocabulary Test. He draws attention to the fact that conservation items such as the plasticine ball test and the water in the jar test are limited in content to matters concerning physical events and relationships, where logical and spatial reasoning is required, and suggests that conventional IQ measures and educational achievement tests will be better predictors of success in certain school subjects, especially in language and social studies.

What Tuddenham is saying is that although tests of conservation would have their principal loading on a general factor, there are significant areas of school performance for which they would have little predictive significance.

This seems to be the reasoning behind the construction of the new British Intelligence Scale. The compilers have decided to include items based on the work of Piaget and others so as to obtain scores which also show the *qualitative* level of thinking attained. In discussing the inclusion of such items in the new test, Warburton (1970) states that while logical operations and sequences can be readily discerned in some areas of ability, it is extremely difficult to extend these concepts to all types of ability and to write appropriate items.

Thus Tuddenham seems to be moving towards a position where he sees conservation as a manifestation of "g", while those constructing the new British Intelligence Scale seem to see logical operations as a further group factor contributing a *qualitative* component to a general assessment of intelligence. Both agree, however, that the effect of the progressive development of logical operations or logical structures can be more readily identified as they operate in areas of a logico-mathematical nature and both see the assessment of ability as a multifactor problem.

Tuddenham concludes "the evidence thus far obtained has about extinguished what hope we might once have held that we could place each child on a single developmental continuum equivalent to MA and from this predict his performance on content of whatever kind".

This view then, sees Piaget's tests as useful in assessing one factor or aspect of intelligence. But there is other evidence, discussed below, which does not fit this pattern neatly.

1 THE EVIDENCE LINKING OPERATIONAL INTELLIGENCE TO LANGUAGE AND TO VERBAL REASONING

There are three sources of information of importance here. First, recent research has indicated (Goldschmid, 1967 and McNally, 1971) that there is a moderate correlation between the Wechsler Intelligence Scale for Children Vocabulary Sub-test and total conservation score for first grade children. The correlations are very similar, being ·40 in the Goldschmid study and ·43 in the McNally study. In both studies the mean age was 7·1 years. Second, Piaget claims, with some justification, (see the section on the teaching of language Chapter 7) that the development of logical structures underlies the development of language, a position which seems to be gaining acceptance (Wallace, 1972). Third, the results of the research done by the writer (McNally, 1970, 1971) with respect to verbal reasoning using the Piaget based Peel tests of verbal reasoning (described in Chapter 2) show a clear and distinct relationship between level of reasoning and scholastic performance.

Of particular interest are the results which show a consistent relationship between the percentage of formal reasoners and class level (ability grading) within any grade or form. Three examples will serve to illustrate the point:

1   In one study (McNally, 1970) a total second form (grade 8) and a total third form (grade 9) were tested. It was found that as class ability level

decreased (i.e., 2A, 2B, 2C etc.), the percentage of formal reasoners, relative to concrete reasoners, decreased. This was true for both forms.

2   A further study (McNally, 1971) showed that in three classes of bright sixth grade children (minimum IQ 125) selected to pursue a course of enriched experiences consistent with their brightness, the Piaget-based verbal reasoning tests predicted more effectively to total scholastic performance, including language, than did MA. The correlation between the attainment of the formal level of reasoning and scholastic achievement was ·44, while that between MA and scholastic achievement was —·09.

3   There was a direct (linear) relationship between number of formal reasoners and the grade or form being tested as illustrated by the following graph, which indicates the percentage of formal reasoners by grade or by form.

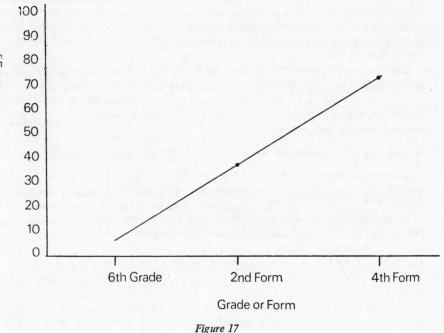

Figure 17

One interesting factor which emerged over the two studies was that the percentage of formal reasoners in the bright sixth grade was approximately equal to the average of third form, which was about 30 per cent. Therefore qualitative reasoning, in Piaget's terms, may be related to the verbal area to a greater extent than is believed by some. This does not mean that the view put forward by Piaget that thought precedes language and that only later does language become important in the development of the logical structures is void. It simply means that there seems to be a closer connection between language and conservation than was first thought. It may mean that Furth (1970) is right in suggesting that greater emphasis be placed on thinking in the early school grades as support to the development of language. (The problem of Piaget's theory in relation to language development is taken up again in Chapters 4 and 7.)

2 THE SEX DIFFERENCES WHICH SEEM TO BE EMERGING WITH RESPECT TO CONSERVATION AND FORMAL REASONING

Several studies (Beard, 1963, Goldschmid, 1967, McNally, 1971) have shown that boys tend to conserve earlier than do girls and at the upper level of reasoning Dale (1970) found that boys tend to reach the formal level of reasoning earlier than girls judged by their performance on the colourless liquids test. There is also an interesting parallel between the Vincents Models Test (a test of mechanical aptitude) and conventional intelligence as measured by the AL/AQ group test of intelligence for tertiary students. While there is usually no significant difference between the intelligence test scores for men and women, there is usually a significant difference in favour of men for mechanical aptitude.

One intriguing possibility is that there is a link between the earlier conservation of boys and the superior performance of men on the mechanical aptitude test in terms of early sensorimotor experience in which one of the important variables would be the kinds of objects that were experienced and handled during that period.

3 THE RELATIONSHIP OF PIAGET'S STAGES TO MENTAL RETARDATION

Inhelder has shown (Piaget, 1950, 154) that conservation of substance, weight and volume occurs in individuals who are only slightly mentally retarded, but that really deficient individuals never reach conservation of volume. Likewise Inhelder was able to distinguish among the mildly retarded, the moderately retarded and the severely retarded by showing that the mildly retarded eventually reached formal operations, the moderately retarded reached concrete operations and the severely retarded reached neither. Indeed it has been suggested (Woodward, 1970) that Piaget's approach provides a fruitful source of tests for the assessment of the mentally retarded.

Consideration of these three points and an examination of the evidence presented above in relation to operational intelligence, language and verbal reasoning, and the sex differences which seem to be emerging and the relationship of Piaget's stages to mental retardation, all indicate that Piaget's work is a potential and relevant source of comprehensive tests of cognitive functioning once its full relationship to performance has been established by research programmes. Elkind in Green, Ford and Flamer (1971) does not agree, however, and concludes that such tests would serve no useful purpose in the classroom because teachers would be unable to interpret them. The answer to this lies in the realm of teacher education, either pre- or in-service, for it would seem that the important contribution made by Piaget to understanding intelligence warrants a considerable amount of time in any modern teacher education programme. It would seem, then, that there is the view which sees Piaget's theory of developmental stages as complementary to the conventional view, but there is also evidence that Piaget's stages are more intimately involved with a much wider spectrum of cognitive and scholastic development than those adopting the complementary view believe.

There is, however, a third view that sees in Piaget's formulations an alternative to intelligence testing. This view is exemplified in the New York experiment which is concerned with exploring "Alternatives to Intelligence Testing", reported by Loretan (1965). Dissatisfied with conventional intelligence tests, Loretan asked how teachers could better understand and assess intellectual development of the entering school child so that every child could be taught more effectively. The answer which evolved was that we can understand and assess the intellectual development of entering school children by presenting them with activities that develop their concepts, and on the basis of these concepts we can assess their present position and perhaps predict the direction in which they must move (Loretan, 1965). The basis of Loretan's view is that in the course of teaching activities a picture is obtained of the child's development and present abilities and then instruction can be planned so that development is facilitated. The best guide as to what the child ought to do in the immediate future is his ability to cope with the present task. This would seem to be a clear instance of the principle which will be stressed repeatedly in the coming chapters: the matching of current cognitive structures to experiences offered, or, the problem of the cognitive match.

CONCLUSIONS

1 There is a distinct and identifiable relationship between Piaget's view and the conventional view which is much greater than some believe.

2 There is a danger of over-emphasising the qualitative versus quantitative distinction, particularly when these are presented as completely contrasting views as they have been in even recent general texts on psychology. Nevertheless, the qualitative-quantitative distinction is a valid one.

3 Piaget, although not interested in individual differences as such, has inspired a great deal of research which has re-emphasised just how important these differences are.

4 This work which emphasises the different rates at which children reach various stages and sub-stages with consequent variation in current cognitive structures suggests the need to match individuals and programs (curricula) where possible for optimum development, the implications of which are taken up in some detail in Chapter 5.

5 It seems possible and necessary to design tests to give a much more comprehensive view of the child for we need to know a great deal more than the IQ.

4. Piaget's View of Knowing, Learning, Development, Language, Memory and the Relationship of Intelligence to these Areas

Chapter 2 traced the development of intelligence from the rudimentary sensorimotor actions to formal operations. This development was primarily the development of increasingly effective logical operations. In this chapter those aspects of Piaget's theory which relate to the development of operational thought are introduced. These are successively treated as: (1) knowing, the figurative and operative aspects; (2) the role of language in thinking; (3) development and learning; (4) memory and intelligence; and (5) summary and conclusion.

KNOWING: THE FIGURATIVE AND OPERATIVE ASPECTS

The first discussion looks briefly at the relationship between operational thought and the known object. There are two main aspects of this new perspective on knowing, referred to as *figurative*, and *operative*.

Figurative knowing is concerned with the states or the static aspects of things as they appear to the senses. What might be referred to as the material aspects of knowing. Operative knowing occurs when the person "operates" on, and transforms, a given situation into something that can be assimilated to available schemas. Operative knowing can be thought of as that aspect of knowing which is the meaning aspect.

At the sensorimotor level, the distinction between figurative and operative knowing is not a meaningful distinction because the infant is at the same time perceiving and acting and the figurative and operative aspects of behaviour are inextricably linked. It is only with the achievement of operational structures that it becomes realistic to distinguish between figurative and operative knowing because it is at this stage that a person becomes able to know without externally acting.

This distinction becomes important at the operational level because a person can know something with varying degrees of understanding. For example, suppose I ask a friend: "Do you know what a car is?" He might reply in terms of shape, size and location of controls. This knowing of a car is largely figurative and is primarily perceptual. On the other hand I might have another friend who answers the question "What is a car?" in terms of combustion transmission, fuel consumption, wheel base, cubic capacity of cylinders etc., related in such a way as to indicate that he knows how a car works. In comparison to the first friend, he exhibits a high level operative knowing.

Again, consider what a "ball" means to children of differing ages. In the sensorimotor period the child will assimilate the ball to a practical *action* schema. At the preoperational level the child will assimilate the ball to an *object* schema for he now knows that there exist such things as chairs, knives, dishes and plates.

From the figurative point of view, the two-year-old child's knowing of this ball will be about as well formed as it will ever be. But during the pre-operational period there will be an increase in the childs "meaning" or operative knowing as he comes to know more of the uses of the ball, how it is made, and some other of its properties.

By the time he has reached the concrete level of operations his operative knowing will have become even more transcendent. Take for example the plasticine ball test referred to above. Here the young child has no trouble agreeing that there are two balls and it might be supposed that this figurative aspect of knowing, perceiving that they are balls, is not very much different from what it was much earlier. This is not so for the operative aspect, for here we see distinct differences depending on the level of logical operations present. If the child can conserve, then he will be able to follow the trans-formation of the plasticine from one form (state) to the other and assimilate this to the schema of conservation whereby he will be able to compensate through reversibility and decentration, and account for the distortion that has taken place. The meaning he gives to the process is dependent on the active assimilation of the transformations to available structures.

This is not so for the intuitive thinker who attends to the various states e.g. ball to sausage and misses the essential transformation in between. He is to a greater extent engaging in figurative knowing than is the conserver. The conserver *knows* the ball (of plasticine) at a different level. Whereas the intuitive thinker sees the deformed plasticine ball (sausage) as a non-ball, the conserver sees it as a ball in another form that can be restored to a ball if necessary. The difference is in the degree of operative or "meaning" knowing, and this meaning is invested by the structures available rather than by the perception or image of the object attained.

This increase in the importance of operative knowing continues to develop and reaches its highest level of manifestation at the formal level. Thus know-ing is not a passive registering of images of what is out there. Rather it is an interactional process by which environmental aspects are transformed and assimilated in relation to the particular structures possessed by the individual.

Operative knowing refers to the transformation of objects and events so that they can be assimilated to current general structures, while figurative knowing relates to the configuration of these specific objects and events. The development of intelligence is therefore primarily a matter of a progressive increase in the influence of operative activity or operative knowing, with figurative knowing playing a subordinate role.

One special problem with which the distinction between operative and figurative knowing is concerned is their role in symbol use. In Chapter 2, attention was drawn to the distinction Piaget makes between symbols and signs both of which were subsumed under the general heading symbolic function. In the discussion which follows, this distinction is blurred by referring to both symbols and signs by the single term symbol. When used in this sense, symbol is equivalent to Piaget's "symbolic function" and refers to "the ability to represent something . . . by means of a 'signifier' which is differentiated and which serves only a representative purpose: language, mental image, symbolic gesture and so on" (Piaget, 1969, 51).

Examples of symbols in this sense would be words, pictures, drawings, movements of objects and people. As symbols they have both figurative and operative aspects. Take the use of words for example. Parents frequently delight in their three-year-old offspring being able to use big words: a young preconceptual child may say "My daddy is an industrial chemist". The word "daddy" is in effect a sound sequence to the child, and as such it has a *material* aspect as a sequence of sounds. It has a *figurative* aspect. It also has an operative aspect as well, because the sound sequence can be assimilated to a structure and given meaning. The child's schema of "daddy" at four years is fairly well formed. This is not the case with the words "industrial chemist". The figurative knowing is present in the perception of the words but there would be very low-level operative knowing because the schema for "industrial" and the schema for "chemist" would hardly exist. But at sixteen, when the formal level of reasoning had been reached, the position would be quite different. The operative aspects by then could be described as high-level because the *meaning* aspect, through assimilation to a well developed operational structure, would be considerable.

What Piaget is suggesting here is of fundamental importance to education. Generally, symbols do not explain knowing in the absence of operative knowing. It is operative knowing which explains symbols. This has far reaching consequences for the education of the child. To take a most important aspect. The development of concepts up to the stage of consolidation of concrete thinking cannot move forward solely on the basis of verbal exercise; by symbolisation alone. Attempts to do so are based on the faulty premise that concepts are formed basically by the interiorisation of perceptual images, and ignore the overwhelming importance of action-based operative aspects of knowing. This theme will be taken up again in later chapters when the more detailed educational implications are discussed.

The picture changes, however, with the advent of the formal level of reasoning. Words become much more powerful tools in the development of reasoning as the *operative* aspects of words as symbols increases. This raises the important and controversial question of the role of language in thinking and it is to this question that attention is now directed.

THE ROLE OF LANGUAGE IN THINKING

The controversy which exists with respect to the role of language in the development of thought does not concern the question of whether language contributes to the development of thought. All psychologists agree that it does. The controversy centres around the stage at which language becomes an effective instrument in the development of thought, and the manner in which it relates to the development of thinking. The view presented here is, of course, the view of Piaget. Readers interested in examining the views of other thinkers in this field should consult the works of Bruner, Vygotsky, Luria, etc.

Piaget's basic position is that language does not effectively contribute to the development of thought (operational intelligence) until the stage of formal operations, or at least until formal operations begin to appear. Piaget's main contention is that the development of logical operations is not closely related to language until the stage of formal operations. This does not mean that language plays no role in the intellectual life of the child. Piaget makes it quite clear that it does. He believes that from the beginning of the pre-operational period language may increase the powers of thought in range and rapidity (1969, 86). On this point he sees three marked advances of verbal behaviour over sensorimotor behaviour, which may be summarised as follows:

1   Through narration and evocation, verbal patterns can represent a long chain of actions very rapidly whereas the child using sensorimotor patterns is obliged to follow events at the same speed as the action.

2   Language liberates the child from the immediate because thought can range over vast stretches of time and space.

3   Whereas the sensorimotor intelligence proceeds by means of successive acts, step by step, thought, particularly through language, can represent simultaneously all the elements of an organised structure (1969, 86).

But Piaget notes that these advantages of representative thought do not belong specifically to language alone, but to the symbolic function as a whole of which language is only one aspect. It will be instructive here to recall how symbols come about and see the similarity in the development of language and other symbols.

Take the case of a very young child watching a trench digger at work. He sees the shovel head bite into the earth, lift, turn and dump the earth into a waiting truck. As he watches, it becomes apparent that he makes certain slight movements as he accommodates to the situation. Close scrutiny will reveal, perhaps, that his fingers and hand are cupped in imitation of the shovel and he may even make digging, lifting and dumping movements with his hand. His representation of the event is in terms of symbolic gestures.

But suppose that the boy's father had been present and had said "That is a big scoop and it is digging a big hole for some water pipes". It would come as no surprise to find that later at his home the boy was observed in his sand

69

pit scooping up sand and dumping it into a toy truck saying "I'm a scoop. I'm digging a big hole."

The child is using the words "scoop" and "hole" as symbols to represent what has happened. These symbols come into being by imitation which is fundamentally accommodation. In a similar fashion, the child's deferred imitation of the scoop as he digs the hole in the sand is fundamentally accommodation. Both the imitation and the language are symbolic to the child, the difference being that the symbolic representation of deferred imitation has been constructed entirely by the child himself, whereas the language symbols have already been arbitrarily defined by society and come to him ready made, although language is certainly as much a part of the physical environment as are people and things.

The crucial question, however, is, "Does *knowing* increase because of symbol representation?" The answer is "Not very much". Symbolic repetition of the event simply replays the child's existing knowledge relative to his level of development. In the case of the hole digging discussed above, "meaning" is given by the operative or action aspect. Symbols get their meaning from the operative structure and not vice versa. Knowing proceeds best in young children through actual contact.

I know a young woman who as a three-year-old child wanted an elephant for a backyard pet. Her parents tried to convince her that you could not keep an elephant in the backyard and in fact the whole idea was impractical. She persisted in her idea and her resolve was strengthened with every encounter with a picture book or TV programme featuring elephants. The parents finally took the child to the zoo where she had been promised a ride on the elephant. When the elephant lurched past, towering above the child, she fled in terror, and when later asked why she had fled exclaimed "Oh it is so big and it smells so awful". Symbols had not served this child well in the advancement of her knowledge of elephants.

A similar situation exists when young children assert unhesitatingly that they are going to become firemen, policemen or engine drivers. Young children spend a great deal of time playing games in which they imitate firemen, policemen and engine drivers. But in doing this the child is, typically, not challenging his operative knowing of the functions of these occupations. When at a later age these same children express no desire to become firemen, policemen or engine drivers we say their "concepts" have changed. And so they have through the considerable advance in operative rather than figurative knowing. Symbolic behaviour does not become operative until the formal level of thinking is reached. Symbols do not carry meaning in themselves, but only in so far as they depend on the knowing scheme of the individual who uses them (Furth, 1970, 62).

These ideas are of considerable importance for the classroom. Teachers spend a great deal of time on what is called concept development. Unfortunately, as many teachers would agree, this time is often wasted in the primary school when teachers try to develop concepts through verbal means. Frequently the solution to the problem of uncertainty with respect to a concept is to use more words. Yet if there is a difference between operative and figurative knowing, if there are limitations to the efficacy of symbols including language to promote growth in thought, and if the child needs experience with the actual material up to the concrete stage, then this solution is wrong.

Concept development proceeds best where the operative aspects of knowing are challenged, and this implies activity in the true sense of the word—a theme which will be taken up later in the chapters devoted to implications for education and teaching.

DEVELOPMENT AND LEARNING

To begin this discussion on development and learning, consider the following answers given to one of the Peel stories, see Chapter 2, by three children aged six, eleven and fourteen. The story is short and simple. The individual words can be understood by the six-year-old because the vocabulary is within his grasp when the story is read to him.

The story is the well known one of how King Alfred burnt the cakes. After reading it or having it read to him the child is asked two questions:

"Could Alfred cook?"
"Why do you think so?"

Answers to this question obtained by the author from three children whose ages were as specified above were:

Six-year-old: "Yes, because he is the king and kings are very strong";

Eleven-year-old: "No, because if he could cook then he would not have let the cakes burn";

Fourteen-year-old: "It is difficult to tell from the story because if anyone could cook and had something on his mind, he might still forget the cakes. However, he probably could cook because as the story says he had to hide from the Danes and he would no doubt have had to fend for himself."

That there are distinct differences between these answers is obvious, and the popular reason given for these would probably be "Oh but there is such a difference in age", and so there is. This is no real explanation but within it lies the germ of an explanation. On the other hand a teacher whose training included a course in the development and measurement of intelligence from the conventional viewpoint might say "Well, this is the kind of difference you would expect on the basis of Mental Age". This explanation too contains the germ of an explanation. Yet neither explanation is sufficient.

The author has administered the "Alfred Test" to some 2 000 subjects ranging from young intuitive reasoners to highly sophisticated university and college students. It is very frequently the case that children of the same MA, say of 14, write answers as different in quality as the eleven and fourteen-year-old above.

71

The reason for the qualitative differences in the answers can be traced directly to Piaget's theory. The same story, the identical words are presented to each of the three children. Therefore as symbols the words whether they are seen or heard present somewhat the same figurative aspects.

For example the figurative knowing of "he came one day to the hut" and "she let him sit by the fire to warm himself . . ." would be much the same for all three children. The difference lies in the operational knowing or the logical structure that has been applied to them. To be sure, the very fact that a child can understand the symbol "woman" means that in addition to a figurative aspect there is also an operative one which gives it its meaning. But basically the difference in the answers given lies in the logical structure or operational knowing that is applied to the story.

Consider the first answer given by a six-year-old boy. The answer he gives is in terms of his cognitive structure. In terms of the meaning he can give to the words presented. But his knowing scheme is clearly intuitive. The child has focused on only one aspect of the data. He has assimilated the story to his schema of "king", which in terms of meaning is at a low operative level. "King" for him means an omnipotent warrior carrying all before him. He is unable to connect cause and effect or to establish simple relationships between two or more aspects of the story.

Clearly, no amount of telling or instruction in relationships between the various aspects of the story would serve any useful purpose. The meaning he gives to the passage is determined by the level of logical operations, or the intellectual structure available, which in his case is intuitive or preoperational.

The second answer, given by the eleven-year-old boy, is qualitatively much better. He says in effect if the king could cook then he wouldn't have burnt the cakes. This is clearly an advance in logical operations for the child now reasons in the form "If A, then B". This is similar to his reasoning in respect to conservation in the plasticine ball experiment. And just as the child's reasoning in that experiment is dependent upon having the plasticine present (concrete operational stage), so the reasoning of the eleven-year-old child remains tied to the data given in the King Alfred story. Nevertheless the meaning given to the story is much better, in the sense of being more advanced than that of the six-year-old.

The answer given by the fourteen-year-old is at a different level again. The operational structure applied in this case is obviously at the formal operational level, and the meaning given by him is poles apart qualitatively from that given by the six-year-old. Here we have evidence of the child taking into account extenuating possibilities, the preoccupation of Alfred. This represents in a sense a going outside of the data and looking at the logical relationships. This mode of reasoning is continued when he concludes that being forced to go into hiding implied that of necessity Alfred would have to learn to cook. Once again it is the application of a superior operational intelligence with its high level of operative or meaning aspect which makes this answer qualitatively superior.

72

This is not to say that the conventional view of intelligence in terms of Mental Age is irrelevant. It plainly is relevant and the links between Piaget's view of intelligence and the conventional view have already been explored in Chapter 3. Nevertheless the fact remains that the qualitative differences in interpretation among the three stories can be readily explained in terms of the progressive availability of operational thought and the corresponding increase in the operative aspect of knowing over the figurative aspect.

So far the discussion has been concerned fundamentally with the role of the *development* of thought as it affects interpretation. The subheading above clearly said Development and Learning. Suppose, to continue in historical vein, an Australian child is taught that Blaxland, Lawson and Wentworth crossed the Blue Mountains in 1813, and in the United States, a child of the same age is taught that in 1775 the British routed the Colonial troops at the Battle of Bunker Hill. Here we have two instances of what many believe school is all about, for each is an example of one kind of teaching learning situation. Obviously the teacher would expect that in each case the child would learn these facts and remember them for some future occasion. If we recall the discussion concerning King Alfred we will know that the "meaning" given to these facts will vary with the developmental level of each child. Each child will know these facts according to the availability of operational structures, according to the framework within which knowing takes place.

Learning on the other hand is concerned with the contents of the things we know. If the two children are at the same developmental level, they have available the same structure to deal with the facts presented, for in Piaget's view of intellectual development, intelligence is best viewed as a general instrument of knowing. If both children are at the concrete operational level, then they cannot interpret the crossing of the Blue Mountains or the Battle of Bunker Hill at a level higher than concrete operational. Learning is concerned with specific aspects. We learn that the letter C comes after the letter B, that the biggest river system in Australia is the Murray-Darling, that Sir Edmund Hilary was the first man to conquer Mt. Everest, that a triangle has three sides and three angles. This requires special experience and what we know in that sense is dependent on where we spend most of our lives.

In a way, the development of operational intelligence is dependent upon specific experiences, but in another it is not. The development of operations cannot take place in the absence of experiences with objects. Yet cross-cultural studies have shown that operations develop even though the environment makes available different objects for the child to experience. The common factor in the development of operations and logical thought is not particular and exclusive experiences but the *formal abstraction* from the general co-ordination of actions, or what Piaget refers to as general experience.[1] A child achieves and consolidates the ability to conserve and

---

[1] Formal abstraction is a term employed by Furth (1969, 66) in preference to Piaget's "reflective logico-mathematical abstraction" so that the same word can be used for sensorimotor and operational forms, where the word "formal" stresses the general form which is progressively abstracted from a particular content.

the capacity to apply it to a wide variety of situations because he has abstracted and assimilated the co-ordinations of actions endemic to many particular instances.

The development of operational intelligence, or the development of the "instrument" for knowing or giving meaning, can be clearly distinguished then from learning where learning is concerned as knowing specifics. But it can also be distinguished by the selective operation of forgetting.

Introductory textbooks on psychology usually treat learning and forgetting as two sides of the one coin. One way to ensure retention is to overlearn material, to learn a task, e.g., a list of French verbs, for a number of occasions after it can be correctly recalled. Piaget has a more detailed view of memory than the basic distinction which is about to be made, and it is presented as the last sub-section in this chapter. Once a child has developed the capacity to conserve it is extremely unlikely that he will forget it. A true conserver will always know that no matter how much the plasticine ball is distorted the quantity remains the same. He will always know that no matter how thin the vessel, the quantity of the liquid remains the same. He might not always know that Blaxland, Lawson and Wentworth crossed the Blue Mountains in 1813. It does not make sense to talk about forgetting conservation and incidentally makes no better sense to the author to talk about "teaching" it. Intellectual development, or the general instrument of knowing, depends upon the provision of suitable experiences at the appropriate time. It depends upon the match. It contains its own motivation and does not, like learning, respond to extrinsic rewards or reinforcement. This does not mean that learning, in the sense of knowing specific facts or content, is a waste of time. This is clearly not so. The maintenance of such a stance would be ludicrous and indefensible.

Piaget is not so much concerned with what is "taught" or "transmitted" as he is with *how* it is taught. He is adamant that the methods of social transmission, "teaching", should be such as take into account, provide for and encourage the development of operational intelligence. To this end he is clearly in favour of true activity methods, a point which is developed in Chapter 5. Let it be understood that it is not being claimed that teachers unfamiliar with Piaget's theory have confused development and learning. Experienced teachers show considerable insight in this respect and develop intuitively the capacity to determine when individual development is sufficiently advanced for the introduction of the next experience.

MEMORY AND INTELLIGENCE

Piaget (1968 (b), 1, 2) begins his discussion of memory and intelligence by accepting that it is usual to represent memory as a system of coding and decoding which, of course, implies a code. What he does challenge is the inference that this code remains the same throughout development. In fact he asserts that it does not and puts forward the hypothesis that the memory code itself depends on the subject's operations and is therefore modified during development.

He tested this hypothesis by a series of experiments one of which is described. The basic approach was to present a stimulus to the subjects who were advised to "have a good look" so that they would be able to reproduce it later. Without re-presentation, the children were asked, e.g., to draw what they had seen after one week and after six months. If Piaget's hypothesis was tenable, then memory for the original model ought to improve with the progress of operations. If there was no substance to his suggestion, then memory would deteriorate or at best remain the same.

The experiment about to be described is the first one reported in Piaget's monograph, *On the Development of Memory and Identity* (1968 (b)). It should be noted that the other experiments reported were more complex and the results not as conclusive, although they all supported the hypothesis. A number of children aged from three to eight were shown an ordered set of ten sticks varying in size from 9 to 15 cm. The sticks were already in order and did not have to be arranged. After a period of one week and then six months, without seeing the sticks again, the children were asked to draw and sometimes to describe verbally what they had been shown before.

Results after one week

Piaget found that what the subject retained after one week was not the perceptual model as such, but the way in which it was assimilated to the operational schema. What was retained depended upon the operational level of each subject. Five patterns of recall were revealed which corresponded roughly with age. These were as follows:

1 Children aged three to four years remember a certain number of sticks lined up but represent them as all of the same length /////.

2 From four to five years, approximately, children recall that there are big sticks and small sticks but only of two sizes as ///₁₁₁ or /₁/₁/₁ .

3 A slightly more advanced level among the four to five year olds was putting the sticks in the form of triplets //₁ //₁ or ///////₁₁₁ .

4 Five to six year olds generally produce a small series of four or five elements.

5 Finally, at around six to seven years, a series like the original of about ten elements is produced.

Results after six months

After six months all subjects from three to eight years claimed to remember well what was originally shown. However, the interesting aspect of the experiment was that the children did not reproduce the same drawing or description. There was not one instance of deterioration of memory in this particular experiment (although there were such instances in other experiments). Seventy four per cent had a better recollection after six months than they had after one week. Progress for each child was gradual, and there were no big leaps. The typical improvement was from one level to the next.

Piaget's Interpretation

First the memory-image is not simply a prolonging of the model as perceived· Rather it seems to act in a symbolic manner so as to reflect the subject's assimilation "schèmes", that is the way in which he understood the model. Piaget emphasises understanding as against "copying".

During the six months of the experiment the operational or preoperational scheme of assimilation referred to evolves as the child continues to compare objects of different size, and to engage in the many related experiences involved in the development of the scheme of ordering. The new scheme of the next level then serves as a code for decoding the original memory, but it is the decoding by a code that has changed. It is now better structured than it was before, and this gives rise to a new image which symbolises the current state of the operational schema, and not what it was at the time when the encoding was done.[2]

Piaget performed other more complex experiments on memory and concluded that where there was a deterioration of memory it was accompanied by a conflict among two or more "schèmes" or the existing "schèmes" were not adequate to support the memory images. He concluded, however, that the experiments showed the tight dependence of memory on the conservation and development of "schèmes" (Piaget, 1968 (b), 15). Piaget does not deny that memory has a figurative aspect, in the sense that it is dependent on perception and mental imagery, but he emphasises that memory is also dependent on operative structure and that memory is therefore in some ways a special case of intellectual activity (operative knowing) applied to the reconstruction of the past.

SUMMARY AND CONCLUSION

The consistent theme which provides the underlying link between the several topics discussed in this chapter is that of the role and importance of operational intelligence. This has been successively considered in relation to "knowing", "language", "development and learning", and "memory". It will be instructive by way of concluding the chapter to summarise the role of operational intelligence in each of these areas.

Knowing

Developmentally, progress which is made in the capacity to know is fundamentally progress in the operative or structural aspects of knowing, the "meaning" aspects of knowing, as against the figurative or configurational

---

[2] This account of memory and the operations of intelligence is based on Piaget's paper "Memory and Operations of Intelligence", pp. 1-16, the first of two papers in J. Piaget, *On the Development of Memory and Identity*, 1968 (b).

aspect of knowing. Things can be "known" in the ultimate only in so far as operational structures permit them to be known.

Language

Symbols do not carry meaning in themselves but only in so far as they depend upon the knowing (operational) "schèmes". From Piaget's point of view, except in the formal stages of reasoning, the effective development of language awaits the development of operativity, in the widest sense; and not the other way round.[3]

Development and Learning

For Piaget development explains learning. The development of Operational Intelligence, that is the development of the "instrument" for knowing or giving meaning, is distinguished from learning in that learning is conceived as knowing specifics. Development explains learning because a thing can only be known to the degree of development of the logical structures.

Memory

As with "knowing", Piaget sees memory as having both a figurative and operative aspect. He does not deny the importance of the figurative aspect, but he emphasises that memory is fundamentally related to existing operative structures and is therefore a special case of intellectual activity applied to the reconstruction of the past.

A final comment

If one of the fundamental aims of education is the development of concepts, then it would seem that the best single guarantee of the eventual achievement of this aim would be the prosecution of an educational programme which would maximise the likelihood of the development of operational intelligence. Even when one considers the classroom scene in terms of conventional aspects of instruction—*memory, learning, development, language, knowledge* and the role of intelligence itself—the central role of *operational intelligence* is undeniable. This is not to deny the existence of other equally worthy educational goals. But it would seem that the underlying importance of logical structure in so many areas should ensure that the development and consolidation of logical structures should remain a continuing goal of child development beyond the stage of the few desultory conservation exercises that characterise many attempts at implementing Piaget's theory of intellectual development.

---

[3] The term "operational" is used by Piaget in a general and a specific sense. As a specific term it refers to the attainment of logical operations beginning at the concrete period. In the general sense it refers to the presence of operative knowing and as such takes in the preoperational period.

5. General Implications of Piaget's Theory for Education and Teaching

In a recent book, *Science of Education and the Psychology of the Child* (1971), Piaget makes it quite clear that he strongly supports what he calls the "new methods of education" and views with disfavour what he calls the "traditional school".[1] He also makes it quite clear that the new methods have their origin in the psychological developments of the twentieth century and that it was the "great movement of modern genetic psychology" that was the source of the new methods (1971, 145). Piaget is, of course, the leading exponent of this movement and, in reaching his conclusion, he traces the development of the new methods through three fairly clearly defined stages. The first concerns the work of Rousseau, Pestalozzi and Froebel. In summing up these early thinkers' contribution to modern education, Piaget notes that generally speaking, although they had anticipated the new methods of education, they failed, despite their intuitive or practical knowledge of childhood, to establish a body of psychology necessary for the working out of educational techniques that are truly adapted to the laws of mental development.

The second stage of the "emergence of the new methods of education" is less clearly stated, but lay in the contribution of such psychologist-educators as Dewey, Claparède and Decroly. The strength of the contribution of this twentieth-century psychology lay in the fact that it was "from the outset, and in all its aspects, an affirmation and an analysis of activity", and that "everywhere we find the idea that the life of the mind is a dynamic reality; intelligence a real and constructive activity" (1971, 146).

But the ultimate source of the new methods, "whatever the connection in the case of each of our principal innovators between child psychology and their key ideas in the field of education", was in the "great movement of modern genetic psychology" (1971, 145). Thus, although Piaget did not specifically conduct his research for the purposes of contributing to educational practice, it is clear that he sees his work as providing support for a particular method and as providing a basis for educational change.

[1] Piaget has, of course, consistently maintained this position.

78

But two points must be clarified before Piaget's particular contributions can be evaluated. The first task is to make clear what differences Piaget sees between the "traditional" and the "new methods". The second is to outline the fundamental tenets of the "new method" as it had developed prior to Piaget's great body of work, and to indicate in so doing the points of agreement and disagreement between that early position and Piaget's present theory. This will amount to a discussion of the work of the experimentalists with particular emphasis on Dewey's ideas, even though Piaget cites the work of Claparède more frequently than he does that of Dewey.

In Piaget's view, "the traditional school imposes his work on the student: it makes him work" and while he acknowledges that a good teacher may teach in such a way as to make provision for genuine activity, nevertheless Piaget believes that "in the logic of the system, the students' intellectual and moral activity remains heteronomous [subject to external law] because it is inseparable from a continual restraint exercised by the teacher" (Piaget, 1971, 151). "The new school, on the contrary, appeals to real activity, to spontaneous work based upon personal need and interest" (Piaget, 1971, 152), although Piaget is quick to point out that this does not mean that active education requires that children should do anything they want.

To Piaget, the distinction is clear. The traditional school imposes certain constraints upon the child while the new methods encourage spontaneous activity based on personal need and interest. To those familiar with the history of educational thought in the twentieth century, this is a very familiar distinction and one that was forcefully emphasised by John Dewey in *Democracy and Education* (1917).

If, then, Piaget agrees with the experimentalists in fundamental terms, a useful way to proceed will be first, to give a synthesis of experimentalist views on man and education, and then to examine more specifically the points where Piaget's views intersect or differ with experimentalism.

THE EXPERIMENTALISTS' POSITION

Experimentalist views mean, fundamentally, Dewey's views because he is experimentalism's leading exponent. But there were other contributors including Kilpatrick and Hullfish. Consequently what follows is a synthesis of experimentalism as it has emerged in the twentieth century. Frequently the term experimentalism and Dewey's name will be used interchangeably.

To the experimentalist, man is a self-directing organism in continuous interaction with the environment. He is not regarded as having passive impulses waiting to be called into play by stimuli from the environment. The organism is active and actively seeks objects and experiences which will serve as instruments for the achievement of its purposes. Thus, the environment is explored by the individual who selects and reaches for environmental factors which bring opportunities for satisfaction and growth. The organism is then purposive, active and goal seeking.

For Dewey, thinking has come about in man in the evolutionary practice of seeking and attaining these objectives because thinking is that which has been found useful, instrumental, in the process of reaching what is "imperiously demanded" for the purposes of growth. Thinking has developed as an aid to the full biological expansion of man. Thinking, for the experimentalist, takes place when man is faced with a situation in which his old habits will not work. When this happens, he attempts to reconstruct his experiences so that he can deal with the new situation. He is forced to consider the factors in the situation so that cognitive reorganisation (mental reorganisation) takes place leading to an emergent line of action which seems likely to lead to a successful solution to the situation or problem. The individual faced with a problem makes use of his past experience to test the possible consequences of his proposed actions. In this way he selects the one which seems to be the most promising and applies it and, if this fails, cognitive reorganisation again takes place and he tries once more. Valuable experience has been gained in the process and this will integrate with the original activity and should a similar problem arise its solution would then be more likely. Thus cognitive restructuring or mental reorganisation will modify the mental activity involved in future problems.

The experimentalist is convinced that the individual in his interaction with the environment and in the course of his purposive goal seeking behaviour typically engages in problem solving, that is thinking, to achieve its ends. Thinking is therefore an instrument which secures for the organism that which he desires in his constant movement towards continued growth.

It is not surprising then that a group who conceived of the organism in this way would favour the method of enquiry and the experimental method as the most appropriate ways to achieve their aim of the progressive development of the ability to think and judge. Education, therefore, is not a routine habit formation or conditioning. It is intelligent enquiry and thought. The experimentalist sees the development of knowledge as residing in doing, in activity, in interacting with the problems of the environment by applying to each problem the scientific method which briefly stated involves:

1 becoming aware of a problem;
2 clarifying the problem;
3 proposing hypotheses for the solution of the problem;
4 reasoning out the implications of these hypotheses; and
5 testing the hypothesis against experience.

With respect to the nature of knowing, the experimentalists adopt a position which has considerable similarity with that of Piaget. To the experimentalist, things are responded to not as things as they *are* but as *meanings*. Knowledge abstracts just those aspects of a thing that suit its purpose. Hence the "object", as taken by knowledge, is not the thing as given in experience but as it is constructed in the *knowing* process. But above all, education as conceived by the experimentalists is conjoint activity. That is, activity which is not just activity but activity which has a social purpose. Therefore, because education is conjoint activity and has a social purpose, school methods must

80

reflect the processes and interelations of society as a whole so that both the school and the community become places where the development of the individual proceeds through interaction with all members of both the school and the wider society. Education, for the experimentalist, is much broader than schooling.

Education is growth, not preparation for the future. Education is the continuous expansion of activity in more fruitful and socially desirable ways and the task of the teacher becomes one of guiding the learner into meaningful activities that inevitably lead to further meaningful activities. Or stated in related terms: education is growth leading to further growth and the problem of education becomes one of how best to guide the interests and capacities of the child in the socially desired direction.

Summary

1 The human organism is a self-directing, purposive, goal seeking organism for whom interest plays a vital role in his interaction with the environment.

2 Thinking developed to aid man to full biological expansion.

3 Knowledge: Things are responded to not as they are but as meanings.

4 Man typically proceeds by problem solving in which cognitive restructuring and profiting from experience through integrating activities plays a dominant role.

5 Education is: (a) The application of intelligent enquiry for the progressive development of the ability to think and judge; (b) Conjoint activity in which individuals interact so that the whole of society is educative; and (c) Growth leading to further growth.

PIAGET, THE EXPERIMENTALIST POSITION AND EDUCATION

Discussion Point 1. Man is an active self-directing, purposive, goal seeking organism who interacts with his environment

On the whole Piaget would agree but there would be some reservations for he would place a different interpretation on some aspects of man's behaviour and development. In Chapter 2, considerable discussion centred around the concept of adaptation. Man, like all biological organisms adapts to his environment. For Piaget, man adapts by accommodating to the pressures of the environment and assimilating the changes that result to his structures so that he is then better equipped to deal with the environment as his structures, through organisation, become more complex, differentiated and capable of greater generalisation. Piaget also stresses the point that man is an active organism who is in dynamic interaction with the world. Initially, this activity is overt as the child in the sensorimotor stage interprets the world by the actions that can be applied to it. Gradually this predominance of overt activity gives way to internalised thought so that at maturity much of the action of the individual is mental activity.

Piaget makes it quite clear that with respect to education he uses the term active in a special sense. He writes:

> the term activity is ambiguous and can be taken either in the sense of functional behaviour based on interest or in the sense of "performance" referring to some external operation of a motor nature. In fact, only the first of these two kinds of activity characterises the active school at every level (for one can be active in the first sense even in pure thought), whereas the second kind of activity is indispensable in the highest degree solely in infants and diminishes in importance with age (Piaget, 1971, 163).

Whether in infancy or maturity, man does not sit around waiting for some stimuli or other to prod him into action and it seems that Piaget and the experimentalists are in general agreement here.

The experimentalist school, in general, accepted the psychology of the Gestaltist-Field Theorists. In particular they accepted the general viewpoint which stressed motives or motivation in terms of goals. Thus the organism with needs sought goals to satisfy these needs. Blockage to the attainment of such goals increased tension resulting in cognitive reorganisation which sought to reduce the tension induced by the blockage. Piaget would not dispute the fact that in his interaction with the environment cognitive re-organisation takes place. His explanation would be in terms of the now familiar adaptation through accommodation and assimilation. Faced with a situation to which he was unable to assimilate, the individual would be forced to accommodate to the novel features and assimilate. But Piaget finds no need to invoke a motivational concept, such as drive reduction or tension reduction, to account for cognitive and intellectual change. The fundamental principle in organismic-environmental interaction is equilibration. Through equilibration of accommodation and assimilation the cognitive structure is brought into dynamic balance so that the organism may again interact and so progressively develop. To Piaget the cognitive structures are self motivating. If the problem facing the child is outside its accommodative grasp, e.g. long division to a six-year-old, then it is a "non-problem". There is no match of current cognitive structure to environment. If the problem is too easy, the child assimilates readily. Optimum development takes place when accommodation and assimilation are in dynamic balance, are equilibrated, and progress is most effective under conditions of moderate disparity of structure and problem. This was referred to in Chapter 2 as the principle of moderate novelty or interest.

With respect to the purposive aspect of man's behaviour, Piaget would agree with the experimentalists if the meaning attached to purposive was: (a) continuous interaction with and adaptation to the environment as a functioning biological organism; and (b) that the concept of purpose as used in this context was, in effect, synonymous with "interest" in the sense that purpose means pursuing a task with interest. Thus Piaget would most likely accept that man is an active, self-directing, purposive organism but he might

82

Plate 1. Attribute blocks from Triad Mathematics Laboratory, Level 1. (Photo: Jacaranda Press)

Plate 2. Concept (classification) development. Triad Mathematics Laboratory, Level 1. (Photo: Jacaranda Press)

Plate 3. Material for the evalution of conservation. Triad Mathematics Laboratory, Level 1. (Photo: Jacaranda Press)

Plate 4. Interpersonal interaction, co-operation, discussion and experiencing. (Photo: Jacaranda Press)

not ▭	big	not small	thin
small	thick	not ▭	not big
not △	not ◣	not big	not ○

Plate 5. Attribute snap cards (words). Concept (classification) development. Triad Mathematics Laboratory, Level 1. (Photo: Jacaranda Press)

Plate 6. Experiences with environmental materials. (Photo: Jacaranda Press)

Plate 7. Structured environment and the opportunity for genuine activity, figurative and operative knowing.

Plate 8. Interpersonal interaction, co-operation, discussion, genuine activity and experience.

Plate 9. Interaction, co-operation and operative knowing.

well have reservations about accepting goal seeking in the full experimentalist sense.

2 Thinking developed to aid man to full biological expansion

Piaget would be sympathetic but, as we have seen, he goes much further in that he says that intelligence (thinking) is biological. The same general mechanisms which underlie physical development, organisation, adaptation (accommodation and assimilation) and equilibration apply equally to the development of thought.

3 Knowledge. Things are responded to not as they are but as meanings

There are two fundamental reasons why Piaget would support this view. First, as was made clear in Chapter 2, when the individual assimilates, i.e., gives meaning to an environmental event (stimulus) the available structures impose their own organisation to that environmental intrusion. Thus the object or event is not simply passively recorded, camera-like, but is transformed by an active process of mediation in the process of being assimilated. The object or event is not copied directly.

Second, as indicated in Chapter 4, Piaget distinguishes between figurative knowing which focuses on the static configuration of things, and operative knowing which is the meaning aspect. Operative knowing can be illustrated, as in Chapter 4, by an example relating to conservation. If a preoperational child, e.g., a four-year-old, is presented with the plasticine ball problem he typically concentrates on the beginning and end states. He looks at the plasticine ball and he looks at the long plasticine snake and says they have different amounts of plasticine. This is largely figurative knowing. Later, at the concrete stage, the child's thinking (knowing) will be dominated by the operative aspects because he will focus on what happens in between, on the actual transformation that takes place. His knowledge of the object will not only be of a figurative kind, but will also be in terms of the greater meaning that his operative structures provide.

Thus while Piaget clearly would agree with the notion that things are responded to as meanings his formulation gets much closer to the reasons why, an aspect of Piaget's theory which was taken up at length in Chapter 4. But there is inherent in this conception of knowledge held by Piaget an affirmation of a distinction made by the experimentalists which is of fundamental importance. Educators down the centuries, particularly since the time of Rousseau, have asserted that the child is not a miniature adult. This is certainly true of the experimentalists and is summed up in the following quotation from Dewey's The Child and the Curriculum:

> Classification is not a matter of child experience; things do not come to the individual pigeonholed. The vital ties of affection, the connecting bonds of activity hold together the variety of his personal experiences. The adult mind is so familiar with the notion of logically ordered facts

that it does not recognise—it cannot realise—the amount of separating and reformulating which the facts of direct experience have to undergo before they can appear as a "study" or branch of learning. (1906, 6)

Experimentalists therefore support the contention that the child is different from the adult and that nowhere is this more evident than in the way in which the child reasons and learns. The child is not a miniature adult because of the qualitative differences which exist in the way in which he interprets the environment. However, while the experimentalist school of thought clearly recognised this and made the child the centre of the educative process, it has remained for Piaget to demonstrate just how precisely the child does differ in his thought and understanding.

In previous chapters we have seen that Piaget begins by proposing that the *functioning* of the mind is the same at all levels (adaptation and organisation) and that this functioning leads to the development of mental *structures* which are characteristic and indeed describe the *stage* of thinking that a child has reached. This has important implications for education because it is a particular view of intellectual development, of child development. And whether it is made explicit or not, all education, all teaching—no matter where or of what kind—is based upon a theory of child development. Any system of education, or for that matter any teacher, who plans day to day experiences for children does so with some idea as to how these experiences might affect the child and with some idea of what is aimed at overall.

Piaget makes it clear (1971, 159-160), that he believes that traditional education regards the child as a small but ignorant adult so that, for traditionalists, the educator's task is not so much to *form* the child's mind as to furnish it though the presentation of subject matter from outside. But, he says, the problem becomes quite different as soon as the hypothesis of *structural variations* is accepted:

> If the child's thought is qualitatively different from our own, then the principal aim of education is to form its intellectual and moral reasoning power. And since that power cannot be formed from outside, the question is to find the most suitable methods and environment to help the child constitute it itself. (Piaget, 1971, 160)

It is quite obvious that Piaget favours educational methods that give due recognition to: (a) the progressive development of logical structures (schemas) i.e., the particular stage of reasoning that has been reached; (b) the realisation that the child literally constructs his own intelligence (logical structures) and therefore his capacity to deal with the environment; and (c) the fact that these structures develop best in appropriate educational (experiential) environments. This view has clear implications for the general organisation of education and teaching, and these are spelt out towards the end of this chapter. For the moment we return to point 4 of the points under discussion.

84

4 *Man typically proceeds by problem solving in which cognitive restructuring and profiting from experience through integrating activities plays a dominant role*

Piaget does not have much to say about problem solving in the classical sense, but it is obvious that his theoretical position is compatible with the experimentalists. Leaving aside Dewey's five steps of thought or the scientific method for the moment, let us look at a typical problem situation. Suppose a child is playing with a ball and it goes over a high fence. The situation can be represented diagrammatically as follows:

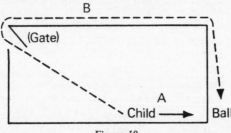

Figure 18

The direct route to the ball is indicated by arrow A but as the fence is too difficult an obstacle for the child to negotiate, the only solution for the child is to detour through the gate. The school of psychology which the experimentalists would support would say that the problem had been solved because the child had perceived the situation, rejected the solution of the direct route, cognitive reorganisation had taken place (a restructuring of the elements of the situation in the mind) and the problem had therefore been solved.

Piaget is much more interested in the development of cognitive structures as such and not quite so interested in their application to everyday problems. But his theories suggest that two comments would be relevant here. Firstly, it would depend very much upon the stage of reasoning (thinking) that the child has reached as to what role the intellectual or cognitive structures would play. Second, his explanation would be in terms of accommodation and assimilation.

Faced with a situation with which the child's available schemas (structures) could not deal, the child (given the appropriate cognitive level) would adapt (accommodate and assimilate) resulting in modification and a more effective response to the environmental demands (the problem). Thus Piaget would agree with the contention that man typically proceeds by problem solving but his explanation of the dynamics of problem solving would differ. Problem solving would, in the main, be regarded as fundamentally the operation of the operative aspects of thinking.[2]

[2] Inhelder and Matalon (1960) warn against the dangers of "adultomorphism" in the discovery of a logical principle, the acquisition of an experimental method and the interpretation of the physical world.

Piaget would probably give qualified approval to Dewey's five steps of thought because it would seem that the successful use of this method would require the kind of logical structure typically found at the formal level of reasoning. This can be illustrated by considering the qualitatively different solutions of concrete and formal reasoners to the verbal reasoning tests described by Peel (1966) of which the following is representative.

In these verbal reasoning tests a simple story is read and the child is asked a simple question and then gives reasons for the answer. One such test describes how Jane, a fifteen-year-old girl, who is preparing for her final examinations is given the task of looking after her younger brother who gets into mischief and makes a mess of himself and his mother's clean washing. The examinee is asked: Was Jane a careless person? Why do you think so?

The concrete reasoner typically answers. "Yes. If she had watched Teddy he would not have wandered." The formal reasoner says something like, "Young children are difficult to watch. Besides she had her examinations to do. Even if she had noticed she still might not have been able to do much in time." It would seem that only in the case of the formal reasoner are Dewey's criteria met. Finally, with respect to "profiting from experience" the comment would be that this is another way of saying accommodation and assimilation leading to the progressive development of cognitive structures.

5 *Education is: (a) The application of intelligent enquiry for the progressive development of the ability to think and judge; (b) Conjoint activity in which individuals interact so that the whole of society is in fact educative; and (c) Growth leading to further growth*

Taking these points one at a time, in so far as they can be separated and dealing first with point (a), it is clear that Piaget's life work has been concerned with "the progressive development to think and judge". This fact has already been established in Chapter 2 and there is no need to reiterate here.

Regarding point (b), Piaget attaches a considerable amount of importance to interpersonal interaction and makes it quite clear (1971, 174) that he disavows the limitation of social interaction characteristic of the constraints of the traditional school. Therefore, from the outset it must be stated that Piaget believes with the experimentalists that social interaction or conjoint activity is fundamentally educative and indeed he gives significant support to their position.

Piaget's thoughts on this can best be discussed under two headings, the two aspects being interrelated: the socialisation of the child; and the effects of interpersonal interaction and discussion on the development of cognitive structures. Piaget starts from the position that the child is social almost from the day of its birth and by the end of the second month smiles and seeks to make contact with others. But he also observes that despite these tendencies to social contact society is external to the individual and to become a socialised person there must be a progressive relationship established between these internal social tendencies and those essential foundations of human society "language, intellectual exchanges, moral or legal action" (1971,

174). But the child although possessing "urges toward sympathy and imitation" has a great deal to learn before he can be considered socialised. As with all other development the child proceeds by adaptation. He assimilates others to himself and accommodates himself to others. Thus he gives meaning to others as specialised objects behaving in various ways and accommodates, that is, changes his structures so that he can fit into the demands of society (the group). But the degree to which he can do this is dependent upon his cognitive or intellectual development, upon the stage of reasoning or thought he has reached.

In Chapter 2 where the progressive development of intelligence was traced, one major achievement of childhood was the development of the concept of the permanence of an object which, as development proceeded, included the child's perception of himself as an object. This latter development is not typically consolidated until the beginning of the concrete reasoning stage, and up to that time the child consistently sees things from his own egocentric point of view believing himself to be the centre of both the social and the physical world. (See Chapter 2.) During the concrete period the child gradually develops the ability to see things from another's viewpoint and to take the role of another. The ability to do this enlarges the child's capacity to develop social relationships on a reciprocal basis and to view society and the group as a system of interacting selves.

In addition to the important role it plays in the socialisation of the child, interpersonal interaction is also of considerable significance in intellectual development. In Chapter 2 it was emphasised that in order to develop the highest levels of logical thought it was necessary for the child to relinquish his egocentric position. Piaget believes that the relinquishing of egocentrism is facilitated by discussion and intellectual exchange. Through argument and discussion, the child comes to realise that his view is not the only view as he becomes aware that others do not share his opinion. General observation plus the insights obtained through the studies of groups in interaction show that group discussion frequently but not necessarily leads to conflict, hostility and argument with the attendant realisation that others are not as tolerant of our views as we are ourselves. In the thrust and parry of discussion the participants must defend and justify, modify, concede or relinquish the position held. In any one of these situations the participant is forced to modify his thoughts; to accommodate and assimilate.

Thus interpersonal interaction serves an important purpose. It helps the child to give up his egocentric view of the world and facilitates cognitive development. The facilitative effects of interpersonal interaction on intellectual development are important for all levels of thought but become particularly important in adolescence with the development of formal thinking. This is because at that stage, language plays its most crucial role in the development of the cognitive structures and the interaction of the child or adolescent with his peers, parents, teachers and other significant adults in society becomes developmentally relevant. Thus in this special sense, which is by no means the only sense, Piaget shows quite clearly that he believes that the whole of society is educative and leaves in no doubt his belief in the educative importance of social influence when he says:

> To educate means to adapt the individual to the surrounding social environment. The new methods, however, seek to encourage this adaptation by making use of the impulses inherent in childhood itself allied with the spontaneous activity that is inseparable from mental development. And they do so, moreover, with the idea that society itself will also thereby be enriched. (1971, 151)

Summing up then, we can say that Piaget's views are consistent with the experimentalist position that "Education is conjoint activity in which individuals interact so that the whole of society is educative", and indeed strengthen the position considerably by indicating how social interaction, within the framework of society, supports not only the notion of progressive socialisation of the child but his intellectual development as well with social and intellectual development being two sides of the one coin.

Finally, with respect to Piaget and the experimentalists, point 5(c) states that: "Education is growth leading to further growth." The central idea here is one of continuous and progressive development as the individual builds on the results of prior experience. What Dewey and the experimentalists would describe as "growth leading to further growth" Piaget would refer to as the equilibration; or the coming into balance of accommodation and assimilation to achieve a dynamic equilibrium. This dynamic equilibrium is, of course, preparatory to a new disequilibrium as the environment and organism interact and the organism is forced to accommodate, assimilate and equilibrate in the continuous process of differentiation and generalisation of the developing cognitive structures. This is, of course, the functional invariant of adaptation discussed in Chapter 2. It would therefore not be too great an intellectual distortion to describe this process as "growth leading to further growth".

But there is inherent in Piaget's conception of progressive development through the equilibration of accommodation and assimilation an implication of fundamental importance to education and the organisation of schools. Piaget, like Dewey, sees the "law of interest" as fundamental to intellectual functioning and like Dewey regards interest and work imposed from outside as antithetical. Piaget puts the matter this way:

> Interest is nothing other, in effect, than the dynamic aspect of assimilation. As Dewey demonstrated with such profundity, true interest appears when the self identifies itself with ideas or objects, when it finds in them a means of expression and they become a necessary form of fuel for its activity. When the active school requires that the student's effort should come from the student himself instead of being imposed, and that his intelligence should undertake authentic work instead of accepting predigested knowledge from outside, it is therefore simply asking that the laws of all intelligence should be respected. (1971, 158-159)

But we have already seen in Chapter 2 that, for Piaget, true interest as it relates to the laws of intelligence depends upon the principle of *moderate novelty*. The child is interested in that which is within his accommodative grasp. Thus the governing factor of what the child ought to experience next is the current state of his cognitive structures, and carried to its logical conclusion, this means that the child's current structures determine which kind of experience will result in optimal cognitive development. This self regulatory principle is the intellectual equivalent of the early cafeteria experiments (Davis, 1928) in which human infants, for periods ranging from six months to four and a half years, were allowed to select whatever food they wanted each day from a wide variety offered. Translated into educational terms this would mean that the child is most likely to modify his cognitive structure when he controls his own learning. This idea is not new for it was fundamental to the early Laboratory Schools run by Dewey and the experimentalists and, unfortunately, was one of the rocks on which the system foundered for reasons which the writer does not think would be impediments today. Nevertheless, Piaget's theory clearly implies that self regulation is most likely to lead to optimum cognitive development in the child. Putting it into practice is another matter entirely and this is discussed at the end of this chapter when ways and means of organising education and teaching which seem to stem logically from Piaget's theory are discussed.

Piaget, the "New Methods" and Experimentalism. Conclusion

Summing up we may say that Piaget supports the "new methods" and disavows "traditional methods" and that, in general, he supports what has been termed the experimentalist position, his work deepening and extending that view.

There are, however several comments which must be made. The experimentalist position was a total conception of education. It began with a theory of man and it had a particular view of his psychological development. This in turn led to specific ideas as to how the child was to be taught and to firm convictions as to what kind of curriculum best suited this view of man.

Piaget, on the other hand, did not set out to contribute directly to education but he does have a view of man, a particular view of his psychological development and has firm convictions as to how the child is to be taught (method). He does not seem to have convictions as determined as the experimentalists as to what should constitute the curriculum or how it should be organised. (This is less true if the curriculum is viewed as including the experiences offered as well as delineating subject content.) He seems to accept (1971, 13) that teachers in most countries are compelled to follow programs laid down by authorities, although he argues consistently for their continual reform. Nevertheless, his chief contribution to educational practice is in the field of method as it is applied to what might be regarded as conventional curricula. Thus while he is concerned to some extent with what is taught, Piaget is much more concerned with methods of teaching and contrasts receptive methods, active methods and intuitive (figurative) methods, topics which are discussed in more detail below.

89

Therefore, while it is appropriate to refer to the Activity School, the Laboratory School and the Project Method, which were total conceptions of method, as particular approaches to teaching, it is inappropriate to speak of "Piaget's Method". As a separate and distinct method it does not exist. Piaget contributed a number of insights which have clear implications for teaching and it is to these further implications that attention is now directed.

IMPLICATIONS OF PIAGET'S THEORY FOR EDUCATION AND TEACHING

The implications of Piaget's theory for education and teaching are divided into three major sections. First, there is the question of the acceleration of development and the role of heredity and environment (Implications A). Second, points which have general relevance to teaching and as such would apply to most classrooms in Australia today if they could be implemented (Implications B). These implications may be categorised further as: (i) Individual differences and readiness; (ii) Curriculum; and (iii) Method (Teaching Strategies). Third are the implications which suggest particular approaches to the organisation of the school and the classroom or imply a particular method (Implications C). Once again, these implications may be seen in the following terms: (i) Implications for a total reorganisation of the educational setting; (ii) Implications for specific subjects which have an identifiable logical structure as in mathematics; and (iii) Implications of a general nature for subjects which do not possess a clearly identifiable logical structure such as social studies.

A   The question of the acceleration of development and the role of heredity and environment

Can development be accelerated? If it can, then this seems to point clearly to programmes of enrichment including preschool education and programmes such as Head Start. But the question is a difficult one to answer. The most obvious place to look for guidance is to Piaget himself. To give an answer from Piaget's perspective it is necessary to look first of all to an important question which is prior to the question of acceleration, the question of heredity or environment, that is the question of the relative roles of maturation and experience.

Piaget is quite clear on this. The development of individual thought should not be considered as comparable to an embryology obeying strict hereditary rules (1971, 166). If this were so, the teacher would be wasting his time and his effort in trying to speed up the development of his students. All he would have to do would be to find out what knowledge corresponded to each stage and present it so that it could be assimilated to structures of the particular stage (1971, 166-7). Similarly, if the development of reason depended uniquely on the influences wielded by the physical and social environment, the teacher could speed up the process of education considerably and identify the child with the adult in the shortest possible time.

Obviously, Piaget takes a position midway between extremes, for he says that the methods of education which have had the most durable success drew their inspiration from the doctrine of the golden mean, allowing room both for internal structural maturation and also for the influences of experience and of the social and physical environment. He elaborates on this position by stating that although the boundaries between the contribution of the mind's structural maturation on the one hand, and individual experience and the influence of the physical and social environment on the other, cannot be fixed with any certainty, we should accept that both factors are constantly at work with development being a product of continuous interaction between the two aspects (1971, 172-3).

For Piaget this has two important implications. First, and this is a constant theme for Piaget, we should take into account the particular interests and needs at each stage of development that results from such interaction. Second, "that environment can play a decisive role in the development of the mind; that the thought contents of the stages and the ages at which they occur are not immutably fixed; that sound methods can therefore increase the students' efficiency and even accelerate their spiritual growth without making it any the less sound" (1971, 173).

Thus Piaget comes down in favour of experiences influencing development although he views with disfavour specific attempts at artificial acceleration.[3] This is an optimistic view yet it is one which is not universally shared. Indeed several authorities on Piaget's work are far more pessimistic about the outcome of intervention and the efficacy of specially designed experiences. Elkind (1969, 335) concludes that "the Piagetian conception of intelligence provides no support . . . for those who advocate formal preschool instruction. . . ." In somewhat the same vein, Kohlberg writes: "Basically, however, the Piaget approach does not generate great optimism as to the possibility of preschool acceleration of cognitive development (or of compensation for its retardation) . . ." (1968, 1056)

What then is the real position? Piaget makes it quite clear (1971, 36) that his fundamental belief is that intelligence develops naturally and spontaneously. Further he believes that these natural and spontaneous processes "may be utilised and accelerated by education at home or in the school, but that they are not derived from that education and, on the contrary, constitute the preliminary and necessary condition of efficacity in any form of instruction" (1971, 36). He reports, for example, the work of Canadian psychologists who tested children in Martinique on Piaget's tests and found a time lag of up to four years in operational development, despite the fact that the primary school programme was identical with that used in France. The inference to be drawn here is that even though the school programme was identical with the programme in French schools, the environment in Martinique had not been of the kind which permitted the natural and spontaneous development of

---

[3] Wallace (1972, 199-200) makes out a case for the continued investigation of acceleration because of the possible benefits it might have for the intellectual development and education of retarded children and believes, despite Piaget's contention, that environmental demands should not be left to dictate the course of cognitive development.

91

structures. This is the important point to be taken here. As stated above, the writer believes Piaget is not so much concerned with what is taught, but with how it is taught. He says:

> Finally, and above all (for it would be impossible to emphasise this point too strongly), each stage of development is characterised much less by a fixed thought content than by a certain power, a certain potential activity, capable of achieving such and such a result according to the environment in which the child lives. (1971, 171-172)

For Piaget, the strength of the "new methods" lies in the way in which experiences are given so that the child can develop optimally according to the demands of his own intellectual structure. Curriculum is therefore important only in so far as it allows structures to develop. It is not important in itself. The sequential development of cognitive structures can be achieved in a particular culture with a variety of content, but proceeds best in an educative environment which stresses true activity and self regulation. Piaget is therefore concerned fundamentally with method and only incidentally with curriculum.

How then can the views of Piaget, Elkind and Kohlberg be reconciled? The answer lies partly in the use of the word accelerated and partly in the research that is available on "acceleration". When Piaget uses the word it is clear that he means the achievement of optimal rates of natural and spontaneous development. As used in the research on training for conservation (Kohlberg 1968, 1032) the term refers to specific effects obtained on, e.g., training which might accelerate the conservation of number. As Kohlberg (1968, 1032-3) points out in summing up this aspect of the literature, children who have conserved "naturally" are more likely to generalise to other conservation tasks, whereas the effects of specific instruction or artificial acceleration seem to have limited generalisation to other areas of conservation with the possibility of regression in conservation suggesting "pseudo" rather than genuine conservation.[4]

There is, however, limited evidence that "some genuine acceleration of conservation may be induced if the instruction methods used follow from the conceptions of cognitive structure and of conflict and match implied by Piaget's theory" (Kohlberg, 1033). This is precisely the approach Piaget would recommend and sees as endemic to the "new methods".

Thus from the foregoing it can be seen that Piaget views the development of intelligence as resulting from the interaction of maturation and experience. It is also apparent that he believes that the generalised experiences available in the culture, depending upon the particular culture, will provide the basis for such development and further he suggests that the natural and spontaneous processes of development can be utilised and accelerated by educa-

---

[4] See I. E. Sigel and F. H. Hooper, *Logical Thinking in Children*, 1968, for a comprehensive survey on research into acceleration to that date. For a more recent discussion consult M. L. Goldschmid, "The Role of Experience in the Rate and Sequence of Cognitive Development", Chapter 6 in Green, Ford and Flamer, *Measurement and Piaget*, 1971. Goldschmid's chapter contains comments by Lovell, Inhelder, Elkind and Beilin.

tion at home or in the school in so far as they take into account the fundamental processes which are at the base of such development.

B Points which have general relevance to teaching and as such would apply to most classrooms today

i Individual Differences and Readiness

Piaget did not set out to contribute directly to individual differences, yet his work has contributed significantly to this aspect of educational psychology. No teacher, or student, who has used Piaget's tests on, e.g., several six-year-old children can fail to be impressed by the significantly different patterns of cognitive development that are typically revealed. Thus one six-year-old may be able to conserve continuous quantity and discontinuous quantity but not number or two dimensional space, while his friend sitting next to him might be the opposite or he might not pass any of the items at all.

Whatever the position it is obvious that for some children in a typical class the material which is being "presented" will provide an ideal match with respect to accommodation, assimilation and current cognitive structure, while for others it will be meaningless and/or useless because it is outside the accommodative grasp or can be assimilated so easily that it is boring.

This is, of course, the perennial problem of *readiness* and it would seem that there is support from Piaget for both Bruner and Ausubel here. Basically Bruner believes that we should adapt the learning content to the child's characteristic way of thinking, while Ausubel emphasises the role of prior learning and experience suggesting that the school can actually assist in promoting readiness. All views stress the importance of the match between current structures and material wherein lies the great problem. With thirty-five to forty children in the class, how is it possible to provide experiences or present material in such a way as to provide for optimal conflict between material and cognitive structure? The task is formidable but is being approached through reorganisation; in some instances of the whole school, in others of the whole grade and in others of the whole class. These potential solutions are discussed below in that part of the discussion designated "Implications C".

ii Curriculum

Implicit in any discussion of matching experiences to the individual is the broad area of curriculum. In the writer's view, curriculum may be viewed as the interaction of child, teacher and material in such a way that the emphasis on the kind of experience the child undergoes is at least as great as the emphasis on the material to be learned. Therefore, in the sense that the curriculum is a set of vital ongoing educative experiences, we are in reality restating what was said above with respect to individual differences and readiness. The construction of an appropriate curriculum, irrespective of theoretical position, clearly implies an attempt to match material and experiences to various developmental levels which is what curriculum committees in fact attempt to do.

Piaget has been criticised because his work has not led to improvements in curriculum (Boyle, 1969, 120). This may be so, but it may also be an unrealistic view based on a misunderstanding of the total problem and Piaget's theory in relation to it. Boyle in making his criticism states that "what emerges most clearly . . . is that improvements to the curriculum have come about as a result of the analysis of the structure of the material to be taught" (Boyle, 1969, 121-122).

Piaget has recently (1971) expressed views about the curriculum and an examination of these indicates that he believes that the curriculum should not be overloaded, the curriculum should be constantly reviewed and that this is a task for educators and teachers. None of these three points depends for its justification on Piaget's theories. They have wide support among educators, psychologists, teachers and curriculum builders of all persuasions. What is of considerable significance is Piaget's insistence that what is presented to the child should match his present cognitive structures and should challenge him in the sense of providing optimal conflict so that, through accommodation and assimilation, cognitive restructuring can take place with consequent development of the cognitive structures.

It is, of course, obvious that an important contributory step toward this very difficult goal must be an analysis of the structure of the material to be taught. If one is going to match the cognitive structures to the material to be presented, then it is highly desirable that the logical properties inherent in the material be known. This is widely recognised with respect to the teaching of number and a good deal of mathematics teaching in the infants and primary school takes into account the level of cognitive development (current cognitive structure) and the logic of the materials presented. Yet even with such logically structured material as mathematics, there still remains the problem of the practicality of the match. Analysis of the structure is only one aspect of a many sided problem because there are at least two other aspects to be taken into consideration—the current intellectual structures of the child and the conditions under which he will experience the number programme.

In a sense, therefore, the implication which Piaget's theory has for curriculum construction is a somewhat forbidding one. If his view of cognitive development is accepted, then curriculum construction and its implementation becomes a very complex task indeed for the process would involve a thorough analysis of the component subskills of a particular subject area, a fairly precise knowledge of the current level of each child's cognitive structure and a mapping of particular materials to particular individuals using methods appropriate for the optimal progress of each child. This is futuristic and fanciful in terms of present technology and educational resources although Computer Assisted Instruction may in some limited way achieve part of such objectives.

For the present it seems that there are two ways in which something can be done to give effect to matching specific developmental level, programme and experiences. First, having worked out in some detail the appropriate structure of a subject area, it is presented to small groups which are "homogeneous"

94

with respect to current cognitive structure, with the mode of presentation (activities-experiences) being such that each child can interact with the material in terms of a reasonable cognitive match. This method of organisation presupposes that the teacher has the time and the experience to give the tests which will accurately ascertain current cognitive structure. Unfortunately, while such information would be valuable, its usefulness would be short lived. One would confidently expect that because of variations in the rate of individual development, there would be a considerable number of changes in cognitive structure if the programme and experiences were effective.

A further problem arises when consideration is given to the structural analysis of subjects in which logical structure is not as apparent as it is in mathematics and for which Piaget's theory has general rather than specific relevance. The solution may not be, therefore, in attempts to match child, programme and experiences individually, but in some total reorganisation of the school, or at least the school day. There is, in fact, increasing evidence that solutions are being sought in this way with such schemes as the "Integrated Day" becoming more widespread. These potential solutions are discussed and illustrated in the section headed "Implications C" below.

iii *Method (Teaching Strategies)*

It has been consistently argued throughout this chapter that Piaget's work has important implications for method. But the concept *method*, like the concept *curriculum*, is complex and many headed. In fact it is current fashion to speak not of method but of teaching strategies or teaching models. The change is more than a change in name because it is motivated by a desire to get away from the traditional notions of specific lesson types with the emphasis on set formulae, rigid lesson plans and rigid lesson steps to a concept which emphasises that the teaching learning process is between all elements of the situation. When method is viewed in this wider sense, Piaget's work has implications at several levels. First, and this has to some extent been discussed in relation to curriculum above, his work implies the need for total reorganisation of the educational setting and this is discussed under the sub-heading "Implications C" below. His work also has implications for teaching particular subjects of the conventional curriculum. The relevance of Piaget's work for some of these subjects is obvious as in the case of mathematics so the section "Implications C" is extended to include the chapter which follows where the subject matter relates entirely to Piaget and the teaching of mathematics, in the infants and primary school. Piaget's work also has implications for other subject areas and the section "Implications C" also includes, by way of a final chapter, discussion relative to other subjects.

C Implications which suggest particular approaches to the organisation of the school and classroom or imply a particular method

The concluding section of this chapter develops the idea that Piaget's theory has clear implications for the reorganisation of the school and classroom and leaves to the following two chapters a consideration of the relationship between Piaget's views to specific subject areas (that is, C ii and C iii).

i *Implications for a total reorganisation of the educational setting*

The most fundamental of Piaget's insights for education is that the child literally builds his own intelligence, that he is in fact the architect of his own growth. This is the keystone of Piaget's ideas for it subsumes all that has been said in preceding chapters. It is the idea to which education must attend if it is to promote the optimal development of the child. Acceptance of this view of development implies that the school must put the child at the centre of the educative process in a way anticipated by Dewey at the turn of the twentieth century, for the evidence is overwhelming. One important consequence is that the organisation of education in many countries today is antithetical to this proposition and would have to be considerably modified to accord with Piaget's conception of how the child develops.

Of the many ways of organising the infants and primary school current today, it is the opinion of the writer that what is known as the "Integrated Day" gives the greatest practical expression to Piaget's ideas. The concept of the integrated day is outlined below and its operation is illustrated by an example from an Australian primary school. The integrated day is, however, more frequently encountered in the infants school although the form in which it operates varies. Following the description of the integrated day the discussion concludes after the writer outlines how he believes the scheme incorporates and gives effect to specific aspects of Piaget's theory of development.

The integrated day is a school day which is combined into a whole and has a minimum of timetabling and covers the whole of the six years of the infants-primary school. The natural flow of activity, imagination, thought and learning which is in itself a continuous process is not interrupted by artificial breaks every 30 or 40 minutes, nor is it constrained by subject barriers. The child is encouraged to commit himself completely to the work he has chosen. If he desires he is given time to pursue something in depth even though this may take a considerable time. As the children work, problems common to various subjects will arise but within the integrated framework they can make easy transition betwee_ any areas of learning. The emphasis is on integration and subject barriers are ignored and no limit is set to exploration which may involve several traditional subject areas.[5]

It should be made clear, however, that the integrated day is a generalised concept and in consequence there are differences when it comes to practical implementation.[6] Even with an integrated scheme, the kinds of experiences available in any one school or section of a school will be limited by the

---

[5] The definition and explanation of the Integrated Day is based on the accounts given in Precious and Brown (1968) and the Dundas Project 1971-2.

[6] Moran (1971, 65) reports that a survey of 181 teachers using the "Integrated Day" in England revealed five major types of practice.

equipment, physical surroundings, personnel available and the particular view of the integrated day accepted by the staff. This should be borne in mind when considering the example which follows.

The illustration concerns the integration of the senior primary fifth and sixth grades at St Patrick's, Dundas, a school run by the Marist Brothers Teaching Order in New South Wales. The scheme at Dundas is regarded by the organisers as a modified integrated day and is the result of blending theory with years of experience in education. It must be emphasised, however, that the scheme as outlined below is being progressively modified in the light of experience and the necessity to fit into the overall organisation of education in New South Wales.

School Organisation. There are 210 pupils in six homerooms with each homeroom under the care of an experienced primary teacher who is responsible for guiding the thirty-five pupils allocated to a room. The groups are heterogeneous and consist of boys who the previous year would have been either in fourth or fifth grade in a conventional school. The scheme specifically rejects the concept of grouping boys according to attainments in the familiar homogeneous or ability grouping. Each homeroom contains equal numbers of "old" and "new" boys. The "old" boys introduce new members to some of the interesting situations and materials and assist the "new" boys to adapt. The school strongly favours the retention of the "one teacher—one class" situation for most of the day so that each child is able to speak of "my teacher". Because the boys have freedom to choose activities, with a consequent encouragement of spontaneous personal involvement, they are encouraged to develop a responsibility for their own behaviour instead of relying on outside authority, direction and control.

CURRICULUM
The definition of curriculum is a broad one and includes all those activities in which children engage under the auspices of the school. There is a shift in emphasis away from instruction towards experience unlike the traditional school which was largely concerned with what the teacher taught and how effective he was in conducting an orderly class.

a As the school is a Catholic school a basic aim of the school is the Christian formation of the boys. Every effort is made to integrate Christian formation into the overall school programme and as part of this there is a real attempt to develop a viable family spirit in the school, through sharing ideas and experiences. The more gifted are expected to help the less gifted in an atmosphere of genuine Christian love.

b *Communications.* The English studies form a pattern of interrelated skills that are all part of the single act of communication and include speaking, listening, writing, reading, acting and watching. As a broader concept communication also involves aspects of social studies and mathematics. There is an emphasis on mass media both as a tool of communication and as an aspect of the environment which requires critical scrutiny.

97

In the classroom the boys are free to have spontaneous and natural conversation. Real discussion is encouraged and children's questions are considered seriously. Teacher's questions are designed to encourage children to think.

The strong emphasis on oral expression leads naturally to written expression as children write when they have something to say. Here the long term aim is to have children talk and write naturally, freely and expressively; to appreciate literature and to have confidence in their ability to cope with language. Typewriters are available for boys who prefer to record in an effective adult way and tape recorders are used for recording pupil expression.

c *Mathematics.* In mathematics the emphasis is on concept development. Children are given te ts to determine and establish level of conceptual understanding and then follow work designed to radiate from core concepts. The approach is based on exploration and discovery and maximum use is made of structured and unstructured materials. A wide variety of multi-level materials are also used. When resources permit it is hoped to make some calculating machines available for further exploration of number and relationships.

d *Social Studies.* The curriculum for social studies has been constructed by the staff and is designed to meet the needs of boys living in the particular local urban area from which the school draws its pupils. Emphasis is placed upon developing the skills and understandings necessary for living in the complete society of today. This includes, in addition to discovering the broad pattern of relationships existing in the region, the development of desirable attitudes to others through appreciation of individual worth and the opportunity of real experiences in interpersonal interaction.

e *Science.* The science programme, based on observation and experiment, is concerned with the study of problems that occur spontaneously to curious boys in their day to day interaction with the environment. In the science programme, emphasis is placed upon a scientific approach to problem solving rather than arriving at full technical answers. With such an approach, there are plenty of opportunities for boys to plan and work together. An array of basic scientific equipment is available for the conduct of "experiments" that may be set up both inside and outside the school.

School Plant. The six homerooms are equipped with some desks, trapezoidal tables and chairs, stools, a low bench, a carpenter's bench and vice, easels and art material, science equipment, a couple of typewriters, display boards and chalkboards. Calculating machines will be added when available. The homerooms are designed as workrooms. The two quiet rooms are furnished with soft floor coverings, curtains, cushions, stools and some indoor plants. These rooms are designed for private study and reading as well as class work in religion, literature, oral expression and poetry. The library in addition to its normal functions is responsible for regular library lessons and co-ordinates with remedial reading programmes.

THE SKILLS DEVELOPMENT CENTRE
The multi-level materials for the development of individual skills such as

Reading, Spelling and Mathematics is located in a specially prepared room in an attempt to make more efficient use of these materials. Emphasis is on easy access and upon a system of storage which will permit the most effective use of these important aids to self initiated learning.

ORGANISATION

In general, the emphasis is on self initiated learning. Much of this would take place on an individual basis, but there are certain tasks which require co-operative effort and discussion in small groups. There is, however, basic work in reading organised around ability levels in such a way as to make remedial reading more easily handled. There are other subject areas such as physical education, art, craft, music-singing, poetry and much of oral expression, e.g., talks or debates, which of their very nature require group experiences and often are most effectively presented in the whole class situation. The integrated day, however, also allows the boys to pursue and develop interest in these areas on an individual basis outside the formal group sessions.

TESTING, EVALUATION AND REPORTING

One important aspect with respect to evaluation is that the scheme itself is being evaluated by the application of appropriate cognitive and affective tests which include tests of attainment, intelligence, test anxiety, attitudes, interpersonal interaction etc. Pupil evaluation is done jointly by the boys and the teacher and provides for self evaluation as well as diagnosis. The process may involve a discussion of the effectiveness of a learning situation, of the degree of participation, suggestions for improvement of work habits or research and discussion procedures or perhaps the use of reference materials. Each homeroom teacher is responsible for keeping records of each pupil's achievement.

Competition, marks and places in class have no place in the school for evaluation of the individual's work is qualitative rather than quantitative. Written reports are sent to parents from time to time but the most valuable reporting takes place at parent-teacher interviews.

AN ANALYSIS OF THE INTEGRATED DAY AT ST. PATRICK'S DUNDAS IN TERMS OF PIAGET'S THEORY

There are two questions which should be asked in this context. The first, "How well does the St. Patrick's scheme accord with Piaget's overall view of education?" The second examines the question of the way in which the scheme reflects specific aspects of Piaget's theory and to what ends.

Quite clearly, Piaget would approve of the scheme as an example of the "New Methods" in education as these are outlined and discussed in the earlier segments of this chapter. Obviously, the Dundas scheme involves considerably more than ideas originating from Piaget's theory for one can see in the scheme much of what experimentalists have thought valuable as well as elements which have their origins in other educational theories. The scheme is eclectic but, by and large, as Piaget would want, "appeals to real activity, to spontaneous work based upon personal need and interest" (Piaget, 1971, 152).

Why then is the scheme a good example of the application of Piaget's theories to education? Fundamentally because it provides the kind of educational environment consistent with the optimal development of cognitive structures. This we will trace in more detail as a series of numbered points, beginning with the concept of generalised experiences.

1 *Generalised Experiences, Self Regulatory Behaviour and the Cognitive Match.* The environment described above takes cognizance of Piaget's contention, supported by relevant literature, that the overall development of logical structures takes place in an environment which provides a variety of tasks appropriate to the development of cognitive structures such that each child, through self regulatory behaviour, contacts that experience which is most appropriate to continued cognitive development.

Thus we can see in the operation of the Dundas project, Piaget's views that education, or cultural transmission, can provide optimum conditions for development when due recognition is given to the interaction of maturation and experience in a situation where the child is free to make the cognitive match between current structure and educational experience, when the problem of environment (learning experience) is such that the child can accommodate and through the application of current structures can give meaning to the situation. This is much more likely to happen where the child is free to choose that which he wishes to interact with next (indeed the optimum development of his cognitive structure demands it) instead of being forced to cope with a problem which is thought might "match" the whole group, as in classroom teaching.

2 *Motivation.* What has been said above concerns the problem of motivation. Piaget believes that real interest ensues when the principle of moderate novelty applies, which occurs when the challenge of the environment is neither too difficult nor too easy for the current structures. When interest is maximised, motivation is maximised and the learning situation is productive. The integrated day with its emphasis on self-selection of activities is more likely to provide the opportunity for genuine interest to develop with a consequent increase in the desire to continue to learn as the child finds he can meet the environment on terms which are cognitively comfortable and which allow him to make progressive integrations in line with the state of his own particular cognitive structures and at a rate appropriate to his own unique development. This process is more likely to take place under a scheme such as the Dundas scheme where competition, marks and places in class have been eliminated in favour of the qualitative evaluation of the child. In the situation the child is freed from the constrictions of the mark oriented view of education and can therefore commit himself wholeheartedly in a choice situation which has for him the ring of authenticity and reality. This view of motivation eschews extrinsic rewards and views with disfavour the creation of "reward dependent" children—for it believes that the context of

100

self regulatory behaviour is the situation which is likely to give point to the assertion that education is growth leading to further growth.

3 *Interpersonal Interaction, Discussion and Cognitive Development*. Earlier discussion in this chapter made it quite clear that Piaget regarded interpersonal interaction as important because of its effects on socialisation of the child and its effects, through discussion, on the development of the cognitive structures, including the relinquishing of egocentric thought in the young child. It is obvious from the programme outlined above, that considerable opportunity exists for interpersonal interaction, co-operative enterprise and discussion in such a way that both the goals of increased socialisation and of cognitive development are promoted.

4 *Activity, Discovery and Concept Development*. The emphasis in subject areas, such as mathematics and science, is on true activity methods. By true activity methods is meant that the essence of activity and discovery (see Glossary) is not seen as consisting solely in manipulating objects and instruments, but includes as well an emphasis on the formal abstraction of relationships which exist among the elements under consideration. True activity in Piaget's terms can simply consist in reflecting on a relationship between two accounts a child has read explaining a certain point at issue concerning a matter of importance to him. Nevertheless, due cognizance is paid to the developmental level of the fifth and sixth grade children in that a considerable amount of both structured and unstructured materials are available. This is of course necessary if the principle of cognitive match and moderate novelty is to operate maximally.

In a situation such as this where the emphasis is on true activity and not simply on the manipulation of materials, it is likely that the desirable goal of an increase in the opportunity for operative as against figurative knowing will be realised. Operative knowing as we saw, emphasised the meaning aspect of cognitive structures, and it is this emphasis on activity, discovery and enquiry on a truly operative plane which is most likely to lay the foundations of meaning upon which the verbal reasoning of the formal stage is based.

The remarks which have been made concerning Piaget's theory and the integrated day have been concerned to show what Piaget's theory implies for the total organisation of the school day. Such schemes are not totally based on Piaget's theory but draw heavy support from it. Therefore, as this was an attempt to show general implications, no effort has been made to indicate the specific way in which Piaget's theory applies to the teaching of subjects such as mathematics within the integrated day. These applications certainly exist and are traced in the chapters devoted to specific subjects. It can be taken for granted that much of what is suggested for specific school subjects would apply in some way when these subjects are contacted in the flexible environment of the integrated day.

CONCLUSION

1 In this chapter it has been shown that Piaget has a particular view of education (close to the experimentalists) and that this and other unique aspects of his theory have implications for education.

2 It has been claimed that his theory, taken to its logical conclusion, implies the integrated day.

3 In general, those broad aspects of Piaget's theory which have implications for the integrated day are: (a) general experience, self regulation and cognitive match; (b) intrinsic motivation, interest and the principle of moderate novelty; (c) interpersonal interaction and discussion as it relates to cognitive development; and (d) genuine activity, discovery and the opportunity to develop real meaning as cognitive structures are built.

4 The integrated day is, however, the exception rather than the rule in Australian schools today and teaching is generally carried on in subject compartments. Therefore, although in the writer's view Piaget's theory finds its best expression in schemes like the integrated day, the theory is nevertheless relevant to the understanding of teaching specific school subjects. There is, however, increasing evidence which stems from the pilot projects in the various Australian states and from the many meetings of school principals, that interest in the integrated day is mounting and I have little doubt that some form of the integrated day will be standard in the infants and primary school in the near future.

6. Piaget and the Understanding and Teaching of Number

This chapter is divided into two parts: the first looks at what is really meant by saying that a child has an understanding of number or of numerical relationships in terms of Piaget's theory of concept development; and the second examines what this means in specific terms for the teaching of mathematics in the infants and primary school. In this way, particular attention is paid to Implications C ii and C iii of the preceding chapter.

From the very early days of infancy, the child is exposed to a world in which number plays a significant part. It is all around him and forms part of the culture in which he has his being. Yet the growth of mathematical understanding, like the growth of the concept of the permanence of objects, is built step by step in the same gradual way with each forward move depending upon the consolidation of previous gains. In Piaget's view the concept of mathematical relationships is a complex one based on the integration and co-ordination of several basic concepts which have already been discussed in Chapter 2: conservation as it relates to classification, ordering and number. But how are these concepts reflected in mathematical understanding? An answer to this question can be found by analysing what is involved in terms of fundamental logico-mathematical understanding when the expression $4 + 3 = 7$ is manipulated.

Suppose a second grade child is asked to manipulate the expression by having to answer the following problem. "A man had four horses and three dogs. How many animals did he have altogether?" To begin the analysis, consider what "knowing" the number four means.

Piaget believes that there is a parallel between the development of logical thought in the child and the logic underlying mathematics. In Chapter 2 it was claimed that classification, ordering, and one-to-one correspondence (numerical correspondence) were fundamental to the child's understanding of number. Therefore the search for an understanding of the development of number begins where the search for the origins of the child's intellectual development begins, in the sensorimotor period. The initial foundations of number are laid down in the sensorimotor period when the child through maturation and experience eventually develops the concept of the permanence of objects and the ability to distinguish among various objects. But the primitive sort of motor classifications of the sensorimotor period when, e.g., the child seemed to classify, by action, a doll on a string as something to swing, are not real instances of legitimate classification but are important precursors. During the preconceptual period—two to four years—the child gradually builds up his ability to classify things. That is, through experience he builds up his capacity to see likenesses and differences among objects. Thus the preconceptual child is able to sort a collection of farm animals into horses, cows and sheep and can put two such classifications together. If, e.g., he has in one group 2 horses, 2 sheep and 3 pigs and in another 1 horse, 2 sheep and 3 pigs, he can combine these into 3 horses, 4 sheep, 3 cows and 3 pigs and is most likely able to tell you that they are all animals. But it is important to note that at this stage the child is merely classifying according to quality. He is not yet interested in how many. The important thing is that the child is building up a general idea of classes which involves an understanding of similarities and differences.

At the same time as the ability to classify is developing the child begins to concern himself with order, with a series. Thus, through experience, he notes that one toy car is bigger than another or that one box is smaller than another. This ability to order objects according to size is also an important element in the development of the concept of number and its relationship is discussed in more detail below.

Finally, the child, in addition to developing the ability to classify and order objects, is also forming ideas of one-to-one correspondence which is promoted by the spontaneous matching experiences that the child has as he matches such things as cups to saucers, spoons to cups and buttons to buttonholes.

Initially the child does not ask the question "How many?" but simply wants to know whether something belongs. But gradually, by matching, he comes to realise that the number of elements or things in one group (set) is more, less or the same as those in another as he compares, e.g., the set of three cars with four trucks. He has moved from a concern with the quality of objects to a rudimentary concern with quantity, an important aspect of which is the ability to regard each element as a unit. When he has reached the stage of being able to regard each element as a unit, to be concerned about more, less or the same number of units and with bigger and smaller in relation to a series, the child is in effect moving towards an understanding of the cardinal and ordinal properties of number.

To effect a discussion of how cardinal and ordinal number develops, we return to a discussion of what the number 4 means in the problem of 4 horses + 3 dogs = how many animals? First of all it means that four (4) is the symbol that has been ascribed to the set of four objects (elements) irrespective of what these elements are. Four in this example happens to stand for four horses but it can stand for the set of any four elements. This is the aspect of number which is known as cardinal number and the number to which the set of four horses gives rise is known as the cardinal number four. It is the property of "fourness" such that all sets of 4 things can be placed in one-to-one correspondence.

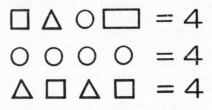

Figure 19

But reference to Chapter 2 will indicate that Piaget has shown that this ability to actually place real objects in one-to-one correspondence develops slowly and that the capacity to conserve numerical correspondence, i.e., the ability to assert unhesitatingly that the number of eggs remains the same as the number of egg cups no matter what their disposition, or that the number of blue counters remains the same as the number of red counters no matter how they are arranged, is not reached in many children until approximately seven years.

One point of importance in this connection is that although children can count before they can conserve numerical equivalence, this facility is no guide to a child's understanding of the cardinal property of number. Conservation of a set of elements, like the initial establishment of the permanence of a single object, represents an important advance in the conceptualisation of the child.

Establishment of a relationship between a set of objects and specific names and symbols does not of itself ensure meaningful manipulation of number. Of equal importance is the correlated concept of ordinal position. When a child counts a row of small cars he is not only setting up a one-to-one correspondence with a set of number names as 1, 2, 3, 4 etc., but he is also naming each car by its position in the row. Car number three is third in the row, car number four is fourth, and so on. When a child touches a car and says "four" he is not necessarily thinking of the four cars he has counted but possibly that the car is the fourth car in the row. His concern is with the position of the car in the series of cars.

Piaget has shown in his experiments on ordinal relations that progress towards being able to order a set of sticks of different lengths is slow and, like the development of numerical equivalence, goes through three fairly clearly defined stages with facility being reached in the concrete operational stage.

For a child to gain a full understanding of number, both cardinal and ordinal aspects are necessary. However, in the early stages of a child's development we have seen that his notions of numerical correspondence and his capacity to seriate are primitive, and it comes as no surprise that his concept of number is rudimentary. Understanding comes when the child, through maturation and experience, co-ordinates the logical operations, thereby providing a frame of reference necessary for the integration of the cardinal and ordinal properties of number. A clear illustration of this gradual progression in the integration or co-ordination of the cardinal and ordinal properties of number is provided in some of the experiments reported in Chapter V of Piaget's *The Child's Conception of Number*, (1952).

In one experiment, a child is given a set of ten dolls which gradually increase in height. In addition, ten walking sticks and ten balls of increasing size are available. The object of the experiment is to have each child match the dolls and the sticks, or the dolls and the balls, so that each doll can easily find its own stick or ball. Piaget found that progress with finding a one-to-one correspondence between two series followed the same stages as that of constructing a single series reported in Chapter 2, approximate ages being, Stage 1 (4-5), Stage 2 (5-6) and Stage 3 (6-7). The experiments showed that at the level at which the child is unable to make dolls and balls correspond he is also unable to form correctly isolated series and that when seriation becomes possible, correspondence also becomes possible.

Stage 1 children found the problem beyond them, but Stage 2 children were able to make the correspondence and arrange the dolls and balls in parallel rows of increasing size so that the one-to-one correspondence between each doll and ball was clear. But the relations discovered in the second stage are only developed at the intuitive level through trial and error. They are not yet operational. In Stage 3 the series is built up without any hesitation or trial and error and most do not find it necessary to seriate the dolls and then the balls. The relations developed in Stage 3 are now free of perception and are truly operational.

Difficulty came, however, when the experimenter displaced the balls slightly so that they were no longer opposite the corresponding doll and asked each child to find the ball belonging to a particular doll. Solution of this problem required the co-ordination or correlation of the cardinal and ordinal mechanisms. An example, from Piaget, of a successful solution by a Stage 3 child will indicate the relationship.

> B o s (6; 6), Question II: "Whose is this ball" (Ball 8)?—(He pointed to Doll 8)—How do you know?—*I can see 3 there* (Ball 10, 9 and 8) *and there* (Doll 10, 9 and 8).—*And this one* (Ball 6)?—*It belongs to that one* (Doll 6) *because before there were 3 and now it's jumped to 6* (so he had counted balls 1-6). (Piaget, 1952, 113)

Children who found difficulty in co-ordinating cardinal and ordinal properties made mistakes which clearly indicated this inability. One child, e.g., was asked to show the ball corresponding to doll number 5 and persistently chose ball 4. The child when asked to explain counted dolls 1 to 4 ignoring doll 5 and then counted balls 1 to 4 and pointed to ball 4, the last one counted.

Piaget notes (1952, 111) that children in this stage constantly make a mistake of one unit and he explains thiş inability to co-ordinate cardinal and ordinal aspects in this way. When a child is asked which stick (or ball) goes with doll five he first has to identify doll five by its position. But in order to determine this position in relation to the sticks the child must estimate the number of elements (positions) which precede it. This results in a dissociation in the child's mind between the position to be found for doll five and the number of preceding terms or positions, dolls one to four. Thus when he is determining the position he does not count five but four, because the numbers one to four represent the set separating doll five from the beginning of the series, but number five represents the position characterising the doll. This explains why the child says "there are four in front" because for him the position does not as yet possess a number of the same nature as those he uses to count preceding terms. When a child is able to co-ordinate the two mechanisms of cardination and ordination, as Bos did in the example quoted above, he can count a row of things so that when he says "five" he is indicating the fifth (ordinal) object, which is the last in a set of objects whose cardinal number is five.

A real conception of the number four in the example $4 + 3 = 7$ involves considerable intellectual progress. However, an adequate concept of three and four does not, of itself, explain the logico-mathematical process in adding four and three or subtracting four from seven. The four operations, addition, multiplication, subtraction and division, are all processes involving the relationship of parts to the whole. Addition and multiplication are concerned with combining whereas subtraction and division are concerned with separating. The acquisition of the part-whole relationship, as the experiments on classification and class inclusion in Chapter 2 show, is a gradual process and parallels the growth of other aspects of logical thinking.

For the sake of exposition, consider what is involved in the addition of four and three and the subtraction of four from seven. The numbers all refer to sets and objects. These can be labelled Sets A, B and C for the set of objects. When we add three and four we are combining Set A with Set B to produce Set C.

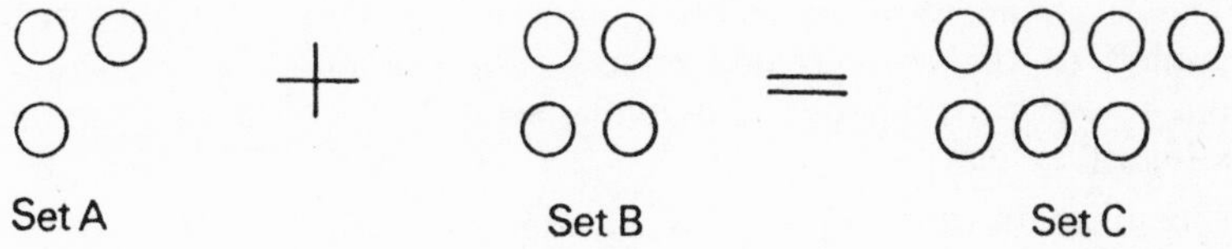

Set A   Set B   Set C

Figure 20

Two subsets are combined to make a larger set which is one perspective of the part-whole relationship. When we subtract 4 from 7 we partition 7 into two subsets such that Set C — Set B = Set A.

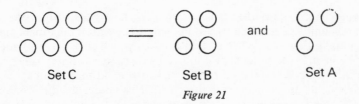

Set C   Set B   Set A

Figure 21

In the absence of structured materials, such as counters or rods, what the child does, in the case of addition, is to involve the operation of closure (Chapter 2) which says that any two operations can be combined to form a third operation. That is, keeping both the concept of 3 and 4 in mind, the child through the application of logical operations (structure) combines these two members to produce a new number 7. In the case of subtraction he holds both Set C in mind, the 7, and Set B, the 4, and removes Set B to form Set A. That is, he applies the operation of reversibility. And because he can also conserve he can hold the concept of 7 elements in mind and move mentally back and forwards between Set C and Set B to remove Set B to form Set A. With experience the two actions of combining and separating come together for complete operational reversibility so that logically the child sees that for any operation there is an opposite operation which cancels it and $4 + 3 = 7$ is seen as equivalent to $7 - 4 = 3$.

Summary

To this stage we have traced the development of an understanding of number in terms of logical operations from the rudiments of classification in the sensorimotor period to the role of conservation and reversibility in the manipulation of the abstract processes of addition and subtraction of number. The steps in this development can be conveniently summarised as a series of numbered points.

1   The logic underlying operational thought has its counterpart in mathematics, but whereas the logic of operations is not consciously present in the child's mind, successful *understanding* of mathematics requires the student to reflect on its structure.

2   The development of the ability to conserve, including reversibility, as it applies to the co-ordinated concepts of classification, ordering and one-to-one correspondence, is fundamental to *understanding* number as a logical system.

3   Classification in the sense of being able to group objects according to the similarities and differences (intension and extension) which is classification in terms of *qualities* is an important precursor to quantitative understanding.

4   Matching and sorting of objects are important experiences for pre-operational children because they lead to the opportunity to classify, to seriate (one-to-one correspondence) and to order.

5   Matching and sorting leads to the formation of sets of objects and to their comparison in terms of gross quantitative judgments such as more, less or the same.

6   In the problem $4 + 3 = 7$, knowing what number 4 means involves knowing: (a) the cardinality of 4 such that 4 = a set of any 4 elements; (b) that these 4 objects are conserved under any transformation; (c) that 4 also refers to the fourth position in a series of objects.

7   Co-ordination of cardinal and ordinal properties of number does not take place until the stage of concrete operations although research suggests that cardination and ordination develop in parallel fashion.

8   Understanding the process of combining (addition) and of separating (subtraction) depends upon conservation and reversibility so that the part-whole relationship becomes a logical reality manipulable in terms of conservation including reversibility.

Implications of Piaget's Theory for the Teaching of Mathematics

Before discussing specific implications of Piaget's theory for the teaching of mathematics, it is necessary to first ask the question "Is conservation (logical operations) related to classroom performance and in particular to mathematics as measured by a conventional arithmetic test?" The answer is a qualified "Yes". Qualified because the relationship is far from perfect and poses problems of interpretation. What follows is a brief report on typical relationships found between conservation and performance in arithmetic with an extended discussion of an Australian study carried out under the direction of the writer (McNally, 1971) which will be referred to as the Westmead (Sydney) study.

Table 3 sets out the correlations between conservation and arithmetic in several studies. The difficulty in comparing these results is that each of the studies used different combinations of tests, both with respect to conservation and arithmetic.

TABLE 3

Correlations between Conservation and Arithmetic in Studies by Almy et al. (1966), Goldschmid and Bentler (1968) and McNally (Westmead) 1971

	ALMY ET AL. (1966)		GOLDSCHMID AND BENTLER (1968)		WESTMEAD (1971)
	Lower Class	Middle Class	Scales A & B	Scale C	
	·38	·53	·52	·39	·48
Grade	K — 1st	K — 1st	1st	1st	1st

Yet the correlations between conservation and achievement in arithmetic are substantial enough to indicate that the child's ability to conserve is relevant to the performance of tasks he encounters in the classroom. Nevertheless, the relationship is far from perfect and indicates that there are other factors involved in the performance of arithmetic. Space does not permit a close examination of all studies but further analysis of the Westmead study suggests what some of these factors might be.

WESTMEAD STUDY, 1971. OUTLINE

The subjects were sixty-nine first grade children from a co-educational infants school, whose mean chronological age was 7·1 years. The children represented the whole of 1st grade at Westmead Demonstration School. There were three classes 1A, 1B and 1C and these were graded according to ability, 1A being the most able class. The conservation tests used were two dimensional space, number, substance, continuous quantity, discontinuous quantity, distance, length and class inclusion. (See Goldschmid (1967) for details of test items.)

These tests were scored for (a) correct response and (b) correct explanation. The maximum possible score for total conservation (response plus explanation) was 76. Test materials were prepared according to Goldschmid's (1967) specifications and the procedure for testing and scoring was the same. The teacher made tests of reading and arithmetic, and also the Vocabulary subtest of the Wechsler Intelligence Scale for Children was given. A table of correlations relating each test to every other test was calculated as were means and standard deviations for all tests. (Correlations for all tests appear in Appendix A.) Partitioning of the results by class and comparing mean age, mean total conservation, mean vocabulary and mean reading scores yields Table 4 and some interesting and informative comparisons.

TABLE 4

Means by Class for the Variables, Age, Conservation, Vocabulary, Arithmetic and Reading

	CLASS	AGE	CONS.	VOCAB.	ARITH.	READING
	1A	6·74	55·7	23·1	73·2	79·8
	1B	6·80	45·5	18·6	61·5	68·3
	1C	8·24	43·5	17·4	58·6	65·9
Possible Maximum		*	76	—	100	100

* Decimal Ages

Class 1C are the older and duller children, approximately 1·4 years older than the 1A and 1B who constitute the upper and lower ability levels of the normal stream. Nevertheless, Table 4 indicates that when each of the three classes is considered as a whole, the average ability to conserve is related to

110

ability to do arithmetic, to read and to vocabulary level. This result can be interpreted in three ways. First, it can be taken by those who believe that language, as reflected by the reading and vocabulary tests, is related directly to the development of thought as providing some confirmation of their position. Second, it can be taken by those who assert that the development of operational thought provides the structure or basis for the progressive development of language as supportive of their position. Thirdly, it can be taken to indicate that there is a general "ability" function which underlies all intellectual functioning which is the view put forward by the author in Chapter 3 and which is another more inclusive way of putting the essence of the second proposition. But wherever the truth lies it is certain that Table 4 offers support for the influence of conservation on classroom performance.

Further support for a relationship between conservation and performance in arithmetic comes from an analysis of the results by comparing mean performance in arithmetic of the top and bottom 20 per cent of the sample on the basis of performance in conservation. This result is shown in Table 5 below.

TABLE 5

Comparison of Mean Arithmetic Scores for the Top and Bottom 20 Per Cent of First Grade Classified on the Basis of Conservation

	N	MEAN ARITHMETIC SCORE (Possible 100)	MEAN CONSERVATION
Top 20 per cent	15	75·3	72
Bottom 20 per cent	15	48·5	5

The results suggest that the inclusion of the middle range of scores for conservation masks the real relationship which exists between conservation and arithmetic for first grade. There were, however, a few children, as the size of the correlations suggest, who conserved poorly and yet did reasonably well in arithmetic. Take, e.g., the case of K.S. aged 6·5 whose individual conservation results were as shown in Table 6 and whose score on the arithmetic test was 79 (grade mean 65·4).

From this set of results it is obvious that K.S. gave the correct response to number, substance, continuous quantity, discontinuous quantity and length but could only explain the conservation of number (numerical equivalence). The interesting thing about K.S's performance was that she scored 0 in the Wechsler Intelligence Scale for Children vocabulary sub-test. In fact, a feature of the whole test situation with this child was the great difficulty in establishing rapport, for the child was extremely timid and her response minimal. Yet the fact that she gave the correct responses to five items makes it quite probable that she had developed the logical structures necessary to understand the

TABLE 6

Responses of K.S. aged 6·5 to Conservation Tests as Listed

TEST	CORRECT RESPONSE	CORRECT EXPLANATION
Two-dimensional space	No	No
Number	Yes	Yes
Substance	Yes	No
Continuous quantity	Yes	No
Discontinuous quantity	Yes	No
Distance	No	No
Length	Yes	No
Class inclusion	No	No

arithmetic of 1st grade.[1] There were, nonetheless, other children with poor scores on arithmetic for whom no mitigating circumstances could be found.

Then again, there were some children who had high conservation scores and yet who had poor arithmetic scores such as N.I. who had a conservation total of 64 out of a possible 76 and whose score on arithmetic was only 43, the sixth lowest score of the 69 first grade children.

Thus what the evidence shows overall is that children who conserve, that is, who demonstrate a relatively high degree of co-ordination of logical operations, perform best in conventional classroom arithmetic at first grade. There is however clear evidence that children can successfully manipulate number and do well in arithmetic tests at the first grade level without this extremely important natural base, but they are in the minority and probably depend on verbal rote methods.

In any event, it is difficult to know what such verbal learning indicates in the way of mathematical understanding in the absence of concrete operations for many studies such as Dodwell (1968), Kofsky (1968) and Wohlwill (1968) have confirmed Piaget's contention that concrete operations develop as a natural base for arithmetic learning. But it must be stressed that what the development of logical structures provides for mathematics is a *base* for mathematical understanding not necessarily mathematical competence in the form of symbol manipulation. Piaget has put the matter succinctly when he says:

> In fact, the operational structures of the intelligence, although they are of logico-mathematical nature, are not present in children's minds as conscious structures: they are structures of actions or operations which certainly direct the child's reasoning but do not constitute an object of reflection on its part. The teaching of mathematics, on the other hand, specifically requires the student to reflect consciously on these structures,

---

[1] There is, of course, the problem of various difficulty levels among **conservation tests**. For a discussion of this problem see Goldschmid and Bentler, 1968.

though it does so by means of a technical language comprising a very particular form of symbolism . . . (1971, 44-45)

Dienes, who has made what many regard as the most fundamental translation of Piaget's ideas to mathematics teaching, speaks about the ability to engage in mathematical activity as having two aspects: disentangling the conceptual structure or the ability to understand, and acquiring and using techniques involved in operating and applying the structure (Dienes, 1965, 2). He believes, and many would support him, that most emphasis in schools has been on handling techniques.

Two important points emerge here. First, that the development of logical structures in the absence of specific experiences in the techniques of manipulating mathematics will not lead to number facility. Second, that emphasis on calculation and manipulation of symbols, unrelated to conceptual structure, provides only superficial mathematical experience. Piaget sums the position up by saying "In a word, the central problem of mathematical teaching is that of reciprocal adjustment between the spontaneous operational structures proper to the intelligence and the programme or methods relating to the particular branches of mathematics being taught" (1971, 45).

If research has in general established that progress in conservation leads to a better understanding and performance with arithmetic, what is the best way to proceed so that conservation and number facility will develop maximally? At the outset it should be made clear that attempts to provide for the acceleration of logical operations by specifically designed mathematics programmes, e.g., Almy (1970), have been less than rewarding. This emphasises a point made in Chapter 5 that the development of cognitive structures takes place as a result of generalised experiences based on self regulatory behaviour and the cognitive match as the individual interacts with persons and materials. What is required then are mathematical programmes that will encourage the natural development of cognitive structure and logical operations in a way in which, at the same time, makes full use of the developing cognitive structure to provide maximum mathematical understanding and number facility.

Fundamentally, in terms of the stance taken in Chapter 5, this means that organisers of mathematical programmes must adapt the ideas put forward in favour of the integrated day to mathematics teaching. In addition to generalised experience, self regulatory behaviour and cognitive match, such a concept would need to emphasise intrinsic motivation through interest and the principle of moderate novelty; interpersonal interaction and discussion; genuine activity, discovery and the opportunity to abstract real meaning at the operative level as the structures develop. This implies schemes which are broad in conception and take into account the interrelationship between the various aspects of developing structures and kinds of experience necessary to promote mathematical competence which includes both understanding and technical competence.

Two approaches which are in line with the principles outlined above are the Dienes approach and the Triad Mathematics Laboratory scheme. There are no doubt other worthy schemes of a similar nature but these two are cited because of their particular relevance to the stance taken in this chapter and they are fundamentally Australian in origin. Dienes, who accepts Piaget's basic position and who has made significant original contributions to the understanding of mathematical concepts and to mathematics teaching, developed a multi-model method of teaching mathematics. This was based on the use of a variety of structural materials. Structural material is material designed to illustrate logical structures by reference to several qualitatively different models or analogues. This material differs from Cuisenaire and Stern material (rods or blocks) which provide children with a "provisional concrete, coding system . . ." (Dienes, 1966, 60). Dienes refers to the use of Cuisenaire and Stern material as "uni-model methods".

The "multi-model" method developed by Dienes shows promise of developing both understanding and mechanical ability in children. This was shown in a survey conducted by the National Foundation for Educational Research in England and Wales (Unesco, 1966) which evaluated methods of teaching arithmetic using the criteria of the development of a better understanding of and more favourable attitudes to arithmetic and mathematics in general. The methods investigated were:

1   Traditional methods defined as those that stress rote learning of symbolic data and in which little attempt is made to illustrate and to make understood the logical structure of arithmetic. Such methods are characterised by much drill, mechanical work, extrinsic reward systems and generally an authoritarian mode of presentation.

2   Structural Methods: Two different structural methods were evaluated: uni-model and multi-model.

3   Motivational methods: These are methods which do not use specifically structured physical models as such, but rely on "real life" environmental situations and emphasise arousing and maintaining the child's interest in number situations.

The survey was conducted in two parts. The first investigation involved over 4 500 ten-year-olds attending primary schools in England and Wales. In this investigation traditional, uni-model structural and motivational methods were compared in terms of performance on mechanical, problem and conceptual tests, as well as emotional reaction to arithmetic.

The best uni-model results came from children with the highest intelligence (boys only) otherwise there was virtually no difference between uni-model and traditional methods both with respect to performance and attitude. Motivational (environmental) methods were as effective as other methods when the former were used in the infants school but consistent use of motivational methods throughout the infant and junior departments produced very poor performance scores.

The multi-model (Dienes) method was investigated in only one school over a two year period. Children taught by the multi-model method were matched individually with control children who had been traditionally taught. The Dienes-taught children were significantly superior to the controls in mechanical and concept arithmetic and also had a much more favourable attitude to the subject. Dull children derived the greatest benefit from the method.

The overall results of the study are suggestive only but the International Study Group for Mathematics Learning reached the following tentative conclusions:

1. Uni-model methods (the Cuisenaire and the Stern) do not seem to provide the conditions necessary for a conceptual understanding of arithmetic any better than those provided under already existing traditional schemes; neither do they appear to bring about emotional attitudes to the subject that are any more favourable than those created under traditional methods. Although there was some evidence that the provision of a single concrete coding system was useful computationally, this kind of structuring does not appear to be radical enough to lead to the development of understanding except in those favourable cases of boys of high intelligence.[2]

2. The cultivation of generalised mathematical coding systems, and thus of genuine understanding, seems to depend, in average and particularly in dull children, upon experiences that are best provided by multi-model methods, i.e., those in which a variety of perceptually and qualitatively different but logically isomorphic experiences are provided. (Dienes, 1966, 61-62)

Thus the research reported supports the fact that this multi-model method or generalised experiences method developed by Dienes leads to genuine understanding and mechanical competence. It will therefore be instructive to examine the conception which underlies the construction of this method and explore in what ways it is compatible with the implications for the teaching of mathematics which were seen to flow from a consideration of Piaget's theory. Not all of the ideas Dienes put forward are discussed below, for discussion is confined to those ideas that seem most relevant in the context; even so the analysis is a rather long one.

One of the ideas upon which Dienes based his system was his contention that the greater degree of generality at which a concept is formed, the wider is the field in which it may be applied (1965, 3). In Piaget's terms this is

[2] D. McN's note. Piaget (1971, 49) has drawn attention to the fact that the Cuisenaire method does not exist as a unified entity but is a plurality of methods ranging from excellent to very bad. It is excellent when it gives rise to active manipulations and discoveries by the child himself and follows the line of spontaneous operational development. Teachers sometimes run the risk, says Piaget, of giving the configurations greater importance than the operations. That is, the *figurative* aspects of perception, imitation and images are stressed rather than the *operative* aspects of thought. See also J. Piaget *Where is Education Heading?*, No. 6, *Series B: Opinions,* International Commission on the Development of Education, Unesco, 1971.

equivalent to the notion of "schème" which is "that part of an action or operation which is repeatable and generalizable in another action or operation".

In achieving this generality of formation, Dienes took into account several factors.

1 Children in their earliest years think mostly *constructively* (Dienes, 1965, 4). In constructive thinking concepts are built out of a broad general picture. Dienes asserts that children must be allowed to build up their concepts in a global, intuitive, constructive way from their own experiences, because *analytic* thinking, the awareness of all possible logical relationships is rarely present before the age of 12, i.e., the beginnings of the formal level of reasoning stage.

2 Children do not learn a concept from one type of experience. The formation of a concept depends upon abstraction (Piaget uses the term *formal reflecting abstraction*) or the seeing of the fundamental relationship among different tasks. In Dienes' opinion it therefore becomes necessary to provide a number of seemingly *different* tasks with the same underlying mathematical structure (Dienes, 1964, 54; 1965, 3). This implies that the concept should be presented so that the individual receives as many different perceptual impressions as possible and this would include visual, tactile and kinaesthetic. For Dienes and Piaget what is abstracted is that which relates all similar examples. Thus the similarity, the sameness or the essential attribute is not in the material as such but in the abstraction of what is common.

3 When a mathematical concept depends upon a certain number of variables each of which may assume a different number of values, it is necessary to vary the sizes of these variables so that the quality aspect will be realised as a result of the variation of the quantities involved. For example: big triangle—small triangle; red triangle—blue triangle; thin triangle—thick triangle from which is abstracted the quality, triangularity, which of course relates in this instance to point 2 above.

4 Dienes also applied what he called the "Dynamic Principle" (Dienes, 1964, 44) which has its origin in Piaget's theory (Dienes, 1959, 6). Dienes' conception of the "Dynamic Principle" has itself undergone modification over the years as a consequence of his work in the field. The exposition of the "Dynamic Principle" proceeds therefore by first outlining Dienes' stated position in 1965 and concludes with his position as reported to a recent conference in New Guinea (1972).

The "Dynamic Principle" in Dienes' earlier work refers to the three stages which a concept must pass through, *preliminary* games; *structured*, "becoming aware" games, and *practice* games.[3] During the preliminary stage the child is given the opportunity to contact the concept in an undirected, seemingly purposeless way that is performed and enjoyed for its own sake

---

[3] It is probable that "play" and "games" as Dienes uses them would translate over to "activities" in other schemes.

116

but which nevertheless provides the basis for the fundamental reality experiences for the development of the concept (Dienes, 1959, 6). In the second or structured stage, the child should be given tasks which will give him experiences similar in structure to the concept to be learned with an emphasis on a variety of experiences. During this stage if the child has not become aware of the concept, then it is possible he needs more preliminary games or alternative games. When a child has gained some insight into the purpose of the activity, then he will engage in practice games which will help to anchor the insight, for the concept will not be fully operational until it can be freely recognised and used in relevant situations. Sometimes the practice game will provide the basis for the next preliminary game.

Dienes' present view of the operation of the "Dynamic Principle" in the learning situation emphasises the following stages:

1 Exploration (play) which Dienes believes is instinctive to the child and necessary for the introduction of any new topic or material.

2 Rule bound games, in which certain concepts are exemplified, should follow with the emphasis on the provision of many games (experiences or activities).

3 Comparison games which lead to an abstract idea of what is common to games played in 2.

4 Graphical representation to enable children to look at what they have learned. That is, pictorial representation enables the child to look at sets of properties and relationships.

5 Symbolic representation—Language. Initially the child may suggest the language or symbols to describe what has taken place, but it eventually becomes necessary to introduce conventional symbolism.

Examination of this more recent conception indicates the presence, in different form, of his earlier principles of preliminary games, structural games and practice games and these have been extended to incorporate the abstraction of mathematical ideas and their relationship with one another. It should also be reiterated here, that Dienes makes considerable use of structured materials as, e.g., attribute blocks and multibase arithmetic blocks as an integral part of his total approach to the teaching of mathematics.

Dienes has made a considerable contribution to the teaching of mathematics in his own right and continues to do so, nevertheless it is apparent that there are in his conception ideas which can be traced directly to Piaget's theory or which would be consistent with Piaget's theory. Notable among these conceptions are: the operation of genuine activity and the importance of operative knowing; a realisation of the importance of concrete material even to the stage of late childhood or early adolescence; the importance of *formal abstraction*; the development of logical relationships among abstractions and the development of generalisable stable concepts with wide specific application.

Finally, Dienes has a particular view on how the classroom should be structured and the experiences presented. In general, learning should take place individually or in small groups of two or three. Children should be free to move from one set of experiences to another in the absence of directions from the teacher. These experiences should be designed so that, e.g., a series of assignment cards, together with available appropriate structured material, would lead to the progressive building up of a concept or to the re-presentation of a concept in parallel form using different material. There should, if possible, be some degree of choice, with great variety to accord with the principles of variability.

The role of the teacher is distinctly different from the traditional role for an authoritarian attitude would not be appropriate in a learning situation of this kind. Here the teacher acts more as a co-ordinator and a resource person whose chief role is to foster a spirit of enquiry and see to it that the child does not flounder, that he has not chosen a task for which he is not ready, which is another way of saying that the teacher's role is to ensure the appropriate "cognitive match" for each child. As Dienes states (1964, 46): "Teachers in charge of such classes act as counsellors and helpers in the children's own efforts to grapple with the problems in front of them."

The second conception of teaching mathematics which embodies the principles implied in Piaget's work is the scheme known as the Triad Mathematics Laboratory scheme. This scheme incorporates the implications from Piaget's work in several ways. First, it is a scheme which provides experiences which attempt to foster the parallel development of number and logical structure. Second, it is a good example of how a curriculum has been constructed to accord with the principles set out in Chapter 5. Third, it exemplifies the concept of generalised experiences in so far as this can be done within the one subject area.

The Triad Laboratory consists of three levels: Level I designed for children aged 5 to 6 approximately, corresponding to the first year of school; Level II, second year at school, ages 6 to 7 approximately; Level III, third year at school, ages 7 to 8 approximately. As the Triad Guide Book (1970, 1) says "The programme represents a synthesis of theory, research and practice. It brings into focus recent developments in elementary mathematics throughout the world. Prominent among these are the vanguard contributions of Piaget, Bruner, Dienes and Gagne . . ." While the influence of all four researchers is readily discernible, it is the writer's belief, after having examined the programme and observed its operation, that it is the work of Piaget which predominates, particularly when one takes into consideration Piaget's direct influence on both Dienes and Bruner.

The programme has three major themes, experiential, number and evaluation, and it is to the first two of these that attention is directed. The experiential and number themes are designed to allow children to explore ideas through both structured and unstructured, including environmental, materials. To give some idea of the scope and content of the scheme, each of the two areas, experiential and number, of the Level I Laboratory will be

118

examined in brief separately. It should be noted that, in addition to the wide variety of materials supplied in the Triad Laboratory, the scheme also uses and integrates material which is usually part of classroom equipment and that it also utilises everyday materials of the child's out of school environment. (Some idea of the nature of the materials contained in Triad can be gained from Plates 1, 2, 3, 4 and 5 although the Triad Laboratory is much more comprehensive than these few pictures show.)

Experiential Theme. In this segment, emphasis is given to those basic properties of the environment which form an integral part of the young child's mathematical experience and development. These are time, length, size, shape, capacity, weight, thickness, position, area, colour, money, other properties such as age and texture, patterns, geometry and logic which includes work on identification of shape, colour, size and thickness, classification, similarities and differences, "not-properties" and part-whole relationships.

In the main, experiences which relate to the work on *logic* are based on the use of structured material (attribute blocks, Plate 1) but is also extended to the attribute snap cards (Plate 5), which, in addition to containing cards with the words big, small, thin, thick, contains cards representing the *not-attributes* associated with size, thickness, shape and colour. The importance of providing experiences which relate directly to *logic* in the development of thought in young children is taken up briefly in the final chapter in the section concerned with language teaching. It should be realised that although the properties of the attribute blocks are to a certain extent idealised, they nevertheless relate directly to the environment, e.g., thick—thin; big—small; triangle—circle. The Triad Guide Book, of course, emphasises the necessity of making the relationship apparent.

The other areas of the experiential theme make use of a variety of materials as e.g. in the activity which gives children the opportunity to play with objects which are different in weight. In a lesson based on the differences in weight the objects are typically such things as foam rubber, stones, empty cardboard boxes, tins, nails, blocks of wood etc. (Plate 6).

Number Theme. Once again two different types of experiences are provided: one with environmental materials, the other with structured materials. The experiences with environmental materials are used to introduce the concepts of number in terms of discontinuous quantities through sets, while experiences with structured materials, i.e. Cuisenaire rods, are used to introduce concepts of number in terms of continuous quantity. These two different kinds of experience are designed to support the development of cardination and ordination with the coming of operational thought.

Specifically, experience with environmental materials in relation to sets encompasses the mathematical ideas of unit; sets and subsets; one-to-one correspondence, equivalence, inequivalence, cardinal and ordinal properties of number; one-to-many correspondence; part-whole relationships and conservation.

The Cuisenaire rods are structured to provide a model of the rational number system and children use this model to explore the system in terms of

119

relationships based on colour and relative length.

This brief description of Triad gives a clear indication of a scheme in which a systematic attempt has been made to structure a mathematics programme, in this case for five- to six-year-olds, which takes into account the parallel development of number and operational thought, and the relationship which exists between the two.

EVALUATION

The concept is continued into the evaluation section of the scheme where provision is made for the on-going evaluation of both number and the development of logical operations which would seem to be an approach clearly implied in Piaget's theory. Plate 3 illustrates this aspect of the scheme by showing first the seals and balls which are part of the equipment used to develop ordinal correspondence. This aspect of the child's conceptual development is evaluated by other devices including a series of seven penguins which have to be matched with hats and walking sticks. It can be easily seen that during the currency of the Triad programme, on-going evaluation would take place with respect to individual children on the basis of their coping with this ordinal correspondence task. The other illustration in Plate 3 shows the egg cups and spoons which are used to evaluate numerical or one-to-one correspondence although the Triad equipment provides for and suggests the use of seven such objects.

The authors of the Triad Laboratory have provided a suggested programme of group lessons and whole class lessons and suggested sequence which the authors believe parallels the development of the child. The Guide Book does suggest, however, that the Laboratory is not intended to restrict the teacher's personal freedom and points out that the in-built, on-going evaluation system permits the teacher to meet the needs of individual children; or, in Piaget's terms, to provide the child with what seems to be material appropriate to the current state of his cognitive structures. In fact, all the way through the scheme, there is emphasis on true activity in the sense that the materials and experiences are designed to permit the child to abstract the relationship inherent in the situation to the extent that his logical structures will allow.

One of the consistent features of many of the Triad-based lessons the writer has observed, in the context of the organisation of the infants classroom, has been the translation of this aspect of the programme into flexible group lessons with frequent opportunity for interpersonal interaction and discussion among children as they compare and discuss in terms of their own cognitive structures. Plate 4 illustrates a situation where in one group the teacher and the children are interacting and discussing outcomes and in the other two children are experiencing interacting and discussing. Both situations seem to provide opportunities for physical experience, formal abstraction, cooperation, interaction and discussion.

Again, the Triad material seems, to the writer, to represent an attempt to analyse the structure of the material to be taught into component sub-skills in a way which will permit a ready mapping of the material to each individual's cognitive structure. This was, of course, one of the implications of Piaget's theory for curriculum construction. It is, of course, recognised by the writer that mathematics carries within it its own logical structure and to that extent such an analysis is more easily made.

Therefore, from this brief exposition of the Triad scheme it can be seen that it has taken into account the necessity for the parallel development of logical structure and mathematical ideas and that it embodies the principle, in so far as a single subject can, of a wide variety of activities in the sense of generalised experiences that seek to use and integrate with environmental experiences and to build on these with an appropriate structured approach.

From a discussion of these two approaches to the teaching of mathematics it can be seen that mathematics can be taught in such a way as to take into account the principles put forward in Chapter 5 for the optimum development of cognitive structure and of mathematical competence. To recapitulate, these principles were generalised experience, self regulatory behaviour and cognitive match; emphasis on instrinsic motivation through interest and the principle of moderate novelty; interpersonal interaction and discussion; genuine activity, discovery and the opportunity to abstract real meaning at the *operative* level as the structures develop. It should be emphasised, however, that although both schemes are related to Piaget's theory, each of the schemes interprets Piaget differently with the Triad scheme adhering more closely to conventional mathematics.

Some Final Points Concerning Piaget's Theory and Mathematics Teaching

Teachers sometimes lament that numbers of children do not like mathematics and where this is so it is probable that this negative attitude influences performance. Both the Dienes and the Triad approaches to the teaching of mathematics have as an important aim the goal that children will enjoy and like mathematics. The research cited earlier indicated that the Dienes approach had generated favourable attitudes towards mathematics and the Triad Guide Book has a section which specifies the affective goals of the Triad scheme in terms of liking and enjoyment of mathematical experiences as part of a general goal of favourable attitudes to school work in general.

There has been much speculation as to why children dislike mathematics and the writer believes that a good deal of the disaffection can be traced to methods and programmes which emphasise the ability to manipulate symbols in the absence of an adequate understanding of the underlying structure. It may well be that schemes based upon the parallel development of logical operations and mathematical facility will go a long way towards remedying this situation.

Role of Drill in Mathematics. Acceptance of Piaget's view does not imply that drill would find no place in the classroom. What is implied is that drill which was not based on a solid foundation of understanding would be largely a waste of time. It is quite obvious that for computational facility it is necessary to develop speed and accuracy in the manipulation of such things as the addition and multiplication tables. There would be a few people who in multiplying 9 by 7 would be concerned about the mathematical properties of the set of 7 objects or the logical operations that underlie their multiplication. If drill is to be used in the classroom, then it would seem that the logic of the situation would demand drill on the basis of prior understanding. Of course this does not mean that drill necessarily implies the use of whole class rote methods but, rather, looks to the use of a variety of experiences in individual and group settings.

The Organisation and Structuring of the Teaching Situation and Discovery

The emphasis on self regulation, true activity and discovery, does not mean that the teacher ceases to instruct and guide the child. While it is true that Piaget stresses that the child builds his own intellectual structure and that the progressive development and integration of this structure depends on the appropriate match, this does not mean that the teacher never tells the child or helps him with relationships. There is nothing in Piaget's theory that says that the teacher should not intervene. Certainly the role of the teacher changes from predominantly verbal methods, for the teacher becomes more of a person who structures the environment. Even in the most flexible form of the integrated day the child does not spend the whole of his time drifting around contacting whatever happens to be there. Certainly his day may begin, at the early infants level, in exploring some interesting object brought to school but in the main the child even when selecting the activity he wishes to pursue will be engaged on activities that have been planned in advance and placed within his environment by the teacher, in the overall design of the prospective experiences thought to be valuable for continuing development. This point will be brought out more strongly in the next chapter in that part of the discussion which centres around the teaching of social studies.

7. The Implications of Piaget's Theory for the Teaching of Social Studies, Science and Language

1 THE IMPLICATIONS OF PIAGET'S THEORY FOR THE TEACHING OF SOCIAL STUDIES

Today there is a considerable amount of rethinking with respect to what should be taught and how it should be taught in Social Studies. One good example of this is what is known as the Taba Approach, as illustrated in Taba *et. al.*, *A Teacher's Handbook to Elementary Social Studies, 1971*. As one would expect, such an approach is concerned with educational objectives, curriculum content, learning activities, teaching strategies and evaluation, to cite but the essential outlines. What is notable about the approach is the important role it gives to thinking and the view of knowledge adopted. In briefly outlining these views on thinking, Taba *et al.* (1971, 11) cite as support Piaget's work and that of Piaget's co-worker Szeminska, although one may question some of the conclusions reached in this connection. Nevertheless, the work of Piaget has had some influence on teaching reform in infants and primary social studies. However, in this segment of Chapter 7 it is intended simply to note this influence of Piaget on those working in the social studies area and to concentrate on outlining what the writer believes Piaget implies for the teaching of social studies. This is done in three parts. The first part continues the argument developed in Chapters 5 and 6 and reports and analyses a method of teaching social studies that follows from the stand taken. The second part outlines Piaget's views of socialisation and social development and shows how Piaget accepts a point of view consistent with that put forward in the first part. The third part examines Piaget's work on the Moral development of the child and raises questions about what emerges in relation to the teaching of social studies.

A Social Studies Experience Unit Consistent with Piaget's Theory

One of the emphases in the new approach to organising the social studies curriculum is upon attempting less, with the aim of moving away from previous situations where attempts to cover many topics led to superficial understanding. This is, of course, Piaget's view (1971, 96) concerning curricula, but it is also important because it allows the teacher to provide experiences which will be more likely to promote both the development of cognitive structure and conceptual growth in social studies. From what was said in earlier chapters this implies a classroom situation with the emphasis on self regulation, and the cognitive match; motivation based on interest and the principle of moderate novelty; interpersonal interaction and discussion; genuine activity and discovery involving operative rather than figurative knowing.

In the pages that follow a method of teaching social studies is illustrated which incorporates these principles but which has its origin in *experimentalism*. It has already been made clear in Chapter 5, however, that experimentalist principles are compatible with the majority of Piaget's views. As the scheme is explained and discussed it will become apparent where the various principles apply. In considering the implications of Piaget's work for the teaching of such subjects as social studies it should be kept in mind that such subjects do not possess an inherent logical structure as does mathematics and therefore the implications are of a more general nature.

The method is based upon structuring the classroom environment so that the basic concepts, generalisations and specific facts are embedded in the material provided. Perhaps the best way to present this method is to outline a unit completed by a 6th grade class in an Australian primary school.[1] The class was co-educational with IQs ranging from 85 to 125 and had a mean IQ of 99.

The topic was Indonesia in which the broad general goals were classified as outlined immediately below, each of which is elaborated briefly following the listing.

Content — Generalisations ⎫
        — Concepts ⎬ Understanding
        — Specific facts ⎭

Attitudes and Values — Self and Others; Social Adjustment and Social Development; Skills and Abilities.

CONTENT

Prior analysis of the topic indicated specifically what would be required in terms of the projected outcomes, above. Thus the generalisations, concepts and specific facts which might lead to the achievement of the outcomes were identified and material was gathered in advance of the presentation which would embody these. The material consisted of Indonesian artifacts such as shadow puppets, beaten silverware, batik cloth, carved wooden statuettes; large pictures which illustrated Indonesian life; maps; books and duplicated notes which contained current information on Indonesia.

ATTITUDES AND VALUES (SELF AND OTHERS)

An important aim of the unit was the provision of opportunities which would contribute to the development of a positive self concept in terms of worth as

[1] The class was taught by the writer in a Sydney school.

a functioning member of a group in a co-operative venture. A second aim was to provide opportunities for developing an attitude towards Indonesians as new neighbours by providing frequent opportunity for discussion among class members and some opportunity to talk to Indonesian nationals. The degree of change was evaluated by attitude scales administered before and after the unit.

SOCIAL ADJUSTMENT AND SOCIAL DEVELOPMENT

Another important aim of the work was the promotion of social adjustment and social development by providing an opportunity for frequent intergroup interaction in an atmosphere which stressed acceptance of others but which provided for legitimate disagreement. Social distance—the amount of positive acceptance as against rejection—in the class as a whole was measured on several occasions using the Horace Mann-Lincoln social distance scale. The same instrument was used to measure individual changes in acceptability.

SKILLS AND ABILITIES

Here the emphasis was on continued development of such skills as map reading; use of library and reference materials; discussion; co-operation in joint activities; use of imagination and creativity.

PRESENTATION

The method is known generally as "The Method of Enquiry" and the method of presentation in this unit consisted of arranging the material, referred to above, in display form so that the child's usual environment (classroom) is restructured. This is done in the absence of the children and in such a way as to provide easy access to the material. This latter point is important because it is essential that adequate opportunity be given to all children to examine the materials provided, both artifacts and written material.

The learning experience begins as soon as the children contact the re-arranged environment for the first time. Usually, the first reaction is a buzz of excitement as the children congregate around the objects, initially as a large group which rapidly changes to small groups of five to six members. (Research on group behaviour shows that discussion is more satisfying to individuals when it can take place in small groups. It is therefore desirable that the room be structured in a way that makes this possible.) Plate 7 shows the initial few minutes of the Indonesian Unit as the children congregate around the various objects. Often the first question asked on such an occasion is: "May we touch the material?" As can be seen from Plate 7, an affirmative response to such a question leads to the emergence of widespread sensori-motor activity as the children through both figurative and operative knowing, though one suspects predominantly through operative knowing, come to know the puppets and the statuettes in a way previously not possible although not yet in the way in which they will know them at the end of the unit.

Soon the questions begin to come and one might expect that the questions relate directly to the scheme of knowing relative to the developmental level of individual cognitive structures. Some of the questions were more sophisticated

125

than others and may well have been indicative of transition to the formal stage of reasoning.[2] Questions ranged in complexity and abstractness from "What kind of food do Indonesians eat?" to "What kind of government does Indonesia have? Is it a Republic?" These questions were recorded either in writing or on a tape recorder for sorting later. When the children seemed to have run out of spontaneous questions discussions were held concerning procedure and the other important goals of increased social acceptance. The writer contends, along with Furth (1970, 134), that the question raising itself is more important than having the child memorise an answer, for as Furth points out, asking questions of the child may elicit merely a low-level operative answer.

Groups were formed of approximately six members on the basis of socio-metric choice, the question asked being "With whom would you like to work on group work?"[3] The children then began the task of answering the

[2] The writer recently concluded research on thinking at the sixth grade level some of which has been published (1970). The tests used were those reported by Peel (1959, 1960, 1966) which are verbal reasoning tests based on Piaget's theory. The studies were carried out on: (a) sixth grade classes for bright children with IQ's of 125 and above; and (b) sixth grade classes which contain the children who remain after the special classes are formed. The results showed that in the sixth classes for children with IQ's of 125 and above, the percentage of children reasoning at the *formal* level was 37, with 41 per cent at the *concrete* level and 22 per cent *transitional* between concrete and formal. In the classes from which the brightest children had been removed, the percentages were *formal* 6 per cent, *transitional* 15 per cent and *concrete* 79 per cent. Therefore although no tests of reasoning were given, it is probable that since some of the children had IQ's at or in the vicinity of 125, there were already children at the formal reasoning stage.

[3] The sociometric test devised by J. Moreno, consists of asking each child to write down the names of children he would prefer under certain circumstances. There is no restriction on the basis or criterion of choice but two of the most frequently used are "With whom would you like to sit?" and "With whom would you like to work?" It is usual, but not necessary, to restrict the number of choices to 3 or 5. From the information gained the teacher can construct a *sociogram* which is a diagram showing choice patterns. For example:

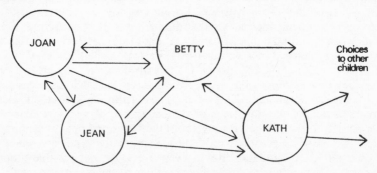

In addition, the number of choices a person receives can be totalled giving a *sociometric status* score which indicates the particular standing of each person in the group. It is from the sociogram that groups can be formed. In general, research shows that children prefer to work with others of approximately similar ability.

questions raised. Initially the children began by seeking answers to the questions raised by the members of their own sub-group but shortly after the initiation of the unit, duplicated sheets covering all questions raised were distributed by the teacher.

Neither the mode by which the children were to answer the questions nor the order in which they dealt with the questions were prescribed. Children were free to explore individually or to pool judgments through discussion and group decision. No restriction was placed on the movement of children within and between groups except that comfortable conditions of work should prevail for all. One of the consistent outcomes of this procedure was the raising of further questions by group members. Again the focus was the operative use of intelligence in the process of thinking. What this meant in practice can be seen in Plate 8 which shows typical intra- and intergroup interaction as the unit progressed. The background in this illustration shows part of the original structured environment.

Sometimes, as happened in this unit, it becomes obvious that the resources available to the children are insufficient to meet requirements in which case the children move out into the environment to use other resources, in this case the museum and Indonesian nationals.

Very little direction was given as to what constituted legitimate activity in the prosecution of the enquiry. Perhaps the most directive part of the total experience was the use of a set of duplicated sheets containing the original questions raised and a place for the child's answers to these questions when either he or the group found them. These sheets, however, were useful in providing a permanent record for the child and the basis for part of the final evaluation at the conclusion. In general, however, the class was free to approach the task in any way considered appropriate.

The result was a wide variety of activities including researching and recording information; illustration (drawing and painting), reading; discussion, including disputation; spontaneous mime; play writing; play production; map making; organising excursions; meetings chaired by the emergent pupil leader at which attempts were made to solve communal problems relating to the unit; and finally meetings and discussion with Indonesian adult nationals.

THE ROLE OF THE TEACHER

In this approach to the presentation of experiences, the teacher's role is considerably different to that which characterises the traditional teacher dominated lesson. In summary the role can be described as follows:

1 The teacher is an analyst in the sense that he analyses the unit to be presented in terms of what will provide for optimal intellectual, social and emotional (including attitudinal) development.

2 He manipulates the environment in that he selects certain materials and plans certain experiences which he believes will promote the outcomes desired.

127

3   The teacher becomes more a guide, expert, adviser and group leader, in the broad sense, in what is essentially a flexible and fluid teaching-learning environment.

EVALUATION

The unit was evaluated in a comprehensive manner. A brief outline of this follows.

1 A formal "academic" test was given to determine how much was "known". This was required for the school records and it also served to give some indication as to how the method measured up against conventional fact oriented teaching. The results were highly satisfactory, although similar results may also have been achieved by traditional class lessons. There were, however, many instances of what could be termed "growth in knowledge" in the Piagetian sense which would not normally show up in the traditional written tests. These were occasions identified by observation and one is outlined below as an example.

One of the objects provided in the unit was an Indonesian shadow puppet, with beautifully enamelled features and attractive costuming (Plate 9). Upon seeing this for the first time one of the girls cried excitedly "Joan, come and look at this beautiful doll!" Three weeks later this girl, together with several class members, presented a play she had written entitled "Indonesian Life" in which the shadow puppet featured prominently in the segment which depicted fairly faithfully the cultural significance that is attached to these puppets in Indonesian life.

In terms of what was said in Chapter 4, this girl's "knowing" of this object was now much more operative and the meaning she had at the end of the unit, when she assimilated shadow puppets to her schema of knowing, would be considerably more advanced than that given by her largely figurative knowing of the puppet in the first instance.

2 Administration of attitude scales showed clear evidence of a very favourable increase in attitudes towards Indonesians but again this might be due to other factors. First, it was obvious from the pre-test that the children knew little or nothing about Indonesians and so the initial poor rating of Indonesians was probably simply the rating given "unknown" people. Secondly the same gains may have been made using the traditional method. Nevertheless, attitudes changed remarkably and statistical tests showed that the gains were significant at the ·01 level.

3 There were also substantial gains in social acceptance of the group as a whole as measured by the Horace Mann-Lincoln Social Distance Scale such that there was an increase in the amount of acceptance and a corresponding decrease in rejection. The increase in acceptance and the decrease in rejection were significant at the ·01 level.

It has been made quite clear that the Method of Enquiry is not wholly based on Piaget but is experimentalist inspired in many ways. Nevertheless, the method does accord well with Piaget's views on education and with his theory of cognitive development.

Analysis of the enquiry method of teaching social studies reveals that it has a number of features that are also characteristic of the integrated day. There is, in a sense, an opportunity for general or overall experience within the framework of the on-going experiences. It is, of course, not as general as the experiences which the same children would have in interaction with their own environment yet it is much more general than is usually provided in the "chalk and talk" social studies lessons.

The type of classroom experience provided by the "Method of Enquiry" does, however, give to each child the opportunity of making the cognitive match between his current structures and the immediate environment because the relatively unstructured situation, in the sense of undirected, means that, through self-regulation, he contacts that which is most suitable for the continued growth of his cognitive structure. It follows from this, in terms of Piaget's theory, that individual interest will be high as the child selects that which is moderately novel to engage his attention. In this situation, interest does not depend on some form of external reward but resides in the "function pleasure" generated by matching cognitive structure to available objects and experience.

Of particular importance is the fact that the "Method of Enquiry" provides for numerous opportunities for interpersonal interaction which means frequent opportunity for discussion. The writer believes that this is one of the fundamental strengths of this approach to the teaching of social studies for two reasons. First, it provides for continued social development including social adjustment, an area frequently not included as a projected outcome of traditional social studies lessons. Second, as outlined in Chapter 5, discussion, including disputation, plays a considerable role in the progressive development of cognitive structure.

Piaget's Views on Socialisation and Its Relationship to Classroom Learning

Piaget's beliefs with respect to discussion and intellectual development have already been canvassed, but his views on social development and socialisation are not as well known. Yet he holds equally firm views on socialisation and believes that the type of classroom organisation outlined above promotes it best. Piaget believes that the affective and social development of the child follows the same general process as cognitive development "since the affective, social and cognitive aspects of behaviour are in fact inseparable" (1969, 114).

He considers that the child from the point of view of inherited behaviour is social almost from the day of its birth in that it smiles at people in its second month and seeks to make contact with others (1971, 174). But as well as these internal tendencies there is also the society that is external to the individual

129

which is in essence a system of relationships established from the outside and includes such things as language, intellectual exchanges, and moral or legal action transmitted from generation to generation (1971, 174).

Thus the child, although possessing urges toward sympathy and imitation from the very first, must learn everything (1971, 174). Initially, the child knows nothing of rules or signs and so must proceed by a process of gradual adaptation—that is, assimilation of others to itself and accommodation of itself to others—to master the essential properties of external society which are mutual comprehension based on speech and communal discipline based on standards of mutual agreement. Initially the child is unaware of its differentiation from the group but in the second half of the first year begins to imitate others, i.e. to accommodate. On the other hand the child is also constantly assimilating others to itself because he is unable to penetrate below the surface of their behaviour and motives and so reduces them to his own point of view to understand them, and as with symbolic play (Chapter 2) projects his own thoughts and desires into them. Gradually the child comes to understand others in the same way as itself and becomes able to appreciate the viewpoint of another making possible the acceptance of rules initially external to him. In Piaget's words the child "succeeds simultaneously both in emerging from itself and in becoming aware of itself, in other words, in situating itself from the outside among others while at the same time discovering both its own personality and that of everyone else" (1971, 175).

The ability to situate oneself outside among others and to take the anticipated feelings of others into account has been shown by Moreno (1942), Taguiri (1958), Parsons (1951) and Goslin (1962) to be important in the development of social acceptance of the individual and in the effectiveness of the operation of the group as a social system. This, of course, includes taking into account the feelings of adults and other authority figures. In fact Goslin (1962, 283) suggests that the accuracy of the predictions of how individuals in a social system (e.g., family or school class) are going to behave is directly related to the effectiveness of the social system and believes that the individual will be alienated from the system if he makes very many mistakes in his guesses about how he is perceived by others.

Piaget recognises the importance of these interpersonal relationships which exist in a social system such as the classroom group for he notes that children are "individually aware that parallel to their classroom discipline and more or less clandestine in nature, there exists a whole system of mutual aid based upon a 'special understanding' . . ." In this connection Piaget notes that "the new methods all tend to employ these collective energies rather than ignore them or allow them to become transformed into hostile forces" (1971, 179-180). These ideas accord well with the type of classroom organisation which emphasises group work, the selection of groups on the basis of sociometric choice and an emphasis on interpersonal interaction. It may therefore be fairly claimed that the Method of Enquiry as outlined in the first part of this chapter seems likely to promote both intellectual and social development in a way implicit in Piaget's theory.

130

Piaget's ideas on moral development belong to the early period of his work and a comprehensive statement is contained in *The Moral Judgment of the Child* (1932). But Piaget's enquiries in this area were not concerned with the everyday conception of morality as relating to such matters as lying, stealing or cheating. For Piaget the essential aspect of morality is concerned with the progressive development of the capacity to accept and follow a system of rules and their effect on the regulation of interpersonal behaviour. Basically there are two elements to a moral system; the norms which society has developed about such things as the way in which individuals will interact with others, and each individual's particular understanding of the rules which govern interaction. It was this aspect of the way in which the rules governing interaction developed that was of particular interest to Piaget and he studied this developmentally by observing and analysing the child's conception of the rules governing the game of marbles. The advantage of studying a game like marbles was that, unlike the norms concerning lying, the rules of marbles have been developed largely by children and so reflect the child's thinking, and they also determine how children will interact with one another. In addition the rules have been handed on from one generation to another just as the norms governing moral behaviour in the community at large have been handed on.

Piaget's observations and analysis revealed that moral development, like intellectual development, was characterised by broad stages generally related to intellectual development. Like the stages of intellectual development, the ages at which they occur are approximate and differ according to the aspect of moral development under discussion. A brief outline of the stages of development relating to the three broad areas follows.

a *The Practice of Rules as an Indication of Moral Behaviour*

i EGOCENTRIC STAGE

This stage spans the years from four to seven approximately. In this stage children neither know the rules nor can they follow rules but believe that they do both. But, as would be expected from the discussion in Chapter 5 and Section 2, above, the child cannot follow rules because he is incapable of taking the role or view of another, and will be unable to do this until he relinquishes his egocentric position and realises he is but one person with one point of view among several other points of view. Thus children in this stage often play "together" in the sense of playing with someone else yet without each really needing the other. There is therefore little genuine co-operation because each does not understand the rules of the other and there is no notion of winning in the accepted sense of the term. Winning for the child is synonymous with enjoying himself.

ii INCIPIENT CO-OPERATION (7 to 10/11) years

In this period, the child has a much better grasp of the rules but it is clear that he does not know all of the rules. This is reflected in the conflicts which arise, for the game is often interrupted by differences in relation to procedure. Nevertheless he co-operates, in the sense of agreeing to rules and abiding by them in so far as his knowledge of the rules and his ability to interpret them will allow, although he now competes with his playmate and his idea of winning is now much different from his earlier view.

Interaction with another player is now much more effective as he begins to take the point of view of another and to appreciate that others may view the game from a different perspective. This improvement in interaction is assisted by the development of language because whereas in the egocentric stage the child's speech was frequently directed from himself to himself, the child now begins to anticipate the needs of his listener as he decentres his attention from the self to others while continuing to objectify his view of things, including people, in the environment.

iii GENUINE CO-OPERATION (From 11 to 12 years)

The child in this period not only agrees with others as to how the game shall be played but operates within the framework of the rules laid down, taking a particular interest in interpretation of existing rules, including the anticipation of all possible contingencies. Frequently the participants will extend the rules of the game, for children at this stage seem to be interested in the legalistic form of rules and to enjoy the experience of innovation and the exploration of relationships among ideas that such activity provides.

b *Attitude Towards Violation and Origin of Rules*

In addition to enquiring into the child's knowledge of rules, Piaget also questioned the child about their inviolability. He wanted to know whether the child thought the rules could be changed, and where they originated.

Piaget found that there were two major stages, the first of which could be divided into two parts. It should be remembered in this connection the warning given earlier that these stages are not to be thought of as fixed and immutable but as indications of the course of development. The first stage lasts from about four to five years to about nine to ten years. In the first part of this stage the child believes that the game of marbles was invented by some authority and that the rules are unchangeable. Nevertheless, the child from about four to six years is prepared to accept changes to the rules which is surprising in view of his belief in the absolute nature of the rules. Piaget's interpretation is that the child has such a poor grasp of the rules that he consents to the alterations because he does not really appreciate that they are alterations.

From about six to ten years, the latter part of the first stage, the child's knowledge of the rules improves but he now refuses to accept changes and attests to the unchangeable nature of rules. Rules are still *absolute*.

Beginning at about ten or eleven years comes the second stage where the child agrees that rules can be changed and that they came about through human interaction and he also realises that rules are maintained by agreement among participants, on a basis of equality. The significant difference between this stage and the previous one is that the child will agree to changes in the game so long as he believes it to be fair, and there is mutual consent. He now accepts and follows rules in which he has been involved in changing.

c *The Child's Conception of Morality*

Piaget also studied the child's attitude to such things as lying and justice. For example he posed situations: (a) in which the unintentional action of a child resulted in considerable damage; and (b) a deliberate and improper action that caused negligible damage. In general Piaget found that the criterion of guilt used by younger children was the amount of damage not the intention of the subject. Piaget refers to this as moral realism. Gradually the child alters the basis on which judgments are made in favour of an approach which takes into account the motivation behind the act. Thus in doing damage it is motive behind the act; in lying, it is the intention to deceive.

Implications of Piaget's Views on Moral Development for Social Studies and Teaching in General

Once again we see the interrelationship of the various aspects of the developing child, the intellectual, the social and the moral. One very obvious implication concerns the expectations with respect to the child's understanding of abstract social and political concepts. It is difficult to see, in the face of the discussion so far, how primary school children especially in the early primary grades (third and fourth) could develop anything but a superficial understanding of such concepts as "law and order", and "economic and social interdependence of the community", to take but two aspects of topics recommended by a current Australian Social Studies Curriculum for Third Grade. In fact this curriculum suggests that "Children should be helped to realise that they have a part to play in the class and school organisation similar to the part played by adults in the community outside". When it is realised that some children in that particular state enter third grade at the age of seven plus, and that children at this age are only beginning to appreciate the rules governing the game of marbles, in which all of the physical elements are present, expectations of the amount of real understanding of the role of adults in the community outside must be small indeed.

In fact, one of the criticisms that can be levelled at much of the teaching of social studies in primary schools is that despite the frequent suggestions by various curricula concerning the relevance of experience and activity in building genuine understanding appropriate to the developmental level of the child, abstract political, social and moral concepts are frequently presented in verbal fashion with the remedy for incomplete understanding or lack of understanding simply being to present more words. When Piaget's views on cognitive development are related to his findings on moral and social development the futility of such an approach becomes obvious.

Again, Piaget's views of moral and intellectual development suggest that effective group work in the primary school must of necessity develop slowly in response to the progressive integration of intellectual, moral and social development. The development of the ability to appreciate rules and to co-operate in conjoint activities seems to await the development of the ability to adopt the perspective of another, i.e., to relinquish the egocentric view of the world, just as the full development of concrete operations awaits the co-ordination of perspectives and an objectification of the child's view of the world.

The importance of this relationship between intellectual, moral and social development is being increasingly recognised and is manifest in pilot pro-grammes such as the "moral dilemma" approach currently being tested in selected New South Wales primary schools by the Centre for Research into Learning and Instruction. Basically the approach involves reading a story about a typical situation children face in everyday life embedded in which is a moral dilemma. For example, one story involves a boy who runs away after his cricket ball has broken a neighbour's window. In the discussion that follows the presentation of the story, the children reach their own con-clusions with the teacher clarifying and stimulating discussion where neces-sary.

This is the kind of approach advocated by Furth (1970, 136-137) who considers that in matters of moral judgment the teacher is not there primarily to give information but rather to avoid explicit comparative judgments that call one thing good and another bad because the articulation of value judgments belongs at the end of a person's development not at the beginning. Rather should the child in open discussion among his peers question and work on the value judgments that will eventually be his but which must be understood, for the present, in terms of his own particular level of cognitive development.

A point of particular interest in this programme is that when several different points of view emerge, the children take the roles of the characters involved and act out the alternative solutions.

Flavell (1968, 6) following Sabin, distinguishes between *role enactment* in which the subject actually takes on the role attributes of another and *role taking*, a more covert, more exclusively cognitive process of adopting the perspective or attitude of another. The role situation referred to above in the brief account given is basically role enactment but it seems nevertheless that the incorporation of such an approach provides opportunities in which the relinquishing of the egocentric position will be facilitated with a consequent flow on to the development of social acceptance, the effectiveness of the operation of the group as a social system, communication and the continued development of cognitive structures.

A recent newspaper report of the "moral dilemma" scheme (*Sydney Morning Herald*, 19 October 1972, 15) offers some evidence in support of some of these points when, in a preliminary and tentative evaluation, the co-ordinator of the project suggested that "the method seemed to increase children's ability to talk about their feelings, to identify values different from their own, to solve problems systematically, and to be sensitive to the feelings of others".

Certainly Piaget sees an organic link between these factors because in *The Psychology of the Child* (1969, 118) Piaget notes the "possible analogy" between operations and the process of socialisation and points to the importance of interaction between the cognitive and social in these words:

> The general co-ordination of actions which characterises the functional nucleus of the operations includes interpersonal as well as intrapersonal actions. It is meaningless therefore to wonder whether it is the cognitive co-operation (or co-operations) which engender the individual operations or the other way around. It is at the stage of concrete operations that new interpersonal relations of a co-operative nature are established, and there is no reason why these should be limited to cognitive exchanges. (1969, 118)

It has already been noted with reference to both intellectual and moral development, that Piaget believes that one important means of promoting development in both these areas is interpersonal interaction and discussion. It is clear, however, from his work on moral and intellectual development that the expectations of the teacher with respect to the amount and quality of co-operation within children's groups must be tempered by an appreciation of current levels of development and that in general the teacher must be prepared for a process of gradual development characterised by ineptitude and difficulty before children are able to work with reasonable autonomy in task oriented groups.

2 PIAGET'S THEORY AND THE IMPLICATIONS FOR TEACHING SCIENCE TO INFANTS AND PRIMARY SCHOOL CHILDREN

There are two aspects of importance here: the development of scientific concepts similar to the development of mathematical concepts; and the way in which science teaching should proceed to maximise cognitive and concept development. The discussion therefore continues under two headings which parallel these two aspects.

The Development of Science Concepts

The discussion of the development of mathematical and scientific concepts as separate problems is a matter of convenience. It is quite clear that the development of such concepts as area, volume, space, length, perspective etc. relate just as much to the development of a stable view of the universe, and the laws which govern it, as they do to mathematical competence and understanding. It is not, however, the intention in this segment of the chapter to trace individually the course of development of these various concepts for this has already been done in Chapter 2. Nevertheless, it is necessary to re-emphasise a point made earlier that the best guarantee of the development of the concepts referred to above is the provision of an environment (experiences) which will promote the overall development of the logical structures so that through the generality of application, specific concepts such as classification, ordination, length and area are more likely to be reached and consolidated. It must always be remembered that in reaching this stage the child has had to build these concepts literally through the interaction of maturation and experience in the way that has been outlined in earlier chapters. Yet, as was indicated in Chapter 2, even concrete operations carries the limitations of being tied fundamentally to the present and to concrete situations for as yet the power and sophistication of formal reasoning is not open to the child.

Piaget's Theory and the Teaching of Science

What then does Piaget's theory suggest for science teaching in the infants and primary school? First, and most obviously, it suggests that the attainment of scientific concepts is a gradual one for the child, that all of the concepts do not reach fruition at the same time within any one child and that there are wide inter-individual differences with respect to the achievement of conservation among children. Granted that this is the position, then it seems that the same general principles that were abstracted in Chapter 5 and applied to the teaching of social studies in the earlier part of this chapter are again implied. It is quite clear that one of the important aims of science teaching in the infants and primary school must surely be the achievement and consolidation of concrete logical operations, for two reasons: the development of insightful understanding of scientific concepts depends upon such achievement; and the development of formal operational thought in the secondary school is a gradual transition which proceeds best from a solid base of concrete experiences.

It therefore seems necessary in teaching science to primary school children, including infants, to structure the classroom in such a way as to promote the continued development of the overall cognitive structures. In terms of Chapter 5, this means the provision of a variety of tasks, materials and problems appropriate to the anticipated current cognitive structure of each child so that through self regulatory behaviour the child will make the cognitive match appropriate to his developmental state and will therefore maximise his interest and motivation. Thus while one should keep in mind the development of particular scientific concepts, it is probable that in the long run the specific material provided, although important, is not the crucial side of the equation. It would be quite reasonable to expect under these circumstances that different children would be doing different things, or the same things at different rates which is, in effect, simply restating for a particular subject area one of the important principles of the integrated day which seems so clearly implied in Piaget's work (cf. Chapter 5). Again, in common with the method of enquiry, the structured environment approach implies the opportunity for interpersonal interaction, discussion and disputation. Children ought to be encouraged to share and compare discoveries in the interests of the maximum development of cognitive structures.

Science in the infants and primary school should be essentially activity and discovery, but true activity in the sense that while objects and ideas will be manipulated and hence experienced, providing real opportunities for significant and meaningful sensory experience, children should be encouraged to explore texture, appearance, sound, odour and to sense movement with the emphasis on formal abstraction of attributes and relationships of objects and events. Manipulation of material is essential if structures are to be built to provide the foundation for the eventual development of formal operations.

There is, however, one very important question which must be answered and it is: "How effectively can infants and primary children apply what is commonly known as the scientific method?" The question, of course, cannot be answered in its present form but must be recast to ask how effectively the intuitive and concrete thinkers can apply the scientific method. The answer is—intuitive thinkers not at all and concrete thinkers probably with considerable assistance. To take the problem a step further let us first of all consider what the scientific method, validly applied, means. Fundamentally in its all-embracing form it means the application of formal thought which means as stated in Chapter 2: (a) setting up hypotheses (hypothetico-deductive method); (b) systematically testing these (combinatorial analysis); and (c) propositional thought (ability to reason without direct adherence to the data).

The concrete operational child cannot approximate this without assistance, and the intuitive child cannot approach it at all. What then can be expected from the intuitive child and from the concrete operational child with respect to scientific thought?

SCIENTIFIC THOUGHT AND THE INTUITIVE CHILD

The basic characteristics of the true intuitive thinker are: (a) inability to conserve and therefore inability to apply the logical operation of reversibility and to compensate for the overwhelming influence of perception; and (b) centration. What the intuitive child is unable to do then is to co-ordinate the abstractions (in the sense of formal or reflective abstractions) he makes into the kind of stable concepts he will develop at the concrete operational stage. These "intuitions" are sporadic and isolated cognitive expressions, which, although goal directed and focused, are nevertheless still vulnerable to perception and represent an unsystematic kind of thinking. It is therefore unrealistic to speak about "scientific thought" with respect to the intuitive child, but the period is an important one nonetheless and the accommodations and assimilation of this period form the substrate of the gradually emerging concrete operations.

Therefore the intuitive child, because he is more goal directed and can attend to features of the environment and integrate these into a cognitive structure, however unsystematic this may be, should be encouraged to manipulate, observe and discuss, including discussion with other children as well as with the teacher.

Research evidence shows fairly conclusively that where acceleration of the development of conservation has taken place, the children who benefit most are those who are in the transitional stage between intuitive and the concrete operational stages, a period in which one would expect to find a fair proportion of kindergarten and early first graders. To this end experiences provided by such schemes as the Triad Mathematics Laboratory (Level I) would appear to be especially suited to complement any early infants science programme where there is emphasis on manipulation and experience of objects and the development of vocabulary appropriate to developing mathematical and scientific ideas. (See Plate 4 which shows kindergarten children experiencing "water play".)

SCIENTIFIC THOUGHT AND THE CONCRETE OPERATIONAL CHILD

The concrete operations period can extend for a fairly long time for any one child. A typical child usually demonstrates the ability to conserve at about seven years of age and the period lasts at least until twelve years of age. However, the reasoning of the concrete operational child at twelve years differs from that of the seven year old in that he can conserve in areas that the younger child cannot—e.g., volume—and he is possibly already in the *transitional* stage preparatory to the attainment of formal operations. Therefore, one must distinguish between early and late concrete operations and must take the differences into account when answering the question concerning scientific thought and the concrete operational child.

Despite the advances made with the achievement of concrete operations, the young child is still not in a position to apply the scientific method. The distinct advance the concrete reasoner has made can be summed up by saying that he now has a relatively rich and integrated logical structure available for application to a wide variety of tasks. But his logic is inferior to the formal reasoner, he cannot usually generate hypotheses, test them systematically and reason with propositions derived from but not directly attached to objects, observations and data.

Towards the end of the concrete operational period he will begin to extend his considerations a little from actual situations to a consideration of possibilities that will fall far short of a consideration of all the possibilities in tasks such as the colourless chemicals test. In fact the concrete operational child does not usually set out to solve a problem in its entirety as a formal child might, but is able to solve concrete problems on a relatively unsystematic trial and error basis although he gives explanations in terms of scientific causality. Thus, whereas the preoperational child believes that the sun goes to bed each night, because he believes that everything that moves is alive and conscious (animism), the concrete operational child can give an explanation in terms of the rotation of the earth. Towards the end of the concrete period (transition), however, the child will seek explanations which satisfy his findings but does not usually continue to search for all possible combinations of variables.

One of the difficulties a concrete child has, particularly a young child, is finding elements common to several situations. He can ascertain and isolate some elements or variables in a problem situation but often includes irrelevant as well as relevant information. In addition, he tends to consider only one factor at a time when attempting to find a solution and ignores other variables instead of attempting to control them. As the child approaches the end of the concrete period and moves into the transitional period his ability to ascertain, isolate and discriminate among relevant and irrelevant variables increases, although he still may fall short of testing all combinations of relevant variables and fluctuate between controlling and eliminating unwanted variables.

In earlier discussion (Chapter 2) it was shown that recent research indicated that only about 4 per cent of sixth grade children would be reasoning at the formal level, although 16 per cent were at the transitional stage. This makes 20 per cent at most who are capable of reasoning formally *on occasions*, the majority of whom are among children from the top (most able) stream of the sixth grade.

Evidence suggests that for science teaching there are two major areas with which the teacher is concerned: problem solving, or the provision of "experiments" for children; and generalised experience.

PROVISION OF PROBLEM SOLVING SITUATIONS OR EXPERIMENTS

Children should be encouraged to observe objects, that is actual specimens, wherever possible and because of the child's inability to go outside the data given in problem situations, observations should be directed and the inferences drawn should be related to what has actually been observed. This notion of directing observations should in no way be interpreted as being in conflict with the notion of the structured environment and the principle of the cognitive match. There is nothing in Piaget's theory that says the teacher does not intervene. The situation might arise where the teacher would direct observations by dealing with the whole class, with a small group or with an individual and having done that it would be up to each individual child to accommodate and assimilate to his own particular cognitive structure in terms of the meaning such structure made possible. In other words, in terms discussed in Chapter 4, the child's knowing of the object and/or event would be in terms of the operativity uniquely available to him as an individual and his interpretation could only be in those terms.

Problems for the concrete operational child should be simple and contain a minimum of variables. Yet even so there is still much that the teacher can do to promote the development of an approach which will assist the child later in the development of the scientific method.

Consider the following problem which might be given to an average sixth grade. It is straightforward and contains a minimum of variables. The child is asked to drop a fairly large piece of porous rock into a beaker partly filled with water and to predict what will happen to the level of the water after ten minutes. It is likely that most children would predict, initially, that the water level would rise and this would be confirmed. There may be others, who may perhaps be at either the formal level or the formal transitional stage, who would note the porosity of the rock and would correctly predict that the water level would initially rise and then fall.

Suppose, however, that the group of children doing the experiment do not make the correct prediction and give answers such as "The water will go higher and stay there because the rock is solid" or "The soft rock will dissolve and the water will stay like it is". This is the kind of situation which gives the teacher the opportunity to assist the child, no matter how slowly, towards the eventual development of the scientific method. First, he must realise that the answers given are tied to the current structures of each individual. Second he must realise that he has to take the child at his present position, accept his conceptions as valid inferences and by one step questions focus attention on the relevant variables in the problem, remembering always that the kinds of abstractions and conclusions available to the child are limited by his structures. Therefore, while the emphasis should be on problems which typically require only one step to be taken and do not require the child to abstract from several variables or follow a long chain of events, the primary school child can be provided with experiments and problem situations which will challenge his growing conceptualisation and prepare him for the eventual emergence of a logical structure which will sustain the application of the scientific method as a consistent approach.

It should not be considered, however, that what has been said immediately above implies that the teacher and child should always be in face to face contact for the presentation of problems and experiments. There are ways, particularly for older children, of giving directions and setting up problem situations which do not depend on oral communications or directions. In the fully integrated day or in the activity based science lesson it is possible that much of the directed observation would be by other means and ideally in a manner consistent with the optimum development of the particular child's cognitive structure.

GENERAL EXPERIENCE

But in addition to problem situations, ample opportunity ought to be given for the child to discover for himself, and, by formal abstraction, build his cognitive structure through experience with a variety of objects in which there is no systematic problem posed, particularly with younger children whose logical structures have not yet been consolidated and lack the generality of application which will come with further development and integration.[4]

The question sometimes arises as to what ought to be recorded by children in primary science and the form it should take. Recording can serve several useful purposes in primary science of which the following are merely examples. The kind and extent of recording required of course depends upon the aims of science teaching and will therefore vary considerably:

---

[4] See B. Close, *Teaching Primary Science*, McGraw Hill, Australia, (in press) for specific information concerning the teaching of science to infants and primary school children along the lines suggested in this chapter.

1   Data collection for future use such as reporting back to the group or class for general discussion.
2   Individual recording of observations in the field or classroom.
3   Recording of summaries and conclusions developed and reached by the group through observation and discussion, including such things as tables classifying objects and events, a task well within the competence of the fully operational concrete thinker. In general these would be recorded as a permanent record, perhaps for comparison with later observations and for later discussion.
4   Sketching to indicate certain features or to show a sequence of events, such as those that take place when porous rock is immersed in water. Such sketching in all probability serves to clarify the child's thought and to assist in *formal abstraction*.

In general, recording should be consistent with the needs and conceptual competence of the child with due regard to the nature of thought at the concrete operational level.

There does not seem to be much educational gain, however, in requiring children to copy diagrams and notes from the chalk-board or other sources without prior experiences with the material. While such an exercise might lead to an accretion of a number of "scientific facts", in terms of Piaget's theory of knowledge such knowing must remain largely at the *figurative* level, lacking the solid basis of operativity from which it should get its meaning. Verbal symbols do not serve the development of concepts very well in the concrete period and make little contribution to the development of operational intelligence.

This does not mean that the child is not encouraged to learn and to use scientific terminology but rather that accurate terminology in the absence of experiences with the material and its effects is an ineffective and inefficient way of building scientific concepts in the concrete operational period.

3 THE IMPLICATIONS OF PIAGET'S THEORY FOR TEACHING LANGUAGE

One of the important issues in education today is the question of whether language influences the development of thought or whether thought influences the development of language. The answer to this question has far reaching consequences for the planning and implementation of educational programmes for the infants and primary school in particular, for there is no dispute as to whether language influences the development of thought when the formal level is reached as all agree that it does.

The argument concerning the relationship between thought and language centres around the period of the development of concrete operations, particularly with respect to conservation. Piaget's position, as outlined briefly in Chapter 4, is that it is the operative structural aspect which underlies the development of language and not the other way around. The opposing point of view, represented by Bruner, sometimes called the Harvard view (cf. Wallace, 1972, 127), maintains that the child becomes "operational" because the experiences which promote the development of cognitive structures are brought under the control of organisational principles which relate directly to the rules of language and which therefore allow the child to use language to transform his experience.

At present, the evidence seems to clearly favour Piaget's position that up to the formal operational stage the development of thought (logical structures) influences the development of language. The evidence which supports Piaget comes from a variety of sources and is briefly recounted below.

First, there is the evidence provided by Vincent and by Oléron (Piaget, 1969, 88) and Furth (1966) that deaf children develop operational structures as do normal children although the achievement is delayed from one to two years. When the performance of blind children is considered (Piaget, 1969, 88) the evidence is even more significant for the development of operational structures is delayed by up to four years, yet although the verbal seriations of blind children are normal (A is smaller than B, B is smaller than C) they are unable to deal with typical manipulative problems of order. In Piaget's view the sensorimotor disturbance peculiar to blind children, hampers the development of the sensorimotor schemes and slows down general co-ordinations. Verbal co-ordinations have not been able to compensate for the lack of activity necessary to develop the capacity for operations (conservation).

Again, Piaget argues that if conservation could be explained on the basis of language (syntactical structure) then there is no obvious reason why the conservation of substance should appear at about seven to eight years, conservation of weight at about nine to ten years and conservation of volume at eleven to twelve years. If the language argument held, conservation once attained should apply to all content areas.

Recent experiments aimed at assessing the role of language in the attainment of conservation carried out at Geneva and reported in Wallace (1972, 127) indicated that while language aids in the storage and retrieval of relevant information, there was little support for the contention that language *per se* contributes to the integration and co-ordination necessary for the development of conservation concepts. Wallace concludes (1972, 127-128) that his own study, although not directly related to the question, seems to favour the Genevan position.

What has been consistently found by the Genevan school, and Sinclair in particular is the appearance of more effective language with the achievement of increasingly effective logical structures (Piaget, 1969, 89). Analysis has shown, however, that it is the development of logical structure (conservation) which promotes the development of language and not vice versa. Overall, then the evidence suggests that it is not the development of thought which depends on language, but language which depends upon the development of thought (operational structure).

Granted that the evidence is running in favour of the development of thought, what does this imply for the teaching of language in the infants and primary school?

Perhaps it implies what at first sight seems the extreme view of Furth (1970) who has quite clear views on the timing of the teaching of reading in particular. Furth asserts (1970, 4) that the message the child who begins school gets is "Forget your intellect for a while, come and learn to read and write; in five to seven years time if you are successful, your reading will catch up with the capacity of your intellect, which you are developing in spite of what we offer you".

Furth's suggestion is to postpone the teaching of reading in favour of providing opportunities for the development of thinking. In summary his argument runs as follows. Elementary school children are capable of operative intelligent thinking well in advance of spoken language and "light years" ahead of what they can read or write. Teaching the child reading and writing in the early years does not expand his thinking. Instead Piaget's work suggests that it is thinking that should be strengthened so that the child can use the verbal medium intelligently.

The school that Furth proposes relegates reading to an elective activity that is encouraged but never imposed and concentrates upon providing an environment in which the intelligent child can grow (Furth, 1970, 146). He believes that the postponement of reading will have no serious effect on the child's eventual capacity to read. This is as yet an hypothesis which remains to be tested but Furth's emphasis on the provision of an environment for the encouragement of thinking certainly follows from Piaget's theories and is consistent with the proposals put forward in Chapter 5.

There would certainly be considerable reaction against such a proposal which may or may not be well founded. In fact the situation could exist where both Furth and those who advocate teaching reading in the early grades of the infants school (as at present) have a valid point. It may well be that learning to read is that kind of skill which develops best if begun when the child is ready, which usually means in the early infants grades. Yet it may also be that there is merit in Furth's contention that not enough effort is spent in the infants and primary school to encourage thought and thinking. Indeed his proposals for the introduction of "Symbolic Picture Logic" (Furth, 1970, 85-104) and other thinking games and activities deserve to be taken very seriously.

What seems to be clear from the work of Piaget and the Genevan school is that the infants and primary school teacher who is concerned to provide the conditions for the optimal development of cognitive structures will at the same time be providing the conditions which will assist in the development of language. It has been consistently argued in the latter part of this book that this development proceeds best under schemes which emphasise: (a) general experience, self regulation and cognitive match; (b) intrinsic motivation, interest and the principle of moderate novelty; (c) interpersonal interaction and discussion as it relates to cognitive development; and (d) genuine activity, discovery and the opportunity to develop real meaning as cognitive structures are built.

Perhaps the most significant feature of the results reporting proportions of formal reasoners in the first four forms (grades) of secondary school (Chapters 2 and 3) is the relatively small proportion of formal reasoners in Forms 1, 2 and 3 of the Australian schools tested. This position obtains whether formal reasoning is assessed on physical-type tests such as the Colourless Chemicals Test (Dale) or the Verbal Reasoning Tests (McNally), although the percentage, of course, rises with successive years (see Figure 17). Should further testing show this situation to apply generally throughout Australian schools, then it is probable that the tendency which Peel noted in England for teachers of early secondary years to assume that thought is more advanced than it really is may very well apply.

Again, research by Case and Collinson (1962) has shown that with respect to verbal material, the appearance of formal thought in adolescents is not uniform across subject matter, in that examinees found history passages more difficult than geography or literature, which Case and Collinson believe may be explained by the difficulties children have in handling time as a variable, especially when ideas appear in sequences other than that in which the events occurred.

This indication of the possibility of differential effects with respect to subjects which are predominantly verbal is of considerable significance when it is realised that the emphasis on verbal material and verbal reasoning increases rapidly from first form (seventh grade) onwards.

Overall, the research which indicates (a) that a relatively small number of children in the early secondary grades reason at the formal level about verbal material, and (b) that ability to reason formally varies with type of verbal material, raises once again and with some insistence the problem of readiness with respect to reasoning about verbal material both as a general problem and within specific subject areas. Already work done by Goldman (1964) suggests that it is likely that the child who has not reached the formal level of reasoning will have considerable difficulty in understanding fully the significance of the parables of the New Testament, and one suspects, much of similar verbal material presented in the early secondary school grades. In fact, it may not be out of place to suggest that at least some of the difficulty with respect to discipline and control which teachers report with respect to some second and third forms may in some part be due to the inability of the concrete reasoner to cope with material at the formal level.

Nor is the position much different in those "non-verbal" secondary subjects such as science which depend extensively upon the use of the "scientific method" and where thought is bound up with the tangible aspects of the environment as well as with verbally derived ideas. The work of Dale and Lovell (op. cit.) suggests quite strongly that even in this situation the child needs considerable assistance in his thinking about relationships from the standpoint of scientific method. Their results indicate the dependence of the early secondary school child on approaches consistent with the concrete reasoning stage and the inability of the majority to apply formal thought which is in practice the "scientific method". The majority of children in the first two years of secondary school cannot concurrently set up hypotheses, reason propositionally nor apply combinatorial analysis systematically to a scientific problem in the way they will be capable of doing in their senior years.

What is equally clear from Australian research is that the transition from concrete operations to formal operations is a gradual one whether such development is traced using methods involving the manipulation of physical entities (Colourless Chemicals) or verbal symbols (Peel Tests). Many of these transitional thinkers are to be found in the early secondary grades.

It again seems clearly implied therefore that classroom and school experiences both in the science-type subjects and the verbal based subjects should be founded on the recognition of the need to provide experiences which will maximise the development of formal operational structures. Here it would seem that the same argument can be applied to the development of formal operations that was applied earlier to the development of concrete operations. The approach referred to would see the development of formal operations as an educational goal at the secondary level in the same way as the development of concrete operations was a goal at the primary level, on the grounds that the development and consolidation of formal operations gives the adolescent a powerful logical structure of wide generality available for the multifarious tasks of reasoning encountered by the high school child and adult. What is difficult is to lay down the way in which this should be done, but research and experience suggests that hypotheses do not spring from nothing but are derived from formal reflective abstraction of previous practical and concrete experiences. What this experience would be for subjects such as science is obvious and has already been referred to in the section dealing with primary science, but mathematics teachers should look seriously at the concept of extending the use of structured materials beyond the primary school, certainly in the less well endowed secondary mathematics classes. History and English are, of course, verbal subjects but even here considerable assistance could be given by appealing directly to personal experience and analogy.

Again, as the formal level of reasoning approaches, language as such becomes an important factor in the growth and development of logical structures. Therefore along with the emphasis on providing concrete and practical experiences should be adequate provision for discussion and disputation as the adolescent subjects his own ideas and thoughts to the critical scrutiny of teacher and peers.

There is, however, the danger of seeing in the suggestions above support for the view that activity consists solely of manual manipulation. This is, of course, completely counter to Piaget's views and he states quite clearly (1971, 68) that "it has finally been understood that an active school is not necessarily a school of manual labour". Even where objects are manipulated in the course of developing concrete logical operations, the cognitive structure is derived not from the manipulation of objects *per se*, but from the co-ordination of the actions of the child. Indeed Piaget asserts (ibid.) "that at other levels the most authentic research activity may take place in the spheres of reflection, of the most advanced abstraction, and of verbal manipulations . . ."

A FINAL COMMENT

One of the problems which besets the translation of Piaget's theory into educational practice is the frequent need to extrapolate from laboratory studies to the classroom. While such studies have provided valuable insights into child development and in consequence illuminated educational thought and practice, there is a lack of comprehensive studies which systematically attempt to determine in an integrated way the classroom experiences which will maximise intellectual and cognitive development. One heartening feature of some current approaches is the de-emphasis on laboratory type studies in favour of comprehensive classroom-oriented research. The question, as the writer sees it, is not whether Piaget's theories have relevance for the classroom but rather, given that Piaget's theories have relevance for the classroom, how can we map theory into practice most effectively.

Appendices

Glossary

Bibliography

Index

Appendix A

TABLE 1

MATRIX OF INTERCORRELATIONS, WESTMEAD INFANTS SCHOOL, FIRST GRADE, NOVEMBER 1971
Main Variables: Age, Conservation, Vocabulary, Number Test.   N = 69   BOYS + GIRLS

	AGE	2D SPACE	CONS. NO.	CONS. SUB.	CONS. DISC. QUANT.	CONS. CONT. QUANT.	CONS. DIST.	CONS. LENGTH	CLASS INCL.	TOTAL CONS.	TOTAL EXPL.	GRAND TOTAL CONS.	VOCAB.	NUMBER TEST
Age		.10	.07	.16	.22	.21	.27	.09	.13	.18	.23	.21	.14	.25
2 Dimens. Space			.52	.61	.59	.61	.33	.36	.09	.73	.77	.76	.35	.25
Conserv. No.				.69	.61	.62	.26	.46	.05	.74	.74	.76	.30	.44
Conserv. Substance					.89	.88	.26	.52	.18	.90	.92	.92	.43	.47
Conserv. Discont. Quantity						.94	.26	.62	.13	.92	.90	.92	.38	.45
Conserv. Cont. Quantity							.30	.56	.11	.91	.91	.93	.31	.41
Conserv. Distance								.25	−.08	.41	.43	.43	.21	.28
Conserv. Length									−.15	.65	.57	.63	.30	.31
Class Inclusion										.15	.18	.17	.05	.19
Total Conserv.											.92	.98	.38	.50
Total Explan.												.98	.44	.46
Grand Total Conserv.													.43	.48
Vocabulary														.26
Number Test														

TABLE 2

COMPARISON OF CORRELATIONS BETWEEN STUDY BY M. L. GOLDSCHMID
(CHILD DEVELOPMENT, Vol. 38, 1967) AND WESTMEAD INFANTS, FIRST GRADE, NOVEMBER 1971

Variables: Conservation & Vocabulary (WISC) Boys and Girls
Goldschmid Study N = 101, Westmead Study N = 69

		2D SPACE	CONS. NO.	CONS. SUB.	CONS. DISC. QUANT.	CONS. CONT. QUANT.	CONS. DIST.	CONS. LENGTH	TOTAL CONS.	TOTAL EXPLAN.	GRAND TOTAL CONS.	VOCAB.
Two-Dimensional Space	WM		.52	.61	.59	.61	.33	.36	.73	.77	.76	.35
	G		(.54)	(.61)	(.53)	(.50)	(.43)	(.31)	(.66)	(.69)	(.69)	(.31)
Conservation of Number	WM			.69	.61	.62	.26	.46	.74	.74	.76	.30
	G			(.61)	(.54)	(.61)	(.43)	(.45)	(.74)	(.70)	(.74)	(.21)
Conservation of Substance	WM				.89	.88	.26	.52	.90	.92	.92	.43
	G				(.72)	(.71)	(.52)	(.44)	(.84)	(.83)	(.85)	(.31)
Conservation Discontinuous Quantity	WM					.94	.26	.62	.92	.90	.92	.38
	G					(.66)	(.56)	(.31)	(.78)	(.79)	(.80)	(.30)
Conservation Continuous Quantity	WM						.30	.56	.91	.91	.93	.31
	G						(.46)	(.40)	(.81)	(.79)	(.82)	(.28)
Conservation Distance	WM							.25	.41	.43	.43	.21
	G							(.31)	(.68)	(.68)	(.70)	(.40)
Conservation Length	WM								.65	.57	.63	.30
	G								(.63)	(.63)	(.64)	(.27)
Total Conservation (correct answers)	WM									.92	.98	.38
	G									(.92)	(.98)	(.38)
Total Explanation	WM										.98	.44
	G										(.98)	(.40)
Grand Total Conservation	WM											.43
	G											(.40)
Vocabulary (WISC)	WM											
	G											

WM = Westmead Study
G = Goldschmid Study

Mean Age Westmead Study = 7.1 years
Mean Age Goldschmid Study = 7.1 years

Appendix B

PIAGET'S POSITION AND THE OXFORD CRITICISM

In 1971 a preliminary report appeared in the Australian press concerning research done on a group of Oxford children under the direction of Peter Bryant. One such report was headed "The Children Demolish Piaget" (*The Bulletin*, 30th October 1971, 47-48). This report indicated that Bryant's work had "undermined . . . the claim that the young child cannot grasp that such fundamental things as number, area and volume remain constant if one changes the appearance" (ibid., 47). This was, of course, a reference to the concept of conservation and indeed the report went on to describe briefly the well known experiments relating to the conservation of continuous quantities (water in the jar) and numerical correspondence (counters test).

Continuing, the report states that "the Oxford experiments have blasted this theory apart by showing that even children as young as three do understand very well that numbers are not changed when only their 'appearance' is altered. Why they give the wrong answers is simply that the child who cannot yet count doesn't know which methods of estimating 'how many' are correct ones and which aren't: a far more trivial failing. When they were taught which methods to use, even very young children in the Oxford experiments did almost as well as adults."

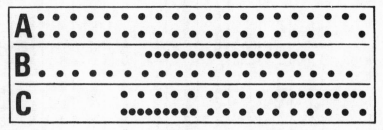

Figure 1

150

Support for this contention was provided by reference to the behaviour of children in response to experimental situations indicated in Figure 1.

Bryant's research indicated that "nearly all the children—even the three-year-olds—knew that the top row in A had more counters than the bottom row. They use a simple 'counting' method which is always correct: all the counters are paired off except one.

"With B, nearly all the children gave the wrong answer: they said the longer row had more counters. This time they were using a second method—'longer means more'—which must have seemed equally valid to them because no one had told them it wasn't.

"With C, the children were completely foxed, roughly half of them saying that the top row contained more counters and the other half the bottom row. This time the children couldn't use any strategy to get the right answer short of counting up each row."

What Bryant found basically was that when pattern A was changed into pattern C, nearly all of the children knew that the numbers had not altered. They were able to do this because they had grasped the principle that number remains constant. When A was changed into B, however, the children performed much more poorly because this principle now clashed with another but stronger one that longer means more. When the children were taught that this was an unsatisfactory method of counting they abandoned it and stuck to the principle that number stays constant. *The Bulletin* commented: "Contrary to Piaget, the child's main problem is to learn which methods for estimating quantity are correct and which aren't." Constancy, according to Bryant, is fixed in the child's mind all the time.

Wallace (1972, 223-225) in discussing the implications of this research points to its similarity with research done by Mehler and Bever, indicating that studies by Achenbach, Bulen, Piaget, and Rothenberg and Courtney have failed to replicate Mehler and Bever's findings while studies by Bever, Mehler and Epstein, and Calhoun obtained results broadly supportive of the position.

Wallace does indicate, however, in his analysis of Bryant's work that he believes that the Oxford group have demonstrated that "the main feature of development is, thus, not the acquisition of conservation but rather learning when it is essential that the conservation principle should take precedence over less reliable quantification principles" (ibid., 225).

Nevertheless in assessing the status of Bryant's findings in the overall context of intellectual development, Wallace is of the opinion that "Rather than totally invalidating the conservation criterion, a parsimonious interpretation of the evidence suggests that the classic Genevan conservation task should be viewed as tapping one aspect of a complex and protracted developmental process" (ibid., 225).

This is a much more favourable view of Bryant's work than that taken by Lunzer (*The Times Educational Supplement*, 11 February 1972, 18) when he says in one place on that page: "But it so happens that Bryant's work misconceives the nature of Piaget's standpoint, and as such it misfires", and

151

in another: "Now these findings will come as no surprise to anyone who is moderately conversant with the relevant literature. Moreover, apart from sundry omissions and distortions, Bryant's novel interpretation coincides with what has been said by Piaget himself and by many others too, Inhelder, Greco, Smedslund, Gruen, Wallace and myself, to name but a few. All would reject the over-simplified 'theory' which he ascribes to Piaget."

In the following number of *The Times Educational Supplement*, (18 February 1972, 19), in response to an interviewer's question concerning Bryant's findings, Piaget said: "Nothing new. It has been done before by American psychologists—Bruner, etc. And it does not contradict our own previous statements about developmental stages. Our interest in the successive stages is that the order is always the same though there may be accelerations, or delays, depending on the culture of the family, or the social structures."

It would seem then that the children have not "demolished" Piaget.

Glossary

ACCOMMODATION: Accommodation in its most specific application, refers to the change in the organism's schemas (schemes) in response to interaction with the environment. Accommodation to each new situation results in the differentiation of a previous structure and therefore the emergence of a new one. Accommodation is thus the modification of internal schemes to accord with reality at a level related to the state of the current intellectual structures.

ADAPTATION: An interaction between the organism and the environment which results in the modification of the organism in a way which is likely to lead to further favourable interactions. When used to refer to intellectual functioning adaptation is an act of intelligence in which assimilation and accommodation are in balance or equilibrium.

ASSIMILATION: Assimilation is the intellectual process in which the individual incorporates incoming stimuli (environmental events) into existing schemas (structures) in such a way as to mould or bend reality to accord with existing structures.

CARDINAL NUMBER: Refers to that aspect of number which identifies the number of elements in a set of objects. E.g., the number 4 always indicates that the set is composed of four elements irrespective of what the elements are or their particular physical arrangement.

CENTRATION: Attention to a specific aspect of a stimulus situation or event resulting in a judgment at variance with objective reality. E.g., the child makes a decision that a plasticine ball rolled into a sausage shape will contain "more plasticine". Here the child *centres* on the length and ignores the compensating factor of a change in thickness.

CONCRETE OPERATIONAL STAGE: The first stage at which the child can think logically (apply logical operations). It is a stage characterised by conservation and reversibility in particular. To say that a child has reached the concrete operational stage is to imply the existence of underlying "groupings" such as

153

classification, seriation and numerical correspondence. Thinking at the concrete operational stage relates to what is directly given whether object, relationship or data, including verbal data.

CONSERVATION: The ability to compensate internally for external changes such as the deformation of a plasticine ball into a sausage or the pouring of water from a wide squat jar into a long thin jar. Essentially conservation refers to the capacity to compensate logically for the perceptual change occasioned by transforming an object or set of objects from one state to another.

DECENTRATION: Used in a specific sense decentration refers to the ability to take into account more than one dimension or aspect at a time. In the conservation of continuous quantities problem (water-in-the-jar problem) this is seen as the ability to take into account both height and width at the same time. In the general sense decentration refers to the ability to take into account such things as the needs of the listener in conversation, the interest of other participants in games and the point of view of another in discussion. It represents a relinquishing of the *egocentrism* of the early years. A child can decentre intellectually and socially.

DISCOVERY: Discovery can be defined in various ways but as used here it refers to the ideas or concepts derived from "formal reflective abstraction" as a consequence of the knowing event. Such a view does not see discovery as involving manipulative experiences exclusively with an absence of verbally presented ideas or data. Nor does it endorse the view that all discovery involves instantaneous and palpable flashes of insight. True discovery often involves laborious and painstaking progress. Again, discovery at the formal level of thinking would be different from that at the concrete level.

EGOCENTRISM: The child's inability to take the viewpoint of another and to make interpretations in terms of his own. The term is in no sense derogatory since the child's inability to take the perspective of another is solely because he cannot, as distinct from those adults who choose not to take the view of another.

EPISTEMOLOGY: The term given to that branch of philosophy or science which is concerned with the nature of knowledge. Piaget believed that the question of the nature of knowledge was open to scientific investigation using the methods of psychology.

EQUILIBRATION: The process by which the changes in the structure of the organism in response to environmental events (accommodation) and modifications made to incoming stimuli by the existing structure (assimilation) are synthesised or balanced.

EQUILIBRIUM: The dynamic balance or state which results from the equilibration of accommodation and assimilation.

154

FIGURATIVE KNOWING: Knowing that is concerned with the static or configurational aspect of an object or event.

FORMAL OPERATIONAL STAGE: The final of Piaget's stages of thinking. The term refers specifically to the ability to reason with the *form* of an argument independent of its content. This aspect of thinking is frequently referred to as propositional thinking. As a general term formal thought refers to the ability to reason hypothetically (set up and test hypotheses), think propositionally and to take into account all possible combinations of variables or aspects of a problem.

FORMAL (REFLECTING) ABSTRACTION: The co-ordinated actions of schemas lead to feedback which in turn enriches the schemas. In this way the general *form* is abstracted from a particular content and through enrichment of the schemas develops the operational structures and hence generalised knowing.

GENETIC EPISTEMOLOGIST: One who studies the problem of the origin and development of knowledge.

INTELLIGENCE: As a general term intelligence refers to the totality of available structures within a given organism and applies to all levels of functioning. It is therefore just as valid to speak of intelligent behaviour at the sensorimotor stage as it is at the formal stage.

INTUITIVE OR PERCEPTUAL STAGE: The later substage of the preoperational period which typically occurs between four to seven years of age in technological societies. The period is characterised by a form of thought in which judgments concerning reality are made on the basis of perception or appearances rather than on logic.

OPERATIVE KNOWING: Knowing that results when a person operates on and transforms a situation, object or event into something that can be assimilated to available schemas. It is that aspect of knowing which is the meaning aspect, the essential generalisable structuring aspect of intelligence; the action aspect.

ORDINAL NUMBER: The sense in which a particular number refers to the position of an object in a series of objects. Thus the number 4 refers to the fourth object in the series.

ORGANISATION: The basic tendency of all organisms to act in an integrated manner. Basically, organisation means that the elements which form the totality are related to one another and to the totality of which they are a part so that in operation the whole is more than the sum of its parts. Organisation also implies intrinsic self regulatory mechanisms.

PERCEPTION: Knowing that is centred on immediate sensations.

PRECONCEPTUAL OR SYMBOLIC STAGE: The earlier substage of the preoperational period which typically occurs between two to four years in technological societies. The period is characterised by an inability to form true concepts and by the development of symbols such as language to represent what is known but not present. This was not possible in the preceding sensorimotor stage.

PREOPERATIONAL STAGE: The stage or period of intellectual development between the sensorimotor stage and the concrete operational stage. It is the preparatory period for the stage of concrete operations. The preoperational stage is frequently divided into the preconceptual or symbolic stage and the intuitive or perceptual stage.

REVERSIBILITY: The ability to mentally return to the starting point of an event and to see that nothing has changed. For example, the child determines that the plasticine sausage could be rolled into a ball again.

SCHEMA(S): The term schema refers specifically to the sensorimotor period and denotes the organised sub-structures which enable the infant to deal with different objects of the same class and with the same objects in various states. The term is, however, extended to embrace structures at any level of mental development although the term most commonly used for the plural in English translations is schemata rather than schemas as is used throughout the present text. In more recent writings Piaget reserves the word schema for the organisation of images and uses the term scheme for the organisation of actions. (Note: it has sometimes been found necessary to use the word schème to give full expression to Piaget's ideas. Where this has been done the word appears in quotation marks.)

SENSORIMOTOR STAGE: The period of development from birth to approximately two years which is sometimes referred to as practical intelligence because the infant's behaviour is basically aimed at getting results. During this period the intellectual structures are built through abstractions from activity, or motor behaviour, and sensory input. The child does not yet have available symbolic representation.

SIGNIFIER: That which signifies something such as language, mental image or symbolic gesture.

SIGNS: Arbitrary or conventional representations that are acquired from external models. In particular words (language) which are transmitted by the culture ready-made and which are collective in nature.

STRUCTURE: A mental system in which the interrelated parts form an organised totality and whose operation is more than the sum of the parts which constitute it.

SYMBOLIC FUNCTION: The ability to represent something such as an object, event or conceptual schema by, e.g., language, mental image or symbolic gesture. Piaget has recently referred to this as the Semotic Function to avoid the confusion which sometimes occurs when the symbol is viewed as only one aspect of symbolic behaviour.

156

SYMBOLS: Representations of objects or events etc., that are formed personally by the individual and are therefore unique to him.

TRANSFORMATION: In relation to the physical world, transformation refers to the changes that occur from one state to another. E.g., a plasticine ball is deformed into a plasticine sausage. As a logical operation or thought process, transformation refers to the ability to compensate for these external changes internally by logical operations resulting in an objective understanding of physical changes.

Bibliography

Almy, M., Chittenden, E. and Miller, P.: *Young Children's Thinking*, Teachers College Press, Columbia University, New York, 1966.

Almy, M.: Longitudinal studies related to the classroom, in M. F. Rosskopf, L. P. Steffe and S. Taback (Eds): *Piagetian Cognitive—Development Research and Mathematical Education*, National Council of Teachers of Mathematics, Washington, 1970, 215-241.

Ausubel, D. P.: The transition from concrete to abstract cognitive functioning: theoretical issues and implications for education, *Journal of Research in Science Teaching*, 2, 1964, 261-266.

Beard, R. M.: The order of concept development studies in two fields, *Educational Review*, 1963, *15*, 105-117.

Boyle, D. G.: *A Student's Guide to Piaget*, Pergamon Press, Oxford, 1969.

Brown, M. and Precious, N.: *The Integrated Day in the Primary School*, Ward Lock Educational, London, 1968.

Burt, C.: The genetics of intelligence, Chapter 1 in W. B. Dockrell. *On Intelligence*, Methuen, London, 1970, 15-28.

Case, D. and Collinson, J. M.: The development of formal thinking in verbal comprehension, *British Journal of Educational Psychology*, 1962, *32*, 103-111.

Chaplin, J. P.: *A Dictionary of Psychology*, Dell, New York, 1968.

Dale, L. G.: The growth of systematic thinking: Replication and analysis of Piaget's first chemical experiment, *Australian Journal of Psychology*, 1970, *32*, 277-286.

Davis, C. M.: Self-selection diet by newly weaned infants, *American Journal of Diseases of Children*, 1928, *36*, 651-679.

Dewey, J.: *The Child and the Curriculum* and *The School and Society*, University of Chicago Press, 1902.

Dewey, J.: *Democracy and Education*, Free Press, New York, 1968, first pub. 1916.

Dienes, Z. P.: *Concept Formation and Personality*, Leicester University Press, 1959.

Dienes, Z. P.: *Building Up Mathematics*, 2nd edn, Hutchinson Educational, London, 1964.

Dienes, Z. P.: *The Arithmetic and Algebra of Natural Number*, The Educational Supply Association, Harlow, 1965.

Dienes, Z. P. (Ed.): *Mathematics in Primary Education*, Unesco Institute for Education, Hamburg, 1966.

Dockrell, W. B. (Ed.): *On Intelligence: The Toronto Symposium on Intelligence, 1969*, Methuen, London, 1970.

Dodwell, P. C.: Children's understanding of number concepts: characteristics of an individual and of a group test, *Canadian Journal of Psychology*, 1961, *15*, 29-36.

Dodwell, P. C.: Relation between the understanding of the logic of classes and of the cardinal number in children, in I. Siegel and F. Hooper (Eds): *Logical Thinking in Children: Research based on Piaget's Theory*, Holt, Rinehart & Winston, New York, 1968, 104-113.

Elkind, D.: Editor's introduction, in J. Piaget: *Six Psychological Studies*, University of London Press, 1968.

Elkind, D.: Piagetian and psychometric conceptions of intelligence, *Harvard Educational Review*, 1969, *39*, 319-337.

Elkind, D.: Two approaches to intelligence: Piagetian and Psychometric, Chapter 2 in D. R. Green, M. P. Ford and G. B. Flamer (Eds): *Measurement and Piaget*, McGraw Hill, New York, 1971, 12-33.

Feigenbaum, K. D.: Task complexity and I.Q. as variables in Piaget's problem of conservation, *Child Development*, 1963, *34*, 423-432.

Flavell, J. H.: *The Developmental Psychology of Jean Piaget*, Van Nostrand, Princeton, 1963.

Flavell, J. H. *et al.*: *The Development of Role-Taking and Communication Skills in Children*, Wiley, New York, 1968.

Furth, H. G.: *Thinking without Language: Psychological Implications of Deafness*, Free Press, New York, 1966.

Furth, H. G.: *Piaget and Knowledge*, Prentice-Hall, New Jersey, 1969.

Furth, H. G.: *Piaget for Teachers*, Prentice-Hall, New Jersey, 1970.

Ginsburg, H. and Opper, S.: *Piaget's Theory of Intellectual Development*, Prentice-Hall, New Jersey, 1969.

Goldman, R.: *Religious Thinking from Childhood to Adolescence*, Routledge & Kegan Paul, London, 1964.

Goldschmid, M. L.: Different types of conservation and nonconservation and their relation to age, sex, I.Q., M.A. and vocabulary, *Child Development*, 1967, *38*, 1229-1246.

Goldschmid, M. L., and Bentler, P. M.: Dimensions and measurement of conservation, *Child Development*, 1968, *39*, 787-802.

Goldschmid, M. L.: The role of experience in the rate and sequence of cognitive development, Chapter 6 in D. R. Green, M. P. Ford and G. B. Flamer (Eds): *Measurement and Piaget*, McGraw Hill, New York, 1971, 103-117.

Goslin, D. A.: Accuracy of self perception and social acceptance, *Sociometry*, 1962, *25*, 283-296.

Green, D. R., Ford, M. P. and Flamer, G. B.: *Measurement and Piaget*, McGraw Hill, New York, 1971.

Hunt, J. McV.: *Intelligence and Experience*, Ronald, New York, 1961.

Hyde, D. M.: An Investigation of Piaget's Theories of the Concept of Number, unpublished Ph.D. thesis, University of London, 1959.

Inhelder, B. and Piaget, J.: *The Growth of Logical Thinking from Childhood to Adolescence*, Routledge and Kegan Paul, London, 1958.

Inhelder, B. and Matalon, B.: The study of problem solving and thinking, Chapter 10 in P. H. Mussen (Ed.): *Handbook of Research Methods in Child Development*, Wiley, New York, 1960, 421-455.

Kaufman, A. S.: Piaget and Gesell: A psychometric analysis of tests built from their tasks, *Child Development*, 1971, *42*, 1341-1360.

Kofsky, E.: A scalogram study of classificatory development, in I. Sigel and F. Hooper (Eds): *Logical Thinking in Children: Research Based on Piaget's Theory*, Holt, Rinehart & Winston, New York, 1968, 210-224.

Kohlberg, L.: Early education: a cognitive—developmental view, *Child Development*, 1968, *39*, 1013-1062.

Loretan, J. O.: *Alternatives to Intelligence Testing*, ETS, Invitational Conference on Testing Problems, 1965.

Lovell, K.: A follow-up study of Inhelder and Piaget's "The Growth of Logical Thinking", *British Journal of Psychology*, 1961, *52*, 143-55.

Lovell, K.: *The Growth of Basic Mathematical and Scientific Concepts in Children*, 5th edn, University of London Press, 1971.

McNally, D. W.: The nature of the Sociometric Choice Process, unpublished Ph.D. thesis, University of Sydney, 1968.

McNally, D. W.: The incidence of Piaget's stages of thinking as assessed by tests of verbal reasoning in several Sydney schools, *Forum of Education*, 1970, *29*, 124-134.

McNally, D. W.: Conservation and Classroom Performance in First Grade, mimeographed report, Westmead College of Advanced Education, 1971.

Moran, P. R.: The integrated day, *Educational Research*, 1971, *14*, 65-69.

Moreno, J. L.: *Who Shall Survive?*, Beacon House, New York, 1953.

Parsons, T.: *The Social System*, The Free Press, Illinois, 1951.

Peel, E. A.: Experimental examination of some of Piaget's schemata concerning children's perception and thinking, and a discussion of their educational significance, *British Journal of Educational Psychology*, 1959, *29*, 89-103.

Peel, E. A.: *The Pupil's Thinking*, Oldbourne, London, 1960.

Peel, E. A.: A study of the differences in the judgments of adolescent pupils, *British Journal of Educational Psychology*, 1966, *36*, 77-86.

Phillips, J. L.: *The Origins of Intellect: Piaget's Theory*, Freeman, San Francisco, 1969.

Piaget, J.: *Judgment and Reasoning in the Child*, Routledge & Kegan Paul, London, 1928.

Piaget, J.: *The Moral Judgment of the Child*, Harcourt Brace & World, New York, 1932.

Piaget, J.: *Le développement de la notion de temps chez l'enfant*, Presses Universitaires de France, Paris, 1946.

Piaget, J.: *The Psychology of Intelligence*, Routledge & Kegan Paul, London, 1950.

Piaget, J.: *The Child's Conception of Number*, Routledge & Kegan Paul, London, 1952.

Piaget, J.: *Six Psychological Studies*, Editor's Introduction, Notes and Glossary by D. Elkind, University of London Press, 1968.

Piaget, J.: *On the Development of Memory and Identity*, Clark University Press, Worcester, Mass., 1968.

Piaget, J.: *Science of Education and the Psychology of the Child*, Longman, London, 1971.

Piaget, J. and Inhelder, B.: *The Child's Conception of Space*, Routledge & Kegan Paul, London, 1956.

Piaget, J. and Inhelder, B.: *The Psychology of the Child*, Routledge & Kegan Paul, London, 1969.

Piaget, J., Inhelder, B. and Szeminska, A.: *The Child's Conception of Geometry*, Routledge & Kegan Paul, London, 1960.

Rawlinson, R. W., Phillips, R. D. and Yabsley, K. B.: *Triad Guide Book*, The Jacaranda Press, Brisbane, 1970.

Rosskopf, M. F., Steffe, L. P. and Taback, S.: *Piagetian Cognitive—Development Research and Mathematical Education*, National Council of Teachers of Mathematics, Washington, 1971.

Sigel, I. E. and Hooper, F. H.: *Logical Thinking in Children*, Holt, Rinehart & Winston, New York, 1968.

Taba, H., Durkin, M. C., Fraenkel, J. R. and McNaughton, A. H.: *A Teacher's Handbook to Elementary Social Studies*, 2nd edn, Addison-Wesley, Menlo Park, California, 1971.

Tagiuri, R. and Petrullo, L. (Eds): *Person Perception and Interpersonal Behaviour*, Stanford University Press, 1958.

Tuddenham, R. D.: A "Piagetian" test of cognitive development, Chapter 3 in W. B. Dockrell (Ed.): *On Intelligence: The Toronto Symposium on Intelligence, 1969*, Methuen, London, 1970, 49-70.

Wadsworth, B. J.: *Piaget's Theory of Cognitive Development*, David McKay, New York, 1971.

Wallace, J. G.: *Stages and Transition in Conceptual Development*, National Foundation for Educational Research in England and Wales, London, 1972.

Warburton, F. W.: The British Intelligence Scale, Chapter 4 in W. B. Dockrell (Ed.): *On Intelligence: The Torcnto Symposium on Intelligence, 1969*, Methuen, London, 1970, 71-98.

Wohlwill, J.: A study of the development of the number concept by scalogram analysis, in I. Sigel and F. Hooper (Eds): *Logical Thinking in Children: Research Based on Piaget's Theory*, Holt, Rinehart & Winston, New York, 1968, 75-104.

Woodward, W. M. The assessment of cognitive processes: Piaget's approach, Chapter 23, in P. Mittler (Ed.): *The Psychological Assessment of Mental and Physical Handicaps*, Methuen, London, 1970, 695-718.

Index

Absent objects, 25
Abstraction. *See* formal abstraction
Acceleration: artificial, 91
  of development, 90, 92, 113, 137
Accommodation, 7-12, 15-16, 18, 21-4, 70,
  81-3, 85-6, 88, 93-4, 130, 137
Active methods: of teaching, 89. *See also*
  new methods
Activity (actions), 9, 11-12, 17-18, 20, 25,
  42, 78-80, 82, 92, 101-102, 112-113, 117,
  120-2, 124, 127, 136-7, 142-3
  co-ordination of, 135
  internalised, 19, 33
  and pure thought, 82
Adaptation, 4-6, 8, 10-11, 81-4, 87-8, 130
  and intelligence, 4-5
  and organisation, 4-6
  and society, 130
Affective development: *See* emotional
  development
Almy, M., *et al*, 109, 113
Animism, 138
Area, 34, 136. *See also* conservation
Assimilation, 7-12, 15-16, 18, 22-4, 67-8,
  81-3, 85-6, 88, 93-4, 130, 137
  biological analogy, 8
  as incorporation, 8
Attitude development, 125
Attribute blocks, 117
Ausubel, D. P., 12(n), 93

Balance (equilibrium), 10-11
Beard, R. M., 64
Beginnings of thought, 18
Beilin, H., 92(n)
Bentler, P. M., 109, 112(n)

Binet, A., 58
Biological: functioning, 5
  states, 10
  structure, 8
Biology: and intellectual development, 4
  Piaget's interest in, 1
Boyle, D. G., 32, 32(n), 51, 94
British Intelligence Scale, 62
Brown, M., 96(n)
Bruner, J., 25, 69, 93, 118, 141
Burt, C., 56-7

Cardinal: mechanisms 106-107
  number, 104-107, 109
Cardinality, 109
Cardination, 109, 119
Case, D., 144
Causality, 18-19
Cause and effect, 15, 19
Centration (centres), 31, 35, 39, 47, 147
Chaplin, J. P., 6(n)
Chronological Age (CA), 58, 60
Claparède, E., 78-9
Class(es), 34-5, 104
  subordinate, 35
  superordinate, 35
Classification(s), 25, 33-4, 36, 39, 49, 83, 103,
  107, 108, 136
  hierarchical, 104
  and intelligence, 61
  motor, 104
Classify, 27, 35-6, 108
Class inclusion, 35-6, 36(n), 107, 110
Clinical method, 2
Close, B., 140(n)

Closure (combinativity), 33
  operation of, 108
Cognition, 2, 6(n)
Cognitive: ability, 56
  development, 48, 50, 59, 87, 89, 91(n),
    93-4, 100-102, 129, 133-5, 143, 146
  growth, 49
  match, 100-2, 113, 118, 121, 124, 129,
    136, 139, 143
  reorganisation, 80, 82
  restructuring, 80, 85, 94
  structures, 7-8, 10-14, 17, 44, 46, 65,
    72, 82, 85-9, 92-5, 100-102, 113, 120-1,
    124, 126, 129, 134, 136-7, 139-140,
    142-3, 145
  and curricula, 65
  and intellectual structures, 6-7
  and the match, 65, 82
  and self-motivation, 11
  See also intellectual structure(s); logical
    structure(s); structure(s)
Collinson, J. M., 144
Combinatorial: analysis, 51-3, 137, 145
  thought, 51
Comparison games, 117
Concept(s), 26-7, 34, 38, 70, 124, 141
  of space, 41-2
  of velocity, 41
  of vertical and horizontal, 45
  See also conservation
Concept development, 70-1, 101, 103, 117,
  135
  formation, 26-7
  See also conservation
Concrete operational: child, 37, 50, 137-9
  stage (concrete operations), 13, 14, 27,
    30, 33-4, 36, 42, 48-9, 51, 60, 67, 71-3,
    83, 87, 105, 109, 112, 126(n), 134-9,
    141, 145
  thinking, 33, 68
    incidence of, 54
Concrete reasoner(s), 31, 49, 50, 63, 86, 137,
  141, 144
Concrete reasoning, 24, 32, 34, 36
Concrete thinker. See concrete reasoner
Conjoint activity, 80
Conscious reflection: on structures, 112
Conservation, 31, 37-40, 41, 42, 48-9, 60-2,
  64, 72, 83, 108-110, 113, 119, 136, 142
  of area, 32, 39-40
  and arithmetic, 110
  and classroom performance, 111
  of continuous quantity, 32, 55, 93, 110
  of discontinuous quantity, 32, 55, 93, 110
  of distance, 110
  and language, 111, 141

of length, 32, 110
  and mental retardation, 64
  of number, 37, 93, 110
  of numerical correspondence, 105
  pseudo, 92
  and reading, 110-111
  score, 63
  of a set, 39, 105
  of substance, 40, 54-5, 64, 110
  and task difficulty, 112(n)
  tasks, 61
  of three dimensional space, 32, 42
  total, 55, 110
  of two dimensional space, 32, 42, 93, 110
  of velocity, 41
  and vocabulary, 110-111
  of volume, 32, 40-1, 64
  of weight, 32, 40, 41, 64
Conserve (conserver(s)), 31-4, 39, 54-5,
  59-60, 64, 67, 74, 108, 110, 137-8
Co-ordinate, 39
  perspectives, 39
  relationships, 49
Co-ordination, 16, 17, 19
  of abstractions, 137
  of actions, 73-4, 145-6
  of horizontal and vertical, 44-7
  of perspectives, 48-50, 134
Cuisenaire rods, 114, 119
Cultural transmission (education), 100
Curriculum (curricula), 65, 89, 90, 92-5,
  118, 121, 124

Dale, L. G., 53-4, 64, 144
Davis, C. M., 89
Decentration, 39, 67
  as logical process, 50
Decentre(s), 31-2, 39, 48, 59, 132
Decroly, O., 78
Deduction, 26
Deferred imitation, 20, 22, 70
Development, 71, 76
  of knowledge (Experimentalist), 80
  and learning, 66-7, 71, 73
  of schemes, 76
Dewey, J., 78-9, 83, 85-6, 88-9, 96
Dienes, Z. P., 113-118, 121
Discovery, 101-102, 113, 121-2, 137, 140,
  143
Discussion, 87, 101-102, 113, 120-1, 124,
  127, 129, 135-6, 143, 145
Disequilibrium, 10, 88
Disjoint. See mutually exclusive
Differentiated signifier, 20
Differentiation, 88

Dodwell, P. C., 60, 112
Drawing, 24, 24(n)
Drive reduction: and motivation, 82
Drives, 11
Dynamic Principle, 116-117

Education, 78 ff.
  as conjoint activity, 80, 86, 88
  as cultural transmission, 100
  as growth, 81, 86, 88, 101
  as intelligent enquiry, 80, 86
  and social purpose, 80, 86
  See also new methods
Educational experience, 100
Egocentric, 15, 17
  stage of moral development, 131
  thought, 101
  view, 49, 87
  view, relinquishment of, 134
Egocentricity, 49
Egocentrism, 34, 48-9
Elements (of a set), 104
Elkind, D., 11, 60, 64, 91, 92, 92(n)
Emotional development, 48-9, 127
Enclosure, 42
Enquiry: and operative knowing, 101
Environment, 4, 7-8, 10-11, 14, 16, 21-2,
  92, 100, 119, 127, 135
  and intellectual growth, 143
  manipulated, 128
  restructured, 125
  and self, 14
  social and physical, 91
Environmental: demands, 9
  stimulation, 8
Epistemologist: genetic, 2
Epistemology, 1
Equilibration, 10-13, 82-3, 88
Equilibrium, 5, 10-12, 88
  psychological or intellectual, 10
Equivalence, 39, 119
Equivalent sets, 39
Euclidean: concepts, 42, 45
  properties, 43
  space, 43, 46
Evaluation (of conservation level, Triad),
  118, 120
Evolution, 3
Experience(s), 92-5, 100, 104, 117-118, 124,
  135, 140
  individual, 91
  influence of, 91
  and maturation, 6, 7, 90
  new, 12
  previous, 12, 88

Experiential: method, 80
  theme (Triad), 118-119
Experimentalism, 79 ff., 124
  summary of, 81
Experimentalist(s), 79, 82-4, 86, 88-9, 99,
  102, 124, 129
  and knowing, 80
  and knowledge, 80
Experimental situations, 139
Exploration play, 117
Extension, 34, 108
Extrinsic: motivation, 11
  rewards, 74, 100, 114

Failed realism, 24
Feigenbaum, K. D., 60
Figurative aspect. *See* knowing
Figurative knowing, 66-8, 70-2, 83, 101,
  124-5, 128
Flamer, G. B., 64, 92(n)
Flavell, J. H., 8, 32, 32(n), 36, 51, 134
Ford, M. P., 64, 92(n)
Forgetting, 74
Formal (reflective) abstraction, 73, 101,
  113, 116-117, 120-1, 137, 140-1, 145
Formal operations: characteristics, 50
  and mental retardation, 64
  stage, 50, 65, 67-70, 72, 77, 86-7, 101, 126,
  126(n), 136-9, 142, 145
Formal reasoner(s) (thinker(s)), 50, 62-4,
  86, 138, 144
  and propositional reasoning, 53
  and reality, 50
Formal thinking, 51-3
  incidence of, 53
  and language, 141, 145
  and verbal material, 144
Fortuitous realism, 24
Froebel, F., 78
Function, 5, 84
Functional invariant(s), 5, 7, 88
Function pleasure, 11
Furth, H., 2, 3, 59, 64, 70, 73(n), 126, 134,
  142, 143

g (general intellectual factor), 56-8, 61-2, 111
Gagne, R. M., 118
Galton, F., 56
General ability, 56
General assimilatory sub-stage, 15
General co-ordinations: and the blind, 142
General (generalised) experience, 73, 92,
  100, 102, 113, 115, 118, 121, 129, 139, 143
Generalisation(s), 88, 124
Genetic epistemologist, 2
Genetic psychology, 78

Genevan position, 142-3
  and language, 142
Genuine co-operation (moral development),
  132
Gestaltist-Field Theorists, 82
Goal seeking behaviour, 79
Golden mean, doctrine of, 91
Goldman, R., 144
Goldschmid, M. L., 54, 60-2, 64, 92(n),
  109-110, 112(n)
Goodenough, F. L., 43
Goslin, D. A., 130
Graphical representation, 117
Green, D. R., 64, 92(n)
Group, as a mathematical term, 32(n)
Group (social), 32
  as a social system, 130
Group factors (conventional intelligence), 57
Grouping(s) (logico-mathematical), 32-3,
  32(n), 36
  structure of, 32-3
Group work, 130, 133

Harvard view (of language development),
  141
Heredity, 4, 90
  and environment (interaction), 4, 90
Hooper, F. H., 92(n)
Horace Mann-Lincoln Social Distance
  Scale, 128
Horizontal decalage, 13, 40, 60
  See also overlaps in extension
Hullfish, G., 79
Hunt, J. McV., 51, 61
Hyde, D. M., 41
Hypothesis testing, 52-3
Hypothetico-deductive thinking, 51, 137,
  145

Identity, 33, 39
Imitation, 9, 20-1, 69-70
Incipient co-operation (moral development),
  131
Individual differences, 12, 65, 90, 93
Induction, 26
Inequivalence, 39, 116
Infralogical, 42
Inhelder, B., 39, 42, 45(n), 50, 52-3, 64,
  85(n), 92(n)
Innate ability, 56
Instinctive behaviour, 3, 4
Instrument of knowing, 74
Integrated day, 95 ff., 101-102, 113, 122,
  129, 136, 140

Intellectual: development, 7, 10-12, 42, 50,
  73-4, 84, 87-8, 127, 129-131, 133-5
  exchange, 87
  functioning, 5, 14, 111
  realism, 24
  structure(s), 5-8, 10, 34, 42, 72, 92, 94,
    122
  See also cognitive structure(s); logical
    structure(s); structure(s)
Intelligence, 1, 14, 96
  as adaptation, organisation, 5
  as biological adaptation, 2, 83
  conventional, 56, 59, 61, 65, 71, 73
  development of, 1, 3, 4, 68
  and evolution, 3
  as a general instrument of knowing, 73
  human, 3
  and knowing, 2
  measurement (psychometrics), 56
  and memory, 66, 74
  operational, 33, 49, 64
  qualitative, 58-9, 61-2, 65
  quantitative, 59, 65
  structure and function, 2
  tests, 56
Intelligence quotient, IQ, 56, 58-61, 65
  constancy of, 59
  and unreliability, 60
Intelligent behaviour, 17-18
Intension, 34, 108
Interaction, 10, 16, 22
Interest(s), 79, 88, 91, 100, 102, 121, 124,
  129, 136, 143
  See also moderate novelty
Intergroup interaction, 125, 127
Internal imitation, 20-2
Internalisation, 19, 27, 42
Internal regulatory factor, 11
International Study Group for Mathematics Learning, 115
Interpersonal: behaviour, 131
  interaction, 86-7, 101-102, 113, 120-1, 124,
    129-130, 132, 135-6, 143
  relations, 49, 130, 135
Intuitive: child, 31, 137
  child and length, 47
  (figurative) methods of teaching, 89
  reasoner(s), 47, 71
  reasoning, 24, 29, 33
  stage, 13, 19, 27, 31, 33, 48, 59-60, 72,
    106, 138
  stage and space, 48
  thinker, 32, 67, 137
Iteration, 33

Juxtaposition, 29

Kaufman, A. S., 60
Kilpatrick, W. H., 79
Knowing, 67, 70, 76, 103, 128
  figurative aspect(s), 66, 68, 72-3, 76
    and intelligence, 66, 115(n), 141
  material aspects, 66
  and operational structures, 77
  operative aspects, 66, 68, 71-3, 76, 83
  scheme(s), 70, 77, 125
  and structural aspects, 76
Knowledge, 4, 70, 123
  biological conception of, 1
  formation and development, 2
  growth in, 128
  and intelligence, 2
  nature of, 1
  Piaget's conception of, 2
  See also knowing
Known object, 66
Kohlberg, L., 6(n), 91, 92
Kofsky, E., 112

Laboratory schools, 89
Language, 20-1, 23, 25, 27, 61, 64, 68-71,
    76-7, 87, 132, 141-3
  development, 142
  and thinking, 66
  and thought, 141
Learning, 14, 71, 73, 76
  and development, 66, 71, 73-4, 77
Length, 47, 136
  See also conservation
Logic, 3, 14, 32, 119, 138
  and understanding, 2
Logical: compensation, 48
  concepts, 26
  development, 60
  multiplication, 59
  operation(s), 40, 62, 66-7, 72, 77(n), 106,
    108-109, 112-113, 120-1, 136-7
  operations and arithmetic, 112, 121
  order, 42
  reasoning, 34, 61
  relationships, 117
  structure(s), 18, 31-3, 39, 40-1, 50, 59-62,
    64, 72, 77, 84, 86, 90, 95, 100, 111-114,
    118, 120-1, 138, 140, 142, 145
  system, 32-3
  thought (see thought)
  See also intellectual structure(s); cogni-
    tive structure(s); structure(s)
Logico-arithmetic operations, 42

Logico-mathematical: nature, 62, 112
  process, 107
  scheme, 32
  understanding, 103
Loretan, J. O., 59, 65
Lovell, K., 41, 43, 53-4, 92(n), 144
Lower Grades Primary Mental Abilities
  Test, 57
Luquet, G. H., 24
Luria, A. R., 25, 69

McNally, D. W., 53-4, 60, 62-4, 109, 144
Man: as active, 81-2
  as goal seeking, 81-2
  as purposive, 81-2
  as self directing, 81-2
Marist Brothers, 97
Matalon, B., 85(n)
Match of cognitive structures, 12, 23, 65,
  74, 93-5, 122, 129
Mathematical: activity, conceptual
    structure, 113
  activity, underlying structure, 116
  relationships, 103
  understanding, 103
Mathematics: and attitudes, 121
  and drill, 114, 121
  and Dynamic Principle, 116
  experiences (method), and multidimen-
    sional approach, 114-115
  experiences (method), and unidimen-
    sional approach, 114-115
  and logical structure, 114
  and reflection on structure, 108
  and teaching, 103
Maturation: and environment, 16
  and experience, 6-7, 42, 90, 92, 100, 104,
    106, 136
  internal structural, 91
Means-end relationship, 17
Measurement, 47
  See also conservation of length
Mediation process, 83
Memory, 66, 74-7
  as coding, 74
  and figurative aspect, 77
  images, 76
  as intellectual activity, 77
  and operative aspect, 77
Mental: activity, 9
  development, 88
  growth, 3
  image, 20, 68
  imagery, 76
  symbols, 20-2

Mental Age (MA), 58, 60-3
Mental retardation, 64
  mildly retarded, 64
  moderately retarded, 64
  severely retarded, 64
Method (teaching strategies), 90, 92, 95
Method of Enquiry, 80, 125, 129-130
Moderate novelty, 11-12, 82, 89, 100-102,
  113, 121, 124, 129, 143
  See also interest
Moral development, 131 ff.
  and social studies, 133
  stages of, 131-3
  and teaching, 133
Moral: dilemma stories, 134
  realism, 133
Moran, P. R., 96(n)
Moreno, J., 126(n), 130
Motivation, 11-12, 56, 74, 100, 124, 136
  Gestalt position, 82
  intrinsic, 102, 113, 121, 143
Motivational methods (mathematical), 114
Multibase arithmetic blocks, 117
Mutually exclusive (disjoint), 34

Needs, 11, 23, 82, 91
New method(s) (of education), 78-9, 88-9,
  92, 99
New school, 79
Non conservers, 54-5
Number, 33, 36-7, 39, 42, 103-106, 112, 118,
  120
  programme, 94
Number theme (Triad), 119
Numerical: concepts, 36
  correspondence, 34, 103, 105, 120
  equivalence, 39, 105
  relationships, 103

Object, 15
  permanence, 14-19, 49, 87, 103-105
  schema, 67
  as self, 15
Objective view, 15
Oléron, P., 142
One-to-one correspondence, 37-9, 103-106,
  108, 119-120, 124-5, 128
Ontogenetic, 2
Operational, 106, 117, 141
  intelligence, 33, 49, 69, 72-4, 76-7, 141
  scheme of assimilation (and memory),
  76
  structure(s), 66, 68, 72-3, 77, 112-113
  structure(s) and the deaf, 142

structure(s) and language, 141
system, 42-3
thinking (thought), 33, 66, 73, 77(n),
  111, 119-120
  See also operative
Operations, 25, 73-5, 112, 115(n), 135, 142
  logic of, 108
Operative aspect. See knowing
Operative: intelligence, 127
  knowing, 66-8, 70-2, 76, 77(n), 83, 101,
  117, 121, 124-5, 128
  structure(s), 70, 76-7, 83
  See also operational
Operativity, 77, 139, 141
Order, 104, 108
Ordering, 103, 108
  See also ordinal, ordination
Ordinal: correspondence, 120
  mechanisms, 106-107
  position, 105
  property, 104, 106, 109
  relations, 34, 36-7, 105
Ordination, 109, 119, 136
Organisation, 4-8, 83-4
  and biological functioning, 5
  of the classroom, 90, 129-130
  and psychological functioning, 5
  of the school, 90
  and structure(s), 6-7
Organised: behaviour, 4
  development, 10
Organism: as active, 79
  as goal seeking, 79
  as purposive, 79
Overlaps in extension, 14
  See also horizontal decalage
Overlearn, 74
Overt representation, 21

Parsons, T., 130
Part-whole relationshp(s), 107, 109, 119
Peabody Picture Vocabulary Test, 61
Peel, E. A., 53, 62, 71, 86, 126(n), 144
Perception(s), 28, 31, 39, 48, 60 , 76, 137
Perceptual (intuitive) stage. See intuitive
  stage
Performance, 109
Permanence of objects. See object per-
  manence
Perspective, 15, 24, 34, 42, 44, 48-9
  development of, 49
Perspectives: co-ordination of, 48, 134
  in space, relativity of, 48
Pestalozzi, J. H., 78
Phillips, J. L., 32, 32(n), 50

Philosophy. *See* epistemology
Piaget, J., 1, 2, 6(n), 10, 12(n), 14, 19, 20, 22-3, 25-6, 29, 30(n), 39, 42, 45(n), 50, 52, 53, 64, 68-9, 75-7, 84, 88-92, 99, 106, 107, 112-113, 115(n), 124, 129, 130-1, 135, 142, 145, 146
Play (playing), 9, 22-3
Precious, N., 96(n)
Preconcepts, 26
Preconceptual (symbolic) stage, 9, 13, 18-19, 25-7, 104
Preliminary games, 116-117
Preoperational: child, 41, 83, 108, 138
    stage, 13, 18-19, 27, 44, 49, 69, 72, 76, 77(n)
Primary Circular Reaction, 15
Primary Mental Abilities, 57
Principle of variability, 118
Problem solving, 139-140
Projective (geometry): concepts, 42
    properties, 43
Propositional thinking, 51-2, 137, 145
Psychological development, 89
Psychological states, 10
Purposive behaviour, 80, 82

Rational number system, 119
Raven's Test of Intelligence (Coloured Progressive Matrices), 61
Readiness, 12, 90, 93
    and verbal material, 144
Reasoning, 26
    concrete, 34
    qualitative, 63
    See also operations, thinking, thought
Recall: patterns of, 75
Receptive method(s): of teaching, 89
Reflective logico-mathematical abstraction, 73(n)
    See also formal abstraction
Reflex(es), 10, 14
    crying, 15
    modification of, 4, 10
    sucking, 4
    sucking, grasping, 15
Reinforcement, 74
Relations, 25, 106
    of objects, 16, 137
Representation, 18, 20, 25, 28, 69
Retarded children, 91(n)
Reversibility, 31, 33, 39-40, 59, 67, 108-109, 137
    operation of, 108
Role(s), 23
    enactment, 134
    taking, 134

Rousseau, J., 78, 83
Rule bound games, 117
Rules: absolute nature of, 132
    development of, 131-2
    and mutual consent, 132-3
    violation and origin of, 132

St Patrick's Dundas: integrated day, 97 ff.
Schema(s), 6-11, 14-17, 20-4, 66, 68, 72, 75, 84-5
    co-ordination of, 16, 19
    grasping, sucking, 6
    of knowing, 128
    reflexive, 7, 15
    of sight, 9
    of sucking, 7, 9
Schemata, 6(n). *See* schemas
Science: concepts, 135
    and Dundas Project, 98, 101
    implications for teaching, 135 ff.
Scientific method (Experimentalist), 51, 80, 85, 137-140, 144-5
Secondary Circular Reactions, 16
Second order factor (intelligence), 57
Self, 17, 23
Self concept, 125
Self regulation, 89, 92, 102, 122, 124, 129, 143
Self regulatory: behaviour, 100-101, 113, 121, 136
    principle, 89
Sensorimotor schemes: of blind, 142
Sensorimotor stage, 9, 13-14, 18, 20, 22, 25, 34, 42, 49, 66, 73(n), 81, 103-104, 108
    activity, 125
    behaviour, 69
    child, 38
    experience, 64
Sequential displacements, 18
Seriation, 34, 39
Series, 104-106
Set(s), 104-105, 107, 109, 119
Sex differences, 64
Sigel, I. E., 92(n)
Signified, 21
Signifier, 20, 22, 68
Signs, 17, 21-2, 25, 68
Sinclair, H., 142
Social: acceptance, 49-50, 126, 128, 130, 134
    adaptation, 23
    adjustment, 125, 129
    development, 48-9, 88, 123
    interaction, 86, 88
    relationships, reciprocal basis, 87
    studies, 66

studies, Piaget's theory and teaching of, 123 ff.
system, 130, 134
transmission, methods of, 74
Socialisation, 129, 135
of the child, 86-8, 101, 123
Society, 129
as a system of relationships, 130
Sociogram, 126(n), 127(n)
Sociometric: choice, 126, 130
status, 127(n)
Space: closed, 42-3
conceptual, 48
co-ordination of horizontal and vertical, 46-7
open, 42-3
perceptual, 49
topological, 42-4
Spatial: conceptions, 44, 49
reasoning, 61
relations, 43
Spearman, C. E., 56, 57
Specific factor(s), 56-7
Stage concept, 12(n)
Stage(s) of intellectual development, 12-13, 59, 61, 85, 92
existence of, 13
and order, 13
preparation and achievement period, 13
and structure(s), 7, 84
Stanford Binet, 58
States (static), 31, 39, 48, 66-7, 83
Stern rods, 114
Structural (structured) materials, 114, 117-119, 145
approach, 121
Structural methods: mathematics, 114
Structural variations, 84
Structure(s), 5-14, 18, 21-3, 25, 34, 67-9, 73, 81, 83-5, 87, 92, 100, 108, 113, 121, 129, 137, 140
development of, 91-2
differentiated, 81
of groupings, 32-3
of materials, 94
and organisation, 81
See also cognitive structure(s); intellectual structure(s); logical structure(s)
Structured: classroom, 124, 136
environment, 124-5, 136
games, 116-117
Subsets, 107, 119
Substance, 34
See also conservation

Symbol(s), 14, 21-3, 68, 70-2, 77, 104-105
manipulation, 112
use, 68
Symbolic: behaviour, 70
function, 20-2, 24-5, 43, 68-9
gesture(s), 20, 68-9
play, 22-4, 130
representation, 21, 70, 117
Symbolic Picture Logic, 143
Symbolic (preconceptual) stage. *See* preconceptual stage
Syncretic, 30
Syntax, 25
Szeminska, A., 39, 42, 123

Taba approach (social studies), 123
Taguiri, R., 130
Tautology, 33
Teacher: as co-ordinator, 118
as resource person, 118
Teaching: models, 95
strategies, 95
Tension: increase in, 82
reduction in, 82
Tertiary Circular Reactions, 17
Thinking, 13, 14, 18, 20, 26, 33, 69, 123, 127, 143
and biological expansion, 80
constructive, 116
and Dewey, 79-80
and direction, 29
and experimentalism, 80
games, 143
intuitive, 32
and language, 66
logical, 107
operational, 33, 73, 143
qualitative, 62
See also operations, reasoning, thought
Thought, 13-14, 18-19, 25-7, 29, 33, 34, 36, 69, 81, 84, 90, 141-2, 144
autonomy of, 14, 33
content, 92
development of, 73, 83, 86
five steps of, 86
and language, 141
logical, 13, 26, 32-3, 73, 87, 103
operational, 66, 108
See also operations, reasoning, thinking
Thurstone, L. L., 56, 57
Time, 16
Topological: relations, 43
space, 43
terms, 43
Topology, 42

170

Traditional: education, 84
  methods, 79, 89
  school, 78-9, 86
  teacher, 127
Transductive reasoning, 26
Transformation(s), 31-2, 39, 48, 67, 83, 109
  invariance under, 61
Transition stage: concrete-formal, 126(n), 138
  intuitive-concrete, 31, 40, 47
Triad Guide Book, 42(n), 118-120
Triad Mathematics Laboratory, 113, 118-121, 138
Tuddenham, R. D., 60-2

Universal order: and Piaget's theory, 2-3

Variables: control of in thinking, 139
Velocity, 34
  See also conservation
Verbal behaviour, 25, 69
Verbal learning, 112
Verbal patterns, 25, 69

Verbal reasoning, 36, 62, 64, 101
  tests, 86
Verbal seriations: and blind children, 142
Vernon, P. E., 57
Vincent, M., 142
Vincents Models Test, 64
Visual: imagery, 21
  perception, 21
  realism, 24
Volume, 34
  See conservation
Vygotsky, L. D., 25, 69

Wallace, J. G., 62, 91(n), 141-2
Warburton, F. W., 62
Wechsler Intelligence Scale for Children, 57-8, 61
  vocabulary sub-test, 62, 110
Weight. See conservation
Westmead Study, 109, 110
Wishes, 25
  See also symbolic play
Wohlwill, J., 112
Woodward, W. M., 64